Lov,
All the Best

MW00596513

Russ

WINNING
WITH
RISK
MANAGEMENT

Financial Engineering and Risk Management

ISSN: 2251-2934

Series Editor: John Birge *(University of Chicago, USA)*

Financial Engineering and Risk Management — Vol.2

WINNING

WITH

RISK

MANAGEMENT

Russell Walker

Northwestern University, USA

 **World Scientific**

NEW JERSEY · LONDON · SINGAPORE · BEIJING · SHANGHAI · HONG KONG · TAIPEI · CHENNAI

Published by

World Scientific Publishing Co. Pte. Ltd.

5 Toh Tuck Link, Singapore 596224

USA office: 27 Warren Street, Suite 401-402, Hackensack, NJ 07601

UK office: 57 Shelton Street, Covent Garden, London WC2H 9HE

Library of Congress Cataloging-in-Publication Data
Walker, Russell, 1972–
    Winning with risk management / by Russell Walker, Northwestern University.
    pages cm
    Includes bibliographical references and index.
    ISBN-13: 978-9814383882
    ISBN-10: 9814383880
    1. Risk management. I. Title.
    HD61.W3543 2013
    658.15'5--dc23
                     2012048836

British Library Cataloguing-in-Publication Data
A catalogue record for this book is available from the British Library.

In-house Editor: Alisha Nguyen

Typeset by Stallion Press
Email: enquiries@stallionpress.com

Printed in Singapore by World Scientific Printers.

This book is dedicated

to my family

Anna, Raymond and Natalie

About the Author

 Russell Walker, Ph.D. is a world expert on the applica-
tion of analytics in business and risk management. As
Associate Director of the Zell Center for Risk Research
and Clinical Associate Professor at the Kellogg School of
Management of Northwestern University, Russell Walker
has developed and taught programs on Enterprise Risk,
Operational Risk, Corporate Governance, and Analytical
Consulting. He is often quoted in the Financial Times, the
International Herald Tribune, the Washington Post, and CNN among other
news media, and has been invited to share his perspective internationally, at
the IESE Business School in Spain, the Sasin Graduate Institute of Business
Administration at Chulalongkorn University in Thailand, and the Indian
School of Business in India. Russell Walker also consults with businesses
on harnessing analytics in their enterprise and developing risk management
solutions. He holds an MBA from the Kellogg School of Management and an
MS and Ph.D. from Cornell University. He lives in Highland Park, Illinois.
Russell Walker can be reached at russell@walkerbernardo.com

Acknowledgement

I would like to thank Joanna Green for her scholarly research and assistance on the various case materials. Special thanks also go to Bob Korajczyk of the Zell Center for Risk Research and the Kellogg School of Management for their kind support on this book and in my endeavors. Last but not least, I would like to acknowledge and thank my wife Anna Walker for her patience and generosity in making this book a reality.

It is difficult to make predictions, especially about the future.
Attributed to many including:

Confucius, Albert Einstein, Neils Bohr, Enrico Fermi,
Winston Churchill, Will Rogers, Mark Twain, Woody Allen,
Groucho Marx, Yogi Berra

Overview

This book develops the notion that companies can succeed on the basis of risk management, much as companies compete on efficiency, cost, labor, location, and other dimensions that provide advantages. However, the striking difference between risk management and these other variables is that the reality of risk and its impact on companies are definite, often catastrophic and a shock to the firm. This is striking, as differences in risk management among firms can be more impactful than a difference in operating efficiencies, for example. Those successful in handling risk stand out and the spoils are more clearly and immediately claimed. Winning with risk management requires discipline and a commitment to using information in decisions. More specifically, it requires recognizing shocks in industries as well as when competitors are poorly prepared so that action can be taken. Winning with risk management also requires protecting owned assets and guarding against threats and reputational risks.

This book will examine how leading firms that compete on risk management have successfully done so. Through select case studies, this book showcases best practices in making risk management a competitive advantage in an enterprise. The cases further suggest that the competitive advantage from risk management also has implication on the capital structure of firms and their organizational formation.

The competitive application of risk management is not simply based on a set of algorithms, but rather encompasses how the enterprise deals with uncertainty, how it gathers data and transforms such data into meaningful risk information. The use of risk information requires that organizations seek and examine disconfirming information and promote a culture for decision-making that is open to such information. This book will also examine how organizations must develop, treat, and communicate risk information for the purposes of winning with risk management.

Introduction

This book seeks to demonstrate that risk management is a competitive advantage, offering firms with better risk management know-how an opportunity in the marketplace. The competitive advantage of risk management is realized not in incremental value, but in quantum shifts in the market, generally precipitated by shocks. Cases studies from select industries are used to highlight the critical dimensions and nature of risk and the most important organizational capabilities in dealing with risk. For each case study, a case review and set of risk management lessons are presented to highlight the key take-away points. Additionally, each case study includes a list of questions that serve to focus how the risk management lessons might be applied to your enterprise. Readers may also find these questions to be opportunities for dialogue on the practice of risk management.

In the first chapter, we examine the origin and notion of risk in business. Critical concepts of volatility and uncertainty are examined. A framework for the dimensions of risk is presented to help the manager identify those risks that may in fact challenge the strategy of the enterprise.

The journey in understanding the features of risk continues in Chapter 2, as we explore risk types and the relationship between severity and frequency. Special emphasis is given to operational risk, given its importance to so many firms. In Chapter 3, we examine how risks, especially operational risks, are manifested as shocks to the enterprise and markets.

In Chapter 4, we examine how operational risks are embedded in many business processes, especially global supply chains. We explore the dangerous features of lean systems. The need for measurement and communicating with risk information is further motivated.

The reliance on technology and automated processes brings new operational risks to many enterprises. In Chapter 5, we examine how such risks are manifested and how digital and electronic systems pose high severity risk to enterprises. As firms adopt and rely on technology more and more, the lessons from this chapter and its case study are sure to touch many firms.

This book also develops the notion that some risks impact the firm over a long period of time and may in fact give rise to further risks. These dangerous features are termed persistence and contagion, respectively. In Chapter 6, we examine a case where a firm invested deeply in systems, its organization, and brand to overcome the persistence and contagion of risk.

A case study from the Financial Crisis of 2008 is presented in Chapter 7. It provides an example of how a leading bank with proactive risk management capabilities outperformed the industry and ended up a winner, after the crisis, in terms of assets owned. We take a deep dive into the organizational capabilities needed to create such a corporate competency with risk management.

Sometimes sound risk management means protecting the firm from itself and its own dangerous decisions. In Chapter 8, we examine a case study that shows how such self-imposed risks are symptomatic of deeper organizational issues. We also note that such lessons are repeated frequently in business, suggesting the challenge is even greater than otherwise thought.

Our examination of organizational capabilities continues in Chapters 9 and 10, as we explore how firms should develop risk management-focused cultures. Risk management-focused cultures do not strictly suggest risk minimization strategies, but risk learning capabilities.

In Chapter 11, we examine the critical vulnerability that operating outside of a firm's country of origin poses in market shocks and operational risks. The case explores how political and legal risks quickly follow operational risks is such settings.

The communication of risk information is examined in cases throughout the books, and we summarize the value of and best practices in communicating risk information in Chapter 12. The broader benefits to the enterprise and its strategy of risk management are specifically outlined in Chapter 13.

The book concludes with a list of risk management lessons, taken from the cases presented. This list of risk management lessons is meant to provide the reader with an easy and convenient checklist of key points and behaviors to reference.

Lastly, I have included various quotes, from various thought leaders, that serve to remind us of the unique properties of risk. Risk appears in all aspects of life, and these quotes point out that reality. These quotes have reminded me of many risk lessons that I have experienced, and I hope these quotes prove equally valuable to you.

Contents

Chapter 1
Introduction to Risk

The fact is that one side thinks that the profits to be won outweigh the risks to be incurred, and the other side would rather avoid danger than accept an immediate loss.
— Thucydides, Ancient Greek Philosopher and Author

What Is Risk?

Risk has been a familiar notion in all civilizations, but as a business concept, has evolved in only the last few centuries. Under modern business it receives great attention. The complexities of commerce and shipping provide much meaning and depth to this word and its concept. Let us consider the concepts embedded in the notion of risk and what it means to the business world.

Linguistic scholars remain divided on the origin of risk in the English language, but the Arabic word *risq* and the Latin word *riscum* are the two of the most heavily recognized linguistic origins of risk. The Arabic word *risq* is meant to convey "anything that has been given to you [by God] and from which you draw profit."[1] The Latin word *riscum* has its origin as a maritime term used to describe the circumnavigation of danger, especially barriers. In the Arabic origin, there is a clear and distinct linkage to prosperity, whereas the Latin origin shows greater focus on negative consequences. Knowing that the Arabic and Latin cultures overlapped in the Mediterranean, it is no surprise that risk has evolved in European culture to have both positive and negative connotations, especially with regard to trade and therefore business.

---

[1]Kedar, B. Z. (1970). Again: Arabic Risq, Medieval Latin Riscum. *Studi Medievali*. Centro Italiano Di Studi Sull Atlo Medioevo, Spoleto.

Most linguists agree that the word *risk* first appeared in the English language in the late seventeenth century and likely came from the French *risqué*, which also is used by English speakers, where danger and some sense of opportunity may be at work. The Arabic origin for risk most certainly influenced the French *risqué* and the Spanish *riesgo*.

Risk developed as a concept in commerce that accounted for those acts of God, *force majeure*, and general danger and peril in commerce, especially maritime commerce. This is perhaps best preserved in the current Spanish phrase, *"por su cuenta y riesgo,"* which is literally by one's cost and risk, or the expression "at your own risk" in English. In fact, the concept of risk first appeared in the English language as part of insurance and shipping terms. This historical reference, in part, is due to the fact that shippers and receivers had to bear the "risk" of loss of cargo in transit. The aversion of each group to this risk gave rise to a highly profitable industry, namely insurance on shipping and was made famous by the rise of Lloyds of London from its humble and unassuming start as a seventeenth century coffee house.

In most of these examples, risk and its origin are tied to a notion of insurance. The use of risk in insurance then and today is still predicated on accounting for losses. In the business of investing, risk is recognized to convey the possibility of losses and gains. In the broader general business sense, risk is a reality of business investments. There is upside and downside in risk. Capturing the upside, containing the downside, and recognizing when risk is changing are the bases for risk-taking in business.

The linkage of risk to cost in origin and concept is profound for business. In business, risk does ultimately involve a cost, justified by an opportunity. Such risks are often encountered during a crisis or during a "shock" to the business. This connection of risk to crisis events or shocks that alter the underlying dynamics of a business is also a key concept and one that is nicely captured in the Chinese word structure for "crisis" which is taken from the combination of "danger" and "opportunity." Danger and opportunity occur together in a crisis. Many great politicians over the years have recognized that a crisis also poses an opportunity. For a business, a crisis in an industry or market is also an opportunity. We will examine that concept more deeply throughout this book.

CRISIS

DANGER   OPPORTUNITY

Chinese characters for crisis

As we look to the financial and scientific communities for guidance on the word risk and its appropriate definition, we see that the concepts of likelihood and probability enter the concept of risk quite directly. Additionally, the impact of outcome of some probabilistic event is also a key concept. A common definition and enumeration of risk is the product of a probability (Pr) and an outcome:

$$Risk = \Pr \times Outcome$$

Although the formula for risk is seemingly straightforward, the terms of likelihood and outcome may be well measured. Additionally in business, we are most concerned about making risk decisions about something that will happen in the future, so risk decisions are implicitly predictions, wrought with all the error that comes with making predictions.

Risk and Uncertainty

Business managers are faced with uncertainty and risk in every business venture. The famous American economist Frank Knight tells us that risk "incorporates more than uncertainty" and that risk (unlike uncertainty) is measurable to the business manager. Consider Frank Knight's thesis in his seminal work, *"Risk, Uncertainty, and Profit"* (1921):

> *Uncertainty must be taken in a sense that is radically distinct from the familiar notion of Risk, from which it has never been properly separated. The term "risk," as loosely used in everyday speech and in economic discussion, really covers two things which, functionally at least, in their causal relations to the phenomena of economic organization, are categorically different. The essential fact is that "risk" means, in some cases, a quantity susceptible of measurement, while at other times it is something distinctly not of this character; and there are far-reaching and crucial differences in the bearings of the phenomenon depending on which of the two is really present and operating. There are other ambiguities in the term "risk" as well. It will appear that a measurable uncertainty, or "risk" proper, as we shall use the term, is so far different from an unmeasurable one that it is not, in effect, an uncertainty at all. We shall accordingly restrict the term "uncertainty" to cases of the non-quantitative type. It is this "true" uncertainty, and not risk, as has been argued, which forms the basis of a valid theory of profit and accounts for the divergence between actual and theoretical competition.*

This provides economists the foundation of Knightian uncertainty, which says that the unknown that cannot be measured and is differentiated from that which can be measured. In the context of business and commerce, this is a deep concept. Businesses can often measure the risk impact of probabilistic events. Business managers must deal with risk of measureable uncertainty and immeasurable uncertainty, as posed by Dr. Knight. Nicholas Taleb Nassim reminds us that "in real life you do not know the odds; you need to discover them, and the sources of uncertainty are not defined."[2] The business manager must be prepared for the well-measured risk and the unexpected shock that alters the business, although the latter is more challenging.

The task of measuring risk and measuring uncertainty in business ultimately revolves around searching for information that defines the risk process and the way specific risks impact the enterprise. New information can

---

[2]Nassim, N. T. (2007). *The Black Swan: The Impact of the Highly Improbable.* New York: Random House.

remove or reduce uncertainty, as Knight would agree. New information also provides the risk manager greater insights into the risks facing the enterprise. The organizational treatment of information and the systematic approach to learning are key competencies that we will explore in this study of risk management as a corporate competency.

Risk and Volatility

Harry Markowitz gave careful consideration to the notion of risk in the context of investments and portfolios of investments. He noted that, "the investor does consider expected return a desirable thing and variance of return an undesirable thing."[3] Indeed for many investors, the variance of return is akin to the volatility in the investment. Markowitz further noted that for many investors of his day, "Usually if the term 'yield' is replaced by 'expected yield' or 'expected return,' and 'risk' by 'variance of return,' little change of apparent meaning would result." Markowitz was suggesting that the investment community of his day used the terms of risk and variance (a measure of volatility) more or less interchangeably. It is true, of course, that risk exists only in the presence or variance of returns, and the confluence of these terms is not unexpected.

Concepts of Risk in Business

Risk, in the business context, involves many concepts that overlap and interact. Let us consider these concepts and how a business manager approaches business risk. Figure 1.1 highlights the major concepts related to risk in business.

Probability of occurrence

Since risk is rooted in some likelihood of an uncertain event occurring, the probability of occurrence from 0 to 100% provides a convenient and mathematically useful measure of likelihood. Probabilities most frequently come from a treatment of historical data, such as understanding the frequency of past events. Probabilities may even come from the survey of experts for their outlook on the future.

---

[3]Markowitz, H. M. (1952). "Portfolio Selection," *Journal of Finance*, 7(1), 77–91.

Figure 1.1. Concepts of risk in business.[4]

The application of statistical theory to historical data brings to light the problems of dealing with real-world data. First, using historical data to estimate what might happen next assumes that the past has some bearing on, or at least similarity to, what will happen next. The challenges in this assumption are many, but generally we concede in our concerns, accepting that the future will look something like the past. Once, we have gained comfort with this powerful leap of faith, it is critical to consider the data in and of itself. It is tempting to treat the historical data as random sequence of events, like the outcome of many rolls of dice. This implies that events are independent and that risk comes from the randomness of the system. However, many real-world situations (physical, financial, and human) defy this second assumption about the independence of risk events. The implications for risk decisions and risk taking in business are profound.

Consider the famous analysis by Harold Hurst on the flows of the Nile River. He spent a great deal of this life studying and designing reservoirs for use on the Nile River. This famous river, being at the cradle of human civilization, has brought bounty in the wake of its floods and great anguish in the wake of its droughts, such that it has been monitored and managed for hundreds of years. Hurst examined annual river levels (in fact annual

---

[4]Adapted from Merna, T. and F. Al-Thani (2006). *Corporate Risk Management.* West Sussex: John Wiley & Sons.

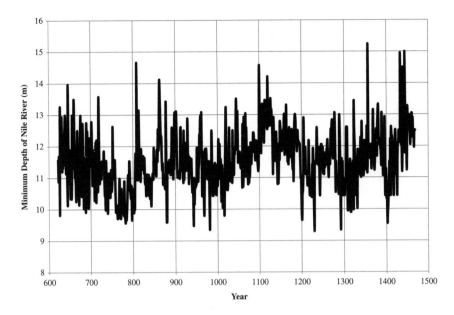

Figure 1.2.   Annual minimum levels of the Nile River (622AD–1469AD).

minimum river levels) over a period of some 800 years (622–1469) to determine the optimal reservoir size to meet the level of water usage by the population. Figure 1.2 shows the annual minimum river level of the mighty Nile, as considered by Hurst.[5]

The sizing of a reservoir is an excellent physical analogy for many risk decisions in business and elsewhere. In this example, the level of the river flow next year is unknown. It is desirable to have sufficient water to meet demand in all years (mostly) and also to trap enough of the water available in surplus years to carry over into the low-water years. Extending this concept to the funding of corporations, pension funds, and even the national treasury of countries is amazingly clear and brilliant. By analyzing the size of surplus years, low-water years, and the time between such years, we can calculate the optimal size of the reservoir. Similarly, in the case of financial systems, we would examine the cash flows (surpluses and deficits), the time between these periods and resolve the needed capital reserves to carry

---

[5]Hurst, H. E. (1951). "The Long-Term Storage Capacity of Reservoirs," *Transactions of the American Society of Civil Engineers*, 116, 770–808.

through a down period. The size of the reservoir is analogous to the cash buffer or capital reserve needed by any of the financial systems mentioned.

Hurst found that the order of the data was especially critical in the analysis and that the river flows were not strictly random. The fact that the Nile River showed a tendency to have low water levels in many years sequentially was more than statistically coincidental. It meant that the optimally sized reservoir must hold surpluses over many years to get through long stretches of low-water years. It also suggested that the data had a structure in time. This was a big revelation. The risk decision regarding the sizing of the reservoir must take into consideration this structure or correlation in time. This analysis by Hurst, first discovered in the field of hydrology, demonstrated the persistence in data and the implication for a risk-based decision. His description of the importance of considering the order of data from a "random process" brought to the forefront the notion that some statistical processes show persistence or memory in the data. This concept has fundamentally altered the view of risk decisions in many disciplines from hydrology to cardiology. The big lesson from Hurst is that the data may show order or persistence and that such structure in the data is critical to making sound risk decisions.

This measurement of the persistence or similarity over time and then distance was used by Mandelbrot to famously consider a host of many other statistical models that call into question the very assumptions of risk analysis and the assumptions of randomness in financial markets.[6,7]

Expert opinions are also used to understand the likelihood of occurrence. Opinions, even from experts, are impaired by the many inefficiencies and biases that challenge us, such as optimism bias and conflicts of interest. So, any assessment of the likelihood or probability of a risk event is subject to error from our human judgment or application of statistical tools.

Impact

The impact or severity of a risk event is a key aspect and involves the cost or loss associated with a risk event or the gain for an upside risk. It is rarely known with precision. However, in business it has limits. For Lloyds

---

[6]Mandelbrot, B. B. (1963). "The Variation of Certain Speculative Prices," *Journal of Business*, 36, 394–419.
[7]Mandelbrot, B. B. (1999). "A Multifractal Walk Down Wall Street," *Scientific American*, 280(2), 70–73.

of London, insuring a trans-Atlantic ship may be limited to the potential loss of its entire cargo. The impact is bounded. For investors, the upside may look unbounded, but generally has some bounds that similarly may not be obvious. Estimation of partial loss from risk events is more complicated, as it requires an understanding of the complexity and path of the risk and how it impacts the business or assets of interest.

Evidence suggests that we, as humans, are generally poor at estimating the impact and likelihood of risk events. In the process of estimating, we suffer from bias and contamination from our previous experiences. We are also familiar with the analysis that airline passengers overestimate airline accidents, just after an accident is reported in the news. That is an example of an overestimation of likelihood due to increased consideration of the recent event in our mental processes for considering uncertainty. When observing a catastrophe such as a car crash, we not only overestimate the likelihood, we are also prone to projecting the results of an observed catastrophe onto our projections of a possible one, especially if it is visual and graphic. These are errors in estimation, of course.

Consider the outlook and financial norms of a person who lived through the Great Depression. My grandparents, like many of their generation, lived with the outlook that another financial crisis would occur and that it would be similar in outcome. The events and severity of the Great Depression changed their outlook forever. We are also prone to optimism bias (thankfully, I guess). At the Kellogg School of Management, I ask MBA students how high interest rates or inflation may rise in the foreseeable future. Answers, not surprisingly, are restricted to the range that they have personally experienced in the past 15–25 years. To them, the notion of 10% interest in mortgages seems impossible. However, their parents would surely have a different outlook.

Unfortunately, there is little we can do about the biases and contamination that impact our outlook other than to constantly and diligently look for new and disconfirming information. Challenging our assumptions and outlook about risk is not only the most important step in managing risk, it may be the most difficult because of our biases.

Complexity and unpredictability

Aside from contending with one's biases, business managers must be cognizant of other aspects of risk, including its complexity in how it impacts the enterprise. We may think of this as the "path of the risk." Risks in business are multi-dimensional and may show relationships and interdependencies with other risks, meaning that the ability to measure a risk (or understanding its impact on the business) is limited by the information available at a point in time and the ability to comprehend the complexity of the risk. The complexity of the risk may overwhelm the ability to predict the outcome, resulting in distaste for the risk by the business. That which is unknown to the business may be considered a risk. However, as Knight demonstrated, risk may be reduced where information and understanding can unravel the uncertainty. In business, uncertainty is common in complex systems. With a movement to greater globalization, interconnectedness, and reliance on automated systems, we can expect greater complexity in business. In many businesses where unraveling the complexity is difficult or impossible, this complexity will be viewed as a risk. Developing an understanding for the complexity is tied to understanding the path and nature of the risk, not simply its statistical properties.

Opportunity to control or influence

A better understanding of an identified risk often leads one to think that a risk can be influenced by certain actions or investments. If the risk cannot be managed or mitigated, hopefully it can be better understood, allowing for more efficient investments. The ability to bring information to a risk decision suggests that learning and discovery are at the core of improving a business' risk position. The risk manager, therefore, looks for information to confirm the hypothesized understanding of the risk and how it is realized in the business. This is the natural approach to identifying the risk that is most attractive to take.

The risk manager may also be concerned about specific risk measures that impact the firm. For example, the time to breakeven, the time to failure, or the time to payment all have specific and critical impacts to the enterprise. It is therefore common, to see time as a component in risk measures. The presence of time is most naturally tied to the decision window for the enterprise. For the entrepreneur, the venture capitalist, and most any business operator, the time to profit, sales, or even payment become aspects of risk. This nuanced view of risk is often critically valuable in defining a risky situation or in sizing the value of an opportunity.

New information is a key differentiator between the Knightian uncertainty and risk. In David Apgar's book *"Risk Intelligence,"* he highlights that some risks, which are "learnable," provide an opportunity for investment and reward.[8] Learning more about a risk than the competition can therefore provide a competitive advantage and even suggest distinctly different business strategies.

When considering these concepts, we can see that risk in the business context involves many concepts beyond likelihood and outcome. Models for addressing the complexity and opportunity for influence are often expressed as changes in the likelihood or impact, conditional on some management activity. However, implementing such complex models and incorporating all of these concepts, especially the resident experience and outlook of the business manager, are unlikely.

The Many Dimensions of Risk

Business decisions require decisions on risk, such as acceptance or avoidance of risk. Risk has many dimensions. Let's consider some of these dimensions in terms of scope and impact. Some examples will assist us in testing this framework.

Explicit risk

First, risk may either be explicit or implicit. An explicit risk is one where the business decisions or investment can be clearly linked and overtly observed to the risk being taken or selected. It is clear that a risk is involved and that the source of the risk is mostly discernable. It does not mean that the enumeration of the risk is easy or that the occurrence of the risk is especially predictable, but rather the presence of risk is not a surprise or hidden to the business manager. Say one buys a contract for December corn delivery. The buyer is explicitly selecting corn and its market volatility as the risk decision.

Implicit risk

An implicit risk is one where the risk being accepted is embedded in a broader or more complex business decision. That is to say, the risk itself is

---

[8] Apgar, D. (2006). *Risk Intelligence: Learning to Manage What We Don't Know.* Boston, MA: Harvard Business School Press.

not obvious. The risk cannot be easily separated from the broader business decision. Quite often, the implicit risk is not realized *a priori*, and its enumeration is often quite complex because it is based on an unknown series of linkages. The business manager, as part of the broader business decision being made, assumes this implicit risk. Again, let us consider a corn contract for delivery in December. Weather delays posed by a December delivery are implicit in selection of the delivery month. Suppose our investor decides to take physical delivery of the corn. In this regard, there is implicit risk associated with the delivery and how weather and transportation might impact the delivery. This risk is implicit in the buying of the contract and cannot easily be removed from the decision to buy corn.

Finite risk

Risks, as manifested at the firm, have different impacts. A finite risk is one that, for the most part, cannot exceed a known amount. Although the enumeration of a finite risk may be challenging because the probability of occurrence may be difficult to assess, the maximum loss is limited to some known amount, usually tied to a level of investment that is transparent. Once this risk is manifested, the loss is finite — complete and known. In the lending of funds, the creditor cannot lose more than the amount lent. In this regard, the risk of loss is finitely described.

Persistent risk

Persistent risks are more troublesome and pose greater concerns. These include those outcomes that continue to impact over a long period of time, such as damage to a brand's reputation or the inability to gain a work permit. The cost of, or loss from, a persistent risk is not a one-time, capped event, but lingers and festers, potentially growing in size and nature over time. Consider how environmental risks come back from years ago. Additionally, consider the risk posed to the installers and manufacturers of asbestos tiles. Persistence is often seen in risks involving liability.

Risk Combinations

Business decisions carry some combinations of the four risk dimensions above. Let us take a look at some common combinations.

Absolute risk

To an enterprise, absolute risk is both finite and explicit, as is one that is recognized in business decisions. The losses or gains from an absolute risk are measurable, quantifiable, and limited in size, which is to say that the risk cannot result in losses beyond the direct investment. In such a decision to invest or not to invest, the risk decision to accept the risk is explicitly made through the investment. Gambling bets are the best example. The investment is capped (finite) and the risk being selected is explicit. Many market-traded assets are fine examples of investments that carry both finite and explicit risks. The buying of a bond is an example. Similarly, purchasing assets and buying inventory in business are transactional events where risk is explicitly accepted and finitely observed.

Many business decisions however pose risks to the enterprise that are not always explicit in the business decision and/or finite in the gains or losses. Such decisions may put the whole or part of the enterprise at risk for some time.

Embedded risk

Embedded risks occur when the risks taken in the business are implicit and the consequence of the decision is limited or finite. Such embedded risks are common in decisions for enterprise operations, where the loss or gain is not tied to the investment. Consider the impacts of compensation structures on employees, especially a sales force. The loss or gain is definite in terms of its realization in rewarding employees for selling more or less product. However what is not definite is the impact to morale — an implicit risk to the business decision of implementing a new compensation plan. Building on this example, the compensation plan implicitly impacts sales of product and the position in the marketplace. These risks may be material and jeopardize the enterprise, and although secondary to the goal, of say, increasing sales, they create a complex decision of risk taking for the business manager. The risks posed by the compensation plan are implicit in the business decision to change the compensation plan.

Similar embedded risks include the decision to form alliances, partnerships, and outsource operations, to name a few. The partner poses risks, some of which may be measurable and detectable, and others that are implicit and perhaps hard to measure or even imagine. Such risks are perhaps the most challenging for the enterprise. These risks are core to the manner of operation and must be owned by the enterprise. Moreover, these risks have few if any natural counterparties and are not easy to trade or sell.

Strategic or industry risk

Operating in any industry poses its own industry risk. Strategic and/or industry risk is explicit in the selection of and the strategy to be in that industry. Consider the print media business in 2011. This industry is under great pressure to compete in the quickly emerging digital space. Virtually every print media company faces this same risk, namely that technology will change the industry. For many participants, this risk endangers the entire enterprise and their ability to produce media going forward. Such a risk is explicitly taken by the selection of being in the print media industry, but the exposure is persistent and encompassing as the risks endanger the entire enterprise. For participants in the media industry, there is a looming and unattractive strategic risk, namely a risk rooted in the industry and their strategy within it.

Infinite risk

Infinite risks are implicit in the business model chosen, and while they might not be realized, subsequent risks may be realized over a longer period of time in many facets. The nature of oil drilling brings the infinite risk of spills and other environmental damages. Consider the two largest oil spills in US history, the Exxon Valdez spill in Alaska and the British Petroleum (BP) Deepwater Horizon oil well explosion. Although Exxon has in many ways, recovered from the spill in Alaska, BP remains in a difficult position. This BP event, unlike the Exxon Valdez event in Alaska, attracted great regulatory scrutiny and even legal and scientific attention that will keep BP liable for environmental losses over many decades. This risk persistance is dangerous and is clearly present for BP. At the time of the Exxon spill, the legal and environmental standards for liability were different. The loss event was in many ways finite for Exxon, limiting not just exposure but the contagion surrounding it.

Tables 1.1 and 1.2 summarize the risk combinations one commonly encounters in business decisions and some examples of these.

Table 1.1. Explicit and implicit risks in an enterprise.

	Explicit	Implicit
Finite (Risk impacts are felt over a short and definite period)	**Absolute Risk** Risk losses are understood and tied directly to the investment made Losses may be limited to the investment	**Embedded Risk** Risk is embedded in the nature of the business operation Risks is not removable from business function
Persistent (Risk impacts are felt over a long and protracted period)	**Strategic or Industry Risk** Risk losses are known Risks are driven less by investment but more by the overall health of the industry Risks are persistent and move with prevailing market forces	**Infinite Risks** Risk losses are not only embedded in operations Risk is spread across business operations, impacting the firm in many unforeseen manners

Table 1.2. Examples of risk types.

	Explicit	Implicit
Finite	**Absolute Risk** 1. Transactional, liquid assets 2. Risk maybe be sellable 3. Counterparty is identified 4. Investment is limited or defined	**Embedded Risk** 1. Losses from operations 2. Hazard losses 3. Failure to execute 4. Supply chain losses
Persistent	**Strategic or Industry Risk** 1. Investments in a brand and company 2. Business model 3. Risk posed by the market or industry of business 4. May be driven by economic or marketplace conditions	**Infinite Risks** 1. Secondary impacts from operational risk 2. Inability to operate or execute from internal processes 3. Follow-on losses due to weakened position

Preferences in Risk Types

In general, economic principles lead us to prefer known outcomes and to shun uncapped losses that may vary widely. As such, the ability of a firm to reduce exposure to infinite risks and separate operational risks embedded in business decisions is a key capability in developing a winning risk management strategy.

Transforming or managing a risk to reduce its unfavorable characteristics is critical. The following Figure 1.3 shows that as a firm works to move a persistent risk to a finite risk, it must gain a better understanding of the enterprise assets at risk. Additionally, steps to limit asset exposure are needed to change a persistent risk to a finite risk. This might be accomplished by moving assets into new businesses or allowing flexibility to consider new business opportunities for assets, as would be seen in transforming a strategic or industry risk to an absolute risk.

As shown in Figure 1.3, in moving from a persistent risk to a finite risk, the firm must be able to change the exposure to the risk and alter how assets are impacted.

In moving from an implicit risk to an explicit risk, the firm needs to understand how the implicit risk is linked to the business decision in order to separate the two. Developing a nearly scientific approach to risk study is key. This is not only an exercise of enumeration but also an altering of

	Explicit	Implicit	Reduction improves the understanding and amount of enterprise assets at risk.
Finite	Absolute Risk	Embedded Risks	
Persistent	Strategic or Industry Risk	Infinite Risk	

Reduction improves ability to pinpoint the source and nature of the risk. Risk become "learnable" and uncertainty is removed or explained.

Figure 1.3.   Risk reduction improvements in moving across risk types.

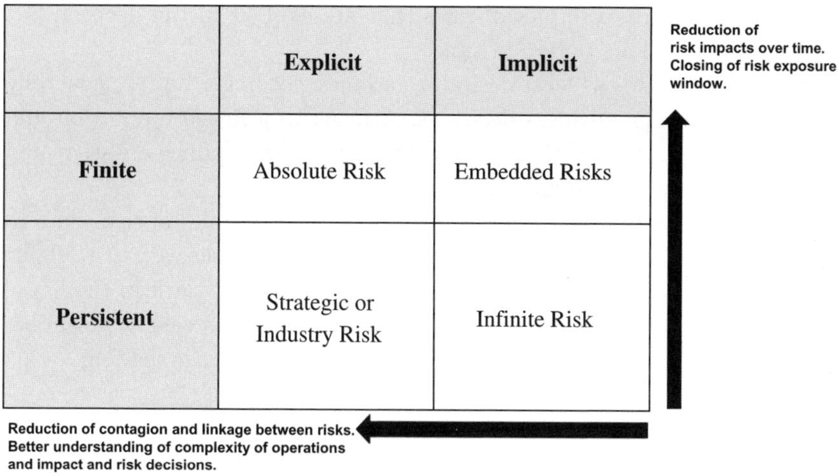

	Explicit	Implicit	Reduction of risk impacts over time. Closing of risk exposure window.
Finite	Absolute Risk	Embedded Risks	
Persistent	Strategic or Industry Risk	Infinite Risk	

Reduction of contagion and linkage between risks.
Better understanding of complexity of operations
and impact and risk decisions.

Figure 1.4. Improvements to the enterprise when transforming risks across risk types.

the business decision to enable such a separation, even though overarching business market forces remain.

Overview of Business Risks

Let us consider how typical risks are mapped to the risk combinations derived from the dimensions of finite, persistent, explicit, and implicit. As noted before, absolute risks (finite and explicit) are those that are directly observed in the investment decision. Obvious examples of absolute risks include market and credit risks, as seen in overt financial transactions. Moving along the finite dimension, we see that as risks become more embedded in the business decision and less separable, they become implicit. This is often referred to as operational risks — risks implicit in operations and inherent to the hazards of business. The risks are often finite in observation, but cannot easily be separated from the business decision.

Persistent risks are those that impact a firm over a longer period of time and are not generally observed as one-time events or even with finite exposure. The selection of any particular industry or strategy will pose a risk. Country risk which refers to operating is a particular country (over another), and technology risk, which refers to using a particular technology (over another), are examples of risks that are explicit in the decision but persistent over a long period of time.

Infinite risks are the least desirable and may not linger but are generally embedded in other business decisions. Attacks to a firm's reputation and changes in business law through regulations are especially persistent and implicit, making these infinite risks in the framework.

The following Figure 1.5 highlights how these examples of risks map to the framework. This is critical as management of these risks vary in available techniques and data support. The shading from light to dark in the figure more or less relate to the severity of poor data support in each type of risk, with infinite risks being the most severe and in the darkest shading.

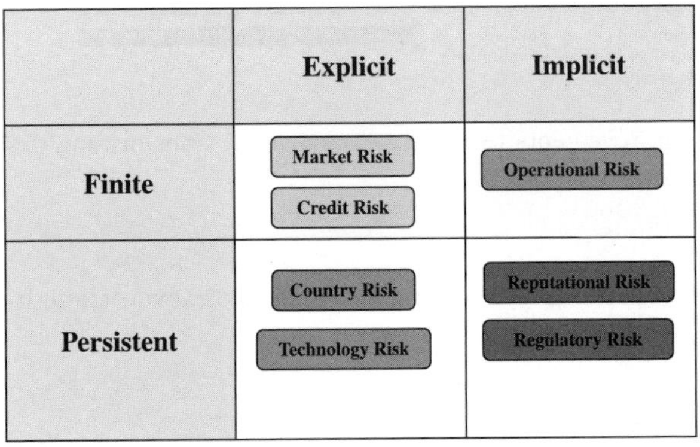

	Explicit	**Implicit**
Finite	Market Risk Credit Risk	Operational Risk
Persistent	Country Risk Technology Risk	Reputational Risk Regulatory Risk

Figure 1.5.   Types of risk encountered and severity of data support.

Recognizing that risks have persistence and may be implicit in a decision is critical, as these risks have the greatest potential to do harm to the enterprise over a long period of time. Such risks are generally related to, or manifested as, reputational attacks or regulatory changes, often as a reaction to a behavior of the firm.

Chapter 2
Overview of Risk Decisions

If you're not a risk taker, you should get the hell out of business.
— Ray Kroc, founder of McDonald's

It comes as little surprise that the word "risk" has its origin in commerce and trade, where both loss and gain are transparent. The duality of loss and gain are at work in every loan made by a bank, providing the need for banks to focus on risk more than in many other industries. Still, risk is a reality for all businesses. As we have seen, risks can be explicit and implicit, and both finite and persistent. Managing risks so that losses are not unexpected and realizing where competitive advantages exist in the marketplace are key. Some forms of risk that are worthy of consideration include: market risk, credit risk, operational risk, regulatory risk, and reputational risk. Figure 2.1 provides high-level definitions for these forms of risk.

Let us dig deeper into the risk types and across the dimensions of explicit, implicit, finite, and persistent.

Market Risk

Market risk is most frequently an explicit and finite risk. The purchasing of any asset involves an investment. The deterioration in asset value is generally covered under market risk, and such an outcome can be dangerous because it can cause contagion. A firm that loses value in assets can expect difficulties in acquiring credit. This was at work during the Financial Crisis, as many banks saw losses in book value and were unable to seek loans or credit due to the concerns of creditors. For many firms that are not in financial services, market risk comes into play when physical assets (such as real estate and physical assets) lose their value. This book will not cover market risk in detail, but we should note its importance in terms of a source of contagion. It is important to note that market risk for especially illiquid assets, such as collectibles or art, can be a problem to

Regulatory Risk Changes in laws, tariffs, taxes, and other politically-driven policy that can alter the business operations and profitability of the enterprise.

Reputational Risk Impact of brand and corporate image of news, rumors, or stories. Generally, driven by business products, practices, or relationships.

Operational Risk Operational Risk is defined as the risk of loss resulting from inadequate or failed *internal processes, people and systems*, or from *external events*.

Credit Risk Probability of not being paid on Accounts Receivable. For banks, this is generally a large function. It is a growing function as others implicitly issue credit.

Market Risk The risk posed by market conditions resulting in the pricing and evaluation of assets. Consider Real Estate and hard to sell assets (art and collectibles).

Risk posed to the enterprise are often interrelated and can be also be strategic risks!

Figure 2.1.   Risk definitions for common risks.

quantify. In such cases, the goal is to better understand market conditions and motivations of buyers. Auction houses actively cultivate particular buyers, knowing that these individuals or institutions have a specific preferences over some forms of art. However, the challenge of understanding markets and buyers is not limited to collectibles and rare art. After the events of 9/11, many airlines found themselves with more aircraft than needed (given that world air travel had precipitously declined). The leasing firms owning the aircrafts found that aircraft were difficult to be re-leased. Who needs an aircraft? Another airline, of course! The fact that airlines across the world were similarly impacted by a drop in travel meant that aircraft assets were not immune to industry specific risks. Market risk models do often consider linkages to economic conditions, but recognizing that buyers are correlated is critical. Similar mass distaste for the buying of mortgage backed securities after the US real estate crisis shows that market risk can have an especially unfavorable behavior of quantum shifts that persist for protracted periods of time.

Market risk models generally build on financial principles about how markets and instruments in such markets should trade. Various models and methodologies exist for pricing a stock or bond, and the famous Capital Asset Pricing Model (CAPM) provides us with a means of relating a particular financial instrument to an overall market. There are models that analyze overall markets and the impact of economic policy and the like on assets. The complexity is overwhelming. At the core of market risk models is the reality that the liquidation price of an asset tomorrow remains uncertain.

Building on Markowitz's portfolio theory and the Black–Scholes equation, the investment community has perhaps the most advanced risk models for measuring the risk in owning financial instruments. It remains a surprise, in spite of these advances, that markets continue to show great volatility. The presence of great volatility is an indication that outlooks are uncertain and that information is desired. The work of risk modeling is never ending.

Credit Risk

Banks are in the business of lending money. For banks, credit risk is definite and explicit. However, many industries end up with credit risk in unexpected ways. Consider the case of any business that takes on account receivables. These are in effect loans against pre-provided services or goods. In reality there are implicit credit risks embedded in the contract for services or goods. Electricity and gas utilities have this problem. The utility provides electricity or gas and is paid in arrears. Implicit in the issuance of service is the acceptance of credit risk. For some utilities, the ability to retract service is strictly limited due to laws, meaning that exposure is not contained. In this case, the risk is not only implicit but may persist for some period of time. Although we will not examine the finer workings of credit risk in this text, it is important to realize and note that credit risk is a common implicit risk and one manifested due to contagion.

Credit risk is focused on predicting and measuring the likelihood of default and the impact to a credit asset (loan) given the default. Most credit risk models separate the modeling of default probabilities from severity, often noted as loss given default. Various models exist and nearly all look to previous loan performance as predictors of default and severity of default. In consumer lending, most banks leverage credit bureau data and relate such data to predict default and its severity in loans. In commercial and sovereign debt, the industry typically looks to the financial health of the borrower, measured in many ways given various economic outlooks.

An interesting nuisance in credit risk is the actual definition of default. It seems easy, but it is not. Rather some conditions are clearly defaults but others may or may not be default. Default is generally a late payment owed to the creditor. However, how late? What if the payment is submitted a few days late? Perhaps that is still an indication of credit risk. Are partial payments partial defaults? And even more complicated is the use of covenance to communicate credit risk. Covenance is the setting of terms of compliance that allow the creditor to monitor and react to changes in the borrower's financial health. Covenance is a recognition that the financial conditions of the borrower can change (for the worse) and new terms are needed in that case. There are few places in business where the terms of a risk related outcome can be negotiated *a priori*. Especially in commercial lending, credit risk is recognized as having increased when and if a rating agency issues a downgrade. Consider the downgrade of US sovereign debt by Standard and Poor's in 2011. The US had not even missed a payment. The range of phenomena that credit risk attempts to measure is indeed a quantum shift. It is movement from payment to no payment. Models are weak in predicting such shifts, so the banking world looks to surrogates like rating agency shifts and complex covenances that are believed (through experience, measurement or argument) to be precursors for credit default. As one would expect, credit risk models can be quite complex and can leverage large amounts of data. It is one of the risk measures that is perhaps most advanced and builds on the most mathematically sounds models available. Surprisingly, many banks and investors missed the subprime crisis and the ensuing credit risk, showing that the best models are indeed flawed by misuse, poor input data, and general imprecision.

Operational Risk

From the financial services industry, we are given the definition that operational risk includes those risks from internal processes, systems, people, and external events. At first glance, operational risk is a catch-all of risks that are not more specifically identified. The origin of the term, operational risk, at least in financial services, is rooted in those risks that are neither classified under market risk nor credit risk, but can impact the firm materially. In this manner, operational risk, at least for financial services, captures risk that is embedded in processes, systems, people decisions, and hazards. It might be finite in exposure, but as we will see from examples, operational risk often is persistent and can cause contagion, mostly in the form of other operational risks.

For firms not in financial services, operational risk is viewed as risk from, or in, operations. It is often tied to supply chain operations or other process-oriented activities. In this regard, the term is similar to that used in financial services. As most firms are not engaged in the process as an end, but rather as a means to accomplishing an end, operational risk is indeed embedded in a broader business decision. There are firms such as UPS and Amazon that have invested so heavily in operations and logistics that process excellence is the standard. For firms like these, operational risk remains present, but its treatment takes on an engineering-level understanding of how processes fail and how to prevent such failures through process improvement. In many ways, excellence in managing operational risk is really about understanding how the risk is embedded in the broader business decision and how it can be separated from the decision for increased benefit. For most firms, the measurement of the means remains less important than the measurement of the ends, which unfortunately relegates operational risk to a poorly understood form of risk, largely embedded in business decisions and a potential source of risk contagion.

Operational risk, as measured and calculated by financial services firms under Basel regulations, is most certainly the least evolved of our risk methodologies. In general, operational risk captures the "mistakes, errors, and hazards" inherent in doing business. But how to measure something that is not supposed to happen and perhaps has never happened before? The risk methodology used by financial services firms looks at data on losses from previous "mistakes, errors, and hazards", and through some statistical scaling and distributional assignment, provides guidance on operational risk levels that are "expected to occur." However, the explanation for the operational risk might not be considered. The path to the error is often not specifically defined. The measure and formulation of operational risk is the least precise and perhaps the most discomforting of the major risks normally calculated. And as operational risks are more or less related to "mistakes, errors, and hazards," it comes as little surprise that operational risk enumeration and management cause great problems for financial service firms and businesses alike. We will look at various cases where operational risk was not only difficult for firms to measure, but also difficult to detect. Operational risk can dangerously lead to large, enterprise-level losses.

Operational risks in business are some of the most challenging to manage and detect, as they are often embedded in a broader business decision. In general, selection of an industry, country, technology, or strategy offers an overt and explicit risk proposition. Operational risks are often the baggage of such a broader decision. Whereas it is possible to test the strategy or measure the industry under various scenarios even before making an investment into the market, it may not be possible to predict operational risk as directly. So, techniques for modeling such industry risk are rather strong, but the data support for the embedded operational risk is the challenge. For instance, answering how a market will respond to a new entrant with a new pricing model requires a projection of data into the future. Modeling for this tests our best economic and risk models. The embedded operational risks are often missed or misunderstood.

Lastly, we are faced with infinite risks, where the manifestation and exposure of the risk are both difficult to measure. Consider the impact to a brand during a crisis or the ability for a firm to operate after new regulation. Modeling such risks requires predicting shocks or quantum changes. It is not only mathematically challenging, it is often that the historical data (similar shocks in the past) are limited or non-existent. In part, infinite shocks are not only the most dangerous by nature, but their nature makes their management and containment even more challenging. This contributes to our inability to adequately measure these. Dr. Knight might even have argued that these risks are more uncertain, where measurement is not possible.

Although many risk managers will question the validity and trustworthiness of credit risk and market risk models in the aftermath of the Great Recession, the reality is that in the world of risk management, our best techniques and data support are generally found in credit and market risk models. Again, it does not mean that the mathematics or exercise of probability prediction is easy, it just means we have the most advanced tools for risk measurement. Beyond that, the tools and data for risk management become weaker, owing generally to the poor understanding of risks in business decisions. Operational risks have gained a great deal of attention in the recent decades (and rightfully so), and great advances have been made to measure and model operational risk. In fact, financial service firms employ Basel-endorsed techniques that ultimately map operational risks to techniques (like value at risk) used in market and credit risk management. However, the drivers of operational risk, and the way operational risk is observed, differ dramatically from credit and market risk. Operational risk requires a near engineering-like understanding of systems, processes and failure mechanisms. In general, businesses do not invest to understand processes and systems to that level, especially when the systems and processes are secondary to the business models or goals. Therefore, in the business world, we see weak operational risk data and generally nascent models for considering operational risk.

The goal of the business manager is therefore to recognize the type of risk facing the organization and make investments in learning about the risk and its nature in order to reduce persistence and remove implicitness as much as possible.

Risk Contagion

It is often said that risks are linked or correlated. Indeed, many economically driven risks happen simultaneously. That phenomena, although troublesome to the business, is called contagion. In operational risk especially, we see that risks, when manifested, give rise to new or additional risks. This is especially true when the risk in question is left unattended.

In some ways the risk contagion might be expected. A shock to an enterprise might weaken its capital position and expose it to additional risks. This is a typical risk contagion. A dangerous feature of risk contagion is that it often gives rise to implicit and persistent risk. As with the example of a weakened firm experiencing new operating or funding risks, the impacts of such are most likely to exist over a prolonged period of time. The risks are implicit in that the firms did not specifically elect to accept them.

Another unfortunate feature of risk contagion is that it often activates a risk that is driven by external forces. In the cases later discussed in this text, we will see various examples of operational risks that give rise to reputational and regulatory risks. The danger of this contagion is that operational risk (to the extent that it is driven by internal processes and systems) is controlled largely by the actions of the enterprise. Once the risks give rise to another risk driven externally through contagion, the control mechanism is lost. The fate of the firm is, in some regard, driven by the actions of others, customers, regulators, investors, etc.

Preventing contagion in risk is a key concept in this text. Not only are business managers required to respond to risk but ensure that the risks do not give rise to additional risks. The ability to do so is a key advantage.

Reputational Risk

When mentioning reputational risk, most firms become quite alarmed. Indeed, there are few things more valuable than trust, promise and commitment built over many years. Firms that have trust and promise as their major assets are especially sensitive to reputational harm. This explains why the accusations against the audit and accounting firm of Arthur Andersen proved so deadly. Other firms rely on reputation too. Most any firm that produces a product that customers consume literally must offer the promise of a safe and high quality product. Financial service firms are entrusted to manage debts and assets of customers. The cataclysmic shifts in real estate prices during the Great Recession of 2008 changed how banks interact with customers in the real estate market. Many banks continue to suffer reputational harm from those actions. Reputational risk is challenging to enumerate, because it is, at least *a priori*, unclear which constituents, and to what degree, they will react negatively to the firm. Investment to overcome reputational harm is generally expensive and, as in the case of Arthur Andersen, may indeed be impossible. Reputational risks linger over a long period of time and of course are implicit in the business operations of the firm.

Regulatory Risk

The recent movement by the US and European governments to consider new regulation in financial services and other consumer facing industries has drawn new attention to the reality of regulatory risk. In many ways, regulatory risk can be viewed as a game changer in the industry. It can help some market participants and harm others. It may not be evenly applied and may even be directed at specific market participants for political or economic reasons. Reversing regulation, although not impossible, is difficult and expensive. Regulation is persistent and therefore poses a persistent risk. The exact impact is even harder to quantify. Indeed, being exposed to regulatory risk is mostly tied to being in a particular industry of unfavorable attention from the government. The specifics that may come under review are in many ways reactions by governments to address constituent outcries. The penalties and concerns in regulation may even appear capricious and serve little in the way of actually directing the industry, meaning that the risks are truly embedded in the operation. We will examine how firms can proactively address regulation and how operational risk can serve as a dangerous source of contagion for both regulatory and reputational risk.

Regulatory and reputational risks share an important and unfortunate similarity. In most instances it is often an offended or motivated constituent seeking to cause the firm some economic harm. Even a customer's decision not to use a product (although not as vocal as an activist) has a negative economic impact. The economic impact of such risks means that firms must manage reputation and regulation through a series of on-going activities. These risks, when manifested, cannot be directly controlled by the firm through internal operations. Seeking information and insights on sources of reputational and regulatory risk will prove important and critical in preventing contagion from other sources.

Risk Severity and Frequency

From our early definition it is clear that risk involves both a likelihood and frequency. It is common to consider risks on a matrix that plots both severity and frequency. Most risk management texts have a similar matrix as Figure 2.2. However, the plot of risk along such a matrix should also lead us to strategies of how these risks can best be handled.

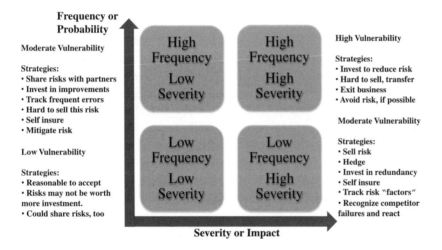

Figure 2.2.   Risk frequency and severity.

Low frequency and low severity

The occurrence of such low frequency and low severity risks is often not even reported or acknowledged by a firm. It is the opinion of many risk management professionals that low severity operational risk is not reported at all. In fact many firms maintain levels of materiality that exclude such tracking for economic reasons. In general, this is probably reasonable and safe. However, as in high frequency and low severity risks, low frequency and low severity risks are a learning opportunity. Examine your insights on how the system or process could fail under low frequency and low frequency risks. Perhaps such risks can even be shared with a business partner who may have better investigative capabilities.

High frequency and low severity

High frequency and low severity risks are those that happen often, yet are not material, but do pose an opportunity for improvement. Consider the problem of a false alarm. We have all experienced it. While at Cornell University, I can recall the older buildings on campus suffering from many false alarms, with each alarm dispatching the Ithaca Fire Department for investigation. The nuisance and inconvenience are obvious. The bill for such "unnecessary" investigation often proved unacceptable. This then suggests that such risks must be understood to ensure they do not grow in severity or lead to other risks. Dealing with high frequency and low severity risks are unattractive for many firms. There are often little incentives for investing to eliminate the risks. Manual overrides or other stopgap procedures may be put into place to ensure that the risk is "not a real one." Such risks can rarely if ever be shared and serve the firm as not only warning signs but also opportunities for process and risk management improvement.

Low frequency and high severity

These are the risks that cause the greatest angst and concern for business leaders. These risks don't happen frequently enough to understand or allow for good prediction of occurrence, but then these risks occur, and the impact is crippling to the firm.

With the exception of natural hazard risk, like fire, most low frequency and high severity (LFHS) risks are not easily transferred. Transfer in the form of natural hazard insurance is possible because natural hazards are not the direct result of management decisions. However, other operational risks such as failures in processes and systems that may be LFHS are indeed due to management decisions and suffer from asymmetric information, meaning that a counterparty will not easily arise to assume that risk, because the underlying information (if known) is available only through an economically motivated party. With the exception of natural hazards, firms should view LFHS risks as opportunities to invest not simply to reduce risks but to protect the profit function of the firm. We will see this competency at work in this text.

It is worth noting that the tenure of executives and even managers at any business impacts how LFHS risks are treated. For CEOs, the average tenure is approximately 4–5 years.[9] This means that the outlook for a LFHS risk event occurring during the tenure is low.

Consider a risk with a 5% of occurrence in a given year. Assume that the risk is independent and stationary (its probability of occurring does not go up over time, nor do events from year to year have any impact on each other). For a 4-year horizon, there is only an 81% chance of the event not occurring at all, and given that businesses make many decisions on an annual basis, the risk is still only 5% chance per year. Building on this simple example, it takes 13 years of exposure to a risk of 5% probability to see a near 50% chance of the risk actually occurring. At 13 years, there is a 51% chance of the LFHS risk occurring. That is nearly 3 times the tenure of the average CEO! For an even rare risk, say 1%, one must experience a tenure of nearly 70 years (68, actually) before the risk of occurrence reaches 50%. For many executives, the temptation is there to disregard LFHS risks. It is not different than gambling in that regard. However, it is the fate of the firm that is in peril.

High frequency and high severity

In many ways, a high frequency and high severity risk is one that will end the business. One might argue that it is not likely. However, the nature of this risk is one that requires the firm to either avoid the risk altogether, as in exiting the business or in changing the nature of the exposure to the risk. Firms that are exposed to such dangerous risk often take a very scientific or engineering-like approach to understanding the details of the risk and then altering some aspect of the business process or system to reduce the severity and or frequency. The key point here is that mathematics and the traditional tools of risk enumeration are insufficient for dealing with

---

[9] *"Why CEO Tenure Varies: Are You at Risk."* Available at http://chiefexecutive. net/why-ceo-tenure-varies-are-you-at-risk.

high frequency and high severity risks. The firm must be investigative, inquisitive, innovative, and ingenious.

Making Risk Decisions and Deploying Capital

Once risks have been identified, it is reasonable to ask what should be done. There are at least five major decisions that can be taken in regards to a known (need not be quantifiable) risk. It may be attractive to avoid the risk or transfer the risk to another party better equipped to handle the risk. If the risk is acceptable, it may be accepted without concern, or mitigated to reduce severity, likelihood, and/or the ensuing negative impact to the firm. Lastly, and a decision that we often forget, the risk may suggest that the firm should exit the business altogether. Such a decision should be made by the senior management of the firm in consultation with the board of directors. Often, the risk decisions are made within business units and at the periphery of the firm.

Once the decision is made, there are clear actions that are necessary — namely, decisions of investment or the deployment of capital (in form of cash and other assets) for supporting the risk decision. Consider the decision to avoid a risk. It must be followed by the action to divest of the activity and/or cultivate alternatives that insure that the risk is avoided. Measurement of this is also critical. Transferring a risk typically involves some payment to a counterparty for taking on the risk. Beyond paying a premium for this right to transfer the risk, a firm must examine the counterparty and know that it is solvent and available to handle the risk manifestation. For many, the term "counterparty risk" came to be known after realizing that an insurer was not guaranteed to be solvent. Counterparty risks are those that involve sharing with business partners. In such arrangements, the business partner is looking for an economic gain and opportunity. Understanding and confirming your partner's strategy and capability are then crucial in transferring risk.

The acceptance of risk is often tied to recognizing that the risk is either embedded in the operations of the firm or inherent in the industry. It is often tempting to then dismiss the risk as "part of doing business." However, the business of risk is not done. The acceptance of risk requires, at a minimum, preparing for its manifestation. This is generally done through self-insurance, but may require more than just capital. Consider a services firm that must remedy a customer impacted from failed service. There is

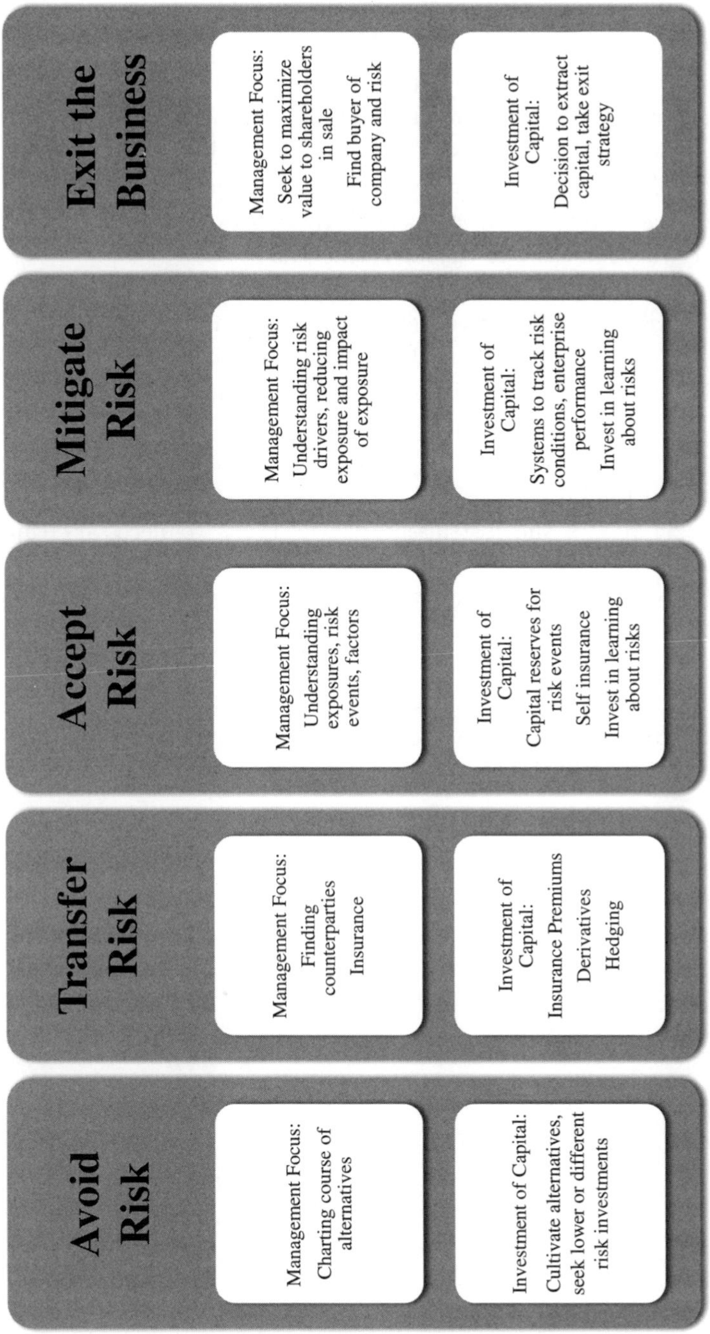

Figure 2.3.   Risk decisions and capital deployment follow-through.

a cost to refund for the failed service, but there may also be a long-term persistent cost in acquiring new or former customers.

Risks are often accepted and subject to mitigation. This requires that the firm invest capital and other resources (e.g., talent, management attention, etc.) on reducing the risk's severity and/or likelihood. When the importance of risk metrics comes up, it is appropriate to ask, "How has the risk changed since the investment?" We will examine the benefits of risk metrics through cases in the later chapters.

Lastly, when the risk is insurmountable or the ability of the firm to manage the risk is unattractive because of the nature of the risk or the capability of the firm, it is fair and reasonable to sell the firm to someone who can indeed manage that risk better. Selling out may seem like a failure and to many it is, but it provides, under those conditions, the greatest return to the shareholders and may in fact allow the firm to best prosper as a division of the buyer.

Figure 2.3 relates the five major risk decisions to necessary capital decisions.

Aligning a firm's risk decision to its readiness for the risk is important and requires a linkage between the focus of management and the allocation of capital in the enterprise. It suggests that the risk managers must be aligned with those making capital allocating decisions. A firm's ability to dedicate capital and resources also suggested risk strategies. Not all strategies are possible and recognizing those that are within the scope, is critical.

Chapter 3

Dealing With Shocks — Large Scale
Risks Impacting Markets
and Industries

Want of foresight, unwillingness to act when action would be simple and effective, lack of clear thinking, confusion of counsel until the emergency comes, until self-preservation strikes its jarring gong — these are the features which constitute the endless repetition of history.

— Winston Churchill, British Prime Minister and Nobel Laureate

In examining risks, it is important to draw attention to the most uncomfortable reality of risk — it can be sudden and catastrophic. Namely, risks can and are often manifested as shocks or quantum shifts, which alter the market conditions and the profit function of the enterprise. These quantum shifts result in long-term persistent changes that are mostly unattractive.

This peculiar property of risk to be manifested through quantum shifts is unlike the moderate change associated with many other processes and forces. The movement from day to night, from young to old is gradual, incremental, allowing one to prepare, take action, and even ponder the change. Sudden shifts offer no preparation and only reward those who were prepared beforehand.

There are many mathematical models for considering shifts and even in measuring such shifts in data. In my experience, plotting data and looking at its behavior shows the reality of shifts in the most powerful manner. Consider the drop in the Dow Jones Industrial Average on October 19, 1987, also known as Black Monday. See Figure 3.1.

This day proved gut wrenching to many investors and traders. As we know now, the events were in many ways precipitated by unforeseen trading

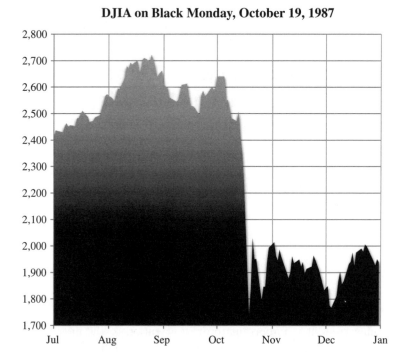

Figure 3.1.   DJIA on Black Monday, 1987.

algorithms that drove automated sell orders. The event was in many ways the first major and modern flash crash. The markets had not known such drop since the Great Depression, leading many to believe that a new depression was imminent. In examining the plot of the DJIA before, on, and after Black Monday, we see the immense challenge in preparing for shocks. What in the data would have signaled this dramatic drop prior to October 19, 1987? In fact, if one were to measure the volatility of the DJIA before the drop, it was relatively modest, historically speaking.

Then we see a dramatic shock, a shift downward. It is not followed by an immediate return to normalcy. The shock is followed by increased volatility, generally a sign of confusion, fear, and misunderstanding in the markets. In all, the availability and trust of information is being questioned. Previous to the shock, market participants believed something about the DJIA and how it operated. The trust was violated. The best information proved to be wrong or incomplete, unknown risks were now visible, and the process for developing new insights, new measurement, and new information started to take root.

For the optimist, the plot of the DJIA is inspiring. With the DJIA hovering about 14,000 at the time of this writing in 2013, in some 25 years, the DJIA has increased by a factor of 7, in spite of these unforeseen risks and perils!

For organizations, predicting shocks should not be the goal. Preparing to survive through the shock is the goal, as even this famous shock showed that prosperity may be ahead. However, as we know, not all firms are able to survive market and industry-wide shocks. There are winners and losers. Markets consolidate and generally reward those best prepared for the shock or at least those least exposed to the shock.

Consider the benefits of being a firm that is financially strong and prepared for market shock. Your competitor falters. Its margins compress, as costs increase. You might consider a price drop to amplify the pressure on the competitor. A buy-out might be an option, whereby you acquire the competitor. And why? Namely, the reward for risk management is generally not manifested in incremental improvements and small changes. Winning with risk management is generally observed as a shock, a positive shock or opportunity that comes as a result not only of fortuitous market conditions but also of preparation and diligence.

Sam Zell, the Chicago billionaire and businessman extraordinaire, has often commented that he has a unique talent in understanding risk. Warren Buffett has commented that he has a unique capability to deploy capital. In considering their respective track records, it might be hard to disagree. However, each has benefited from acquiring assets after negative shocks and then laying claim to gains thereafter. There is a specific realization that risks alter the value of assets, especially during shocks.

More mechanically, it is evident that shocks impact both market participants and firms disproportionately based on their assets and strategy. Shocks amplify the signal and define the fittest. Predicting the shock is not the goal, as we have said, but preparing for a shock, any shock, becomes the goal. Management may take specific actions to reduce its exposure to shocks, reducing the persistence and contagion in risks and preparing for downturns in particular markets. Such action is not simply defensive and protective of company assets but should be followed-up with the realization that opportunities to grow and invest are best after shocks. Claiming those opportunities and being in a position to do so are the goals of winning with risk management.

Case Questions

1. Consider an industry of your interest. What shocks have happened?
2. How have the shocks been realized by the market participants?
3. Why is predicting a shock, mathematically or statistically, so challenging?
4. Reflect on the DJIA movements in 2008 and how the market moved dramatically. What does this tell us about the role of information in markets and propensity for shocks?
5. Did the industry fully recover from the shocks?
6. How long until recovery (if fully achieved) was realized?

Chapter 4
Operations Pose Embedded Risks to the Enterprise

It is not often that a man can make opportunities for himself. But he can put himself in such shape that when or if the opportunities come he is ready.
 — *Theodore Roosevelt, US President and Nobel Laureate*

Risk is often said to be the "cost of doing business." However, in that phrase, it is not expected that the business can be lost forever. The long-term and persistent nature of risk is clearly undesirable. The unfortunate reality is that some business risks are persistent, impacting the firm for a long period of time and impacting the strategy and ability to operate. Such risks are very often observed in operational risk. Let us consider a case that highlights this curious nature of risk. It will highlight some key observations about risk and how it is best handled.

Fire at the Plant — Hazard as a Trigger for Operational Risk

On March 17, 2000, a fire occurred at the Royal Philips Electronics plant in Albuquerque, New Mexico as a result of a power surge. The plant supplied critical semiconductor chips for both Ericsson LM and Nokia Corporation — companies that together received 40% of the plant's chip production. At the time, both companies were about to release new cell phone designs that necessitated the chips.[10] While "smaller than the nail on a baby's pinkie," the chips were of utmost importance as they allowed the

---

[10]Sheffi, Y. (2007). "Building a Resilient Organization," *The Bridge*, 37(1), 30–36.

"mobile phone to do anything from sound amplification to finding radio frequencies."[11]

Operators at Philips initially suggested that chip production would resume within a week of the incident. This information was conveyed quickly within Nokia where managers began to monitor the situation daily and discuss solutions to remediate the situation. At Ericsson, the technician that received the initial report from Philips did not sense the urgency of the matter and failed to pass the information along to his superiors. When Philips later communicated that normal production would be delayed for several more weeks, Nokia was able to expeditiously locate alternative suppliers. Ericsson's management however was unprepared for the news and the further delay. As a result, Ericsson had to postpone the launch of a new phone at a critical point in the cell phone industry, and its market share suffered. The subsequent losses helped bring about Ericsson's decision to exit the independent manufacturing sector of mobile phones and propel Nokia as one of the largest mobile phone manufacturers in the world.

Damage Assessment — Seeking Disconfirming Information

The fire at the Royal Philips Electronics plant lasted less than ten minutes before workers and sprinklers extinguished the flames. While it was certain that the fire destroyed a large stock of semiconductor chips, operators were unsure of the damage within Philips' clean rooms. Clean rooms are essential to semiconductor chip production as they maintain the sterile conditions needed in the manufacturing process. Philips relayed in initial conversations with both Ericsson and Nokia that it would take a week before production would return. However, Philips had underestimated the extent of the damage caused by smoke, soot and water in the clean rooms. Returning the clean rooms to an operational state would take six weeks.

Organizations often underestimate damage in the wake of a catastrophe. The role of post-crisis or post-accident investigation is difficult in that the findings may inherently challenge the optimistic outlook of the enterprise and there are pressures to minimize disconfirming information. In the case

---

[11]Latour, A. (2001). "Trial by Fire: A Blaze in Albuquerque Sets off Major Crisis for Cell-Phone Giants," *Wall Street Journal*, January 29, A1.

of Philips, the role of assessing damage and reporting it was impacted by this organizational bias.

Philips and the Cell Phone Industry — Embedded Operational Risks

In 2000, Philips' semiconductor division "was churning out chips at a rate of eighty million a day; these chips were used in 80% of the mobile phones sold worldwide."[12] Aside from mobile phones, these chips were needed in many other consumer electronic devices that were in demand such as new cars, digital cameras, and mobile memory devices. Owing to this growing demand, surplus capacity was scarce.

Cell phone manufacturers depended on a steady supply of chips to satisfy a customer base that replaced phones often in keeping with the latest trends. Suppliers to the cell phone manufacturers became "increasingly reliant on the replacement market," which meant speed to market became a critical sales factor.[13] The just in time delivery model was at work and principles of lean operation were well entrenched in the manufacturing of cell phone components. This was especially true in an industry with short product cycles of just 18 months, where each shelf week helped the company recoup research and development costs.[14] However, just in time delivery and lean operations by nearly all of the suppliers in the supply chain of cell phone components posed embedded risks for all participants in the industry.

In 2000, cell phone companies saw that cell phones would transform into converged devices with 3G networks that promised wireless mobile access in combination with basic phone functions. Companies invested billions in this vision, creating the infrastructure, establishing 3G licenses and investing in new product design. These investments seemed guaranteed to produce high

---

[12]Mukherjee, A. S. (2009). "The Fire That Changed an Industry: A Case Study on Thriving in a Networked World," in *The Spider's Strategy: Creating Networks to Avert Crisis, Create Change, and Really Get Ahead.* Upper Saddle River, NJ: FTPress.

[13]Brown-Humes, C. and D. Roberts (2001) "Ericsson Nears Surrender in Handset Battle," *Financial Times*, January 26.

[14]Daniel, C. (2000). "Ericsson Faces More Than Just a Test of Fire," *Financial Times*, July 24, 19.

returns since Internet use was doubling every 100 days and there was strong growth in worldwide mobile cell phone penetration.[15]

Nokia Corporation — Background

The Nokia Corporation was founded in 1865 and had started in wood pulp production. By 2000, it was the world's leader in cell phone sales and the largest corporation in Europe by market capitalization. In 1999, Nokia generated $19.9 billion in net sales out of a workforce of 60,000 employees. It had developed a strong brand synonymous with price accessibility and mass appeal for its cell phones, which accounted for 70% of its revenue.[16] It also had a small network sales division that comprised 25% of its revenue.

The transformation from a "stodgy Finnish conglomerate, making everything from rubber boots and cables to lavatory paper and televisions," to the Nokia of today, began in the 1970s when leadership invested in technology and electronics like radiotelephones.[17] When Ericsson's Nordic Mobile Telephone network (the first international network) went up in the early 1980s, Nokia already had presence in basic hardware manufacture; it launched one of the first consumer mobile phones in 1984, the Talkman.

As the Soviet Union collapsed in the early 1990s, so too did trade channels for Nokia's traditional product line. Demand for mobile handsets was increasing. However, Nokia did not have capacity to expand production until the head of the handset division, Jorma Ollila, channeled new resources into the division and one year later as Chief Executive, "bet the company on becoming a mobile-phone pure-play."[18] In 1999, Nokia sold 128 million phones.

Ericsson Corporation — Background

Ericsson was another large and established Scandinavian firm, based in Sweden and founded in 1876 as a telephone manufacturer. In 2000, it had

---

[15] "Beyond the Bubble," *The Economist*, October 11, 2003.

[16] Latour, A. (2001). "Trial by Fire: A Blaze in Albuquerque Sets off Major Crisis for Cell-Phone Giants," *Wall Street Journal*, January 29, A1.

[17,18] "A Finnish Fable EspoO," *The Economist*, October 14, 2000.

100,000 employees and generated net sales of $25 billion. Nokia dominated the handset business, but Ericsson's strength was in network sales.

Ericsson tried to keep pace with its telephone-manufacturing competitors, competing early on in the twentieth century with AT&T. However, by mid-century it took on a more prominent role in telecom technology and landline networks, before pioneering early cellular networks in the 1980s. At the start of the twenty-first century, the company was by "far the world's dominant supplier of mobile networks," with 70% of sales coming from the network division.[19]

Ericsson continued to participate in telephone, now mobile production, despite criticism that the firm focused on uncompetitive upscale models. While the company did experience sales growth in 1999, its handset sales were still below that of Nokia at 43.3 million. Margins were also slim at 1 or 2% for handsets while its network business continued to experience "rapid sales growth and strong margins."[20] The opposite was true for Nokia, whose margins were 24% for hardware while its networks were "weak by comparison, with lower growth and falling margins."[21] Between the criticism and slim margins, Ericsson struggled in the fast-moving handset market. New products were needed to appease the critics and Ericsson hoped the first foray into Bluetooth Technology would do just that.

The Nokia Response — Reacting to the Risk

A few days after the fire, a supply manager at Nokia noticed a flag in the system about chip inflow from Philips. Following a pre-established process, word eventually reached "Tapio Markki, the top component purchasing manager."[22] On March 20, Philips briefed the Nokia team about the incident, which detailed the news about the fire and the estimated week-long delay. Markki sent word of the fire up the chain to Pertti Korhonen, the Senior Vice President of Operations, Logistics, and Sourcing, in Nokia's

---

[19] "Ericsson Gets Alarm," *Financial Times*, October 23, 2000.

[20,21] "Nokia/Ericsson," *Financial Times*, April 29, 2000, 28.

[22] Mukherjee, A. S. (2009). "The Fire That Changed an Industry: A Case Study on Thriving in a Networked World," in *The Spider's Strategy: Creating Networks to Avert Crisis, Create Change, and Really Get Ahead.* Upper Saddle River, NJ: FTPress.

mobile handset division. Korhonen then implemented a series of tracking applications in the system for the five components Philips made at the plant and began placing daily, instead of weekly, calls to Philips about inventory.[23]

On March 31, Philips phoned Nokia with news that the damage to the clean rooms was worse than earlier estimates and that it would be weeks before they could restart production. The Nokia team assessed that the shortage could "prevent the production of some 4 million handsets and could have an impact on 5% of their annual production."[24] The assessment was unacceptable, and a team of 30, including Korhonen and the CEO Jorma Ollila, took action from several angles. First, Nokia engineers re-examined whether a chip redesign would allow Nokia to access alternative suppliers. The team then found new suppliers for three of the five components available independently of Philips — two suppliers in the US and Japan responded with the requisition within five days. Under pressure, Philips secured more inventory from the Netherlands and Shanghai plants after expanding production. By the end of the search, Nokia had their chips and as a bonus, engineers had "developed new ways to boost production at the Albuquerque plant — creating an additional two million chips when the plant came back online."[25]

This global effort resulted in Nokia avoiding production losses because of supply chain disruption, an event which years earlier had cost the firm millions. Owing to the previous setback, Jorma Ollila had "instituted the practice of sending executive hit squads to bottlenecks and giving them authority to make on-the-ground decisions."[26] After the fire, this practice worked in tandem with other company practices, such as an input monitoring system and a clear channel of communication between all personnel levels. As a result, the fire was a minor hiccup for Nokia.

---

[23]Latour, A. (2001). "Trial by Fire: A Blaze in Albuquerque Sets off Major Crisis for Cell-Phone Giants," *Wall Street Journal*, January 29, A1.

[24,25]Handfield, R. (2011). *How Do Supply Chain Risks Occur? A Managerial Framework for Reducing the Impact of Disruptions to the Supply Chain.* Available at http://scm.ncsu.edu/public/risk/risk3.html.

[26]Latour, A. (2001). "Trial by Fire: A Blaze in Albuquerque Sets off Major Crisis for Cell-Phone Giants," *Wall Street Journal*, January 29, A1.

The Ericsson Response — Risks Persists

Ericsson managers did not know about the fire until weeks after the staff technician received Philips' initial message. One-week delays were common and "the fire was not perceived as a major catastrophe," according to an Ericsson spokeswoman.[27] When Philips phoned technicians again on March 31 for revised estimates and to inform them that the short-term supply of chips was uncertain, the top brass at Ericsson continued to remain in the dark about the fire.

It was early April before the Ericsson executive team was informed of the fire. By then, the outlook was bleak because Ericsson had streamlined its supply chain by making Philips its sole provider.[28] Moreover, Nokia had already ordered all extra supplies of chips that existed elsewhere. When Ericsson finally announced the loss to the market, Ericsson shares fell more than 11%.[29]

The component shortage at Ericsson helped delay the launch of the first mobile phone to feature Bluetooth Technology, the T36. Company officials estimated $400 million in direct revenue losses, which insurance would somewhat cover.[30] However, the disruption in the mobile phone division was obvious and the new phone had lost critical shelf time. While Ericsson adjusted its shipping configuration to mitigate future shortages, analysts agree Ericsson's endeavor in mobile handsets was floundering.

By the end of October 2000, Ericsson lost 3 percentage points in global market share to Nokia. By the end of the year, Ericsson had to discontinue mass-market expansion of the T36 citing too short of a market life. The company incorporated it into another model that came out in 2001, the T39 — more than half a year after it had initially announced the T36.[31] The losses were astounding in the annual report, with nearly $1.68 billion

---

[27]Latour, A. (2001). "Trial by Fire: A Blaze in Albuquerque Sets off Major Crisis for Cell-Phone Giants," *Wall Street Journal*, January 29, A1.

[28]Eglin, R. (2003). "Can Suppliers Bring Down Your Firm," *Sunday Times*, November 23.

[29]MacCarthy, C. (2000). "Ericsson Handset Side Hit by Fire," *Financial Times*, July 22, 17.

[30]Latour, A. (2001). "Trial by Fire: A Blaze in Albuquerque Sets off Major Crisis for Cell-Phone Giants," *Wall Street Journal*, January 29, A1.

[31]"Ericsson Gets Alarm," *Financial Times*, October 23, 2000.

lost in the company's mobile phone division, "which the company blamed on a slew of component shortages."[32]

Unlike Ericsson, Nokia's annual report that year made no mention of component shortages or the fire. Moreover, even with the rapid response with which it handled the fire, Nokia continued enhancing its supply chain operation and installed "dynamic visibility systems to track major shipments of all of its major suppliers establishing a thorough risk management assessment of each of its major suppliers, and creat[ing] contingency fallback plans for disaster planning at each location."[33]

The Bubble Bursts — Risks Impact the Industry

The telecommunications bubble coincided with, and was largely a consequence of, the larger dotcom bubble that burst in mid to late 2000. The telecommunications industry experienced mass "fraud, bankruptcy, debt and destruction of shareholder value," in part, because investments were based on incorrect predictions about the growth of the Internet and accompanying goods and services.[34] Some sources believed Internet traffic doubled every 100 days, but in reality it doubled *every year* between 1997 and 2003. Moreover, growth in worldwide mobile phone penetration also peaked in 1999, at 52%, and fell abruptly in 2001 to 29%. Companies had invested billions in fiber-optic networks, 3G spectrum, and sophisticated converged devices. The markets forecasted quick returns coming from consumers demanding the newest replacement phones. In fact, many cell phone manufacturers thought that 3G would bring momentum to the industry and persuade consumers to update their handhelds for the fastest access to a mobile Internet.

However, mobile phone designs did not reflect this vision and failed to incorporate the Internet in an appealing way. As one analyst at Dow Jones said, "Are there really that many people who want to surf the Web on a cell phone's two-inch screen?"[35] Moreover, the bubble and 9/11 stalled

---

[32]Sheffi, Y. (2007). "Building a Resilient Organization," *The Bridge*, 37(1), 30–36.
[33]Handfield, R. (2011). *How Do Supply Chain Risks Occur? A Managerial Framework for Reducing the Impact of Disruptions to the Supply Chain.* Available at http://scm.ncsu.edu/public/risk/risk3.html.
[34]"Beyond the Bubble," *The Economist*, October 11, 2003.

consumer markets in some parts of the world, and companies still needed to invest in more 3G licenses and networks to offer quality coverage. It would be some time before companies would see a return on these heady investments, with 3G networks and useful cell phone designs finally appearing mainstream in 2007.

Post Bubble: Ericsson and Nokia — Different Risk Treatments, Different Fates

The bubble hit Ericsson in early 2001 when the company terminated approximately 20% of its workforce and outsourced its cell-phone production. By April 2001, Ericsson exited the domain of independent manufacture of mobile phones, and created a 50-50 venture with Sony that became Ericsson's new production shop. As of 2009, the Sony-Ericsson brand was the fifth largest producer of mobile phones by sales, with just 4.5% of the market share in 2009 — down from 7.6% in 2008.[36]

The telecommunications industry eventually recovered from the bubble, before again facing slower demand brought on by the global recession in the late 2000's. As of 2010, Ericsson was a much smaller company at 82,500 employees with plans for further reductions. In 2009, net sales were stagnant at $29 billion.

Nokia weathered the telecommunications bubble in the mid to late 2000s better than its competitors by anticipating the downturn; they slowed hiring, shelved new product development, and lowered expenses by outsourcing production.[37] While there were layoffs, they were not as significant. Despite less than ideal growth figures, the company grew considerably since 1999 and continued to maintain its position as sales leader with a 2009 market share of 36.4%.[38] Its nearest competitor in 2009 was Samsung with only 19.5% of market share.

---

[35] Rapoport, M. (2010). "In the Money: Now It's a Wireless Bubble That's Popping," *Dow Jones News Service*, July 27, *Factiva*.

[36] "Top-5 Mobile Phone Vendors Lost Market Share in 2009," *Cellular News*. Available at http://www.cellular-news.com/story/42084.php.

[37] Guyon, J. and P. Hjelt (2002). "Nokia Rocks Its Rivals; Flawless Execution Put Nokia on Top. Will Customer Love Keep It Growing?" *Fortune*, March 4, 145(5), 115.

[38] "Top-5 Mobile Phone Vendors Lost Market Share in 2009," *Cellular News*. Availablle at http://www.cellular-news.com/story/42084.php.

Supply Chain Risk Require Dynamic Capabilities

Nokia's rapid response in managing a supply chain disruption demonstrated to its shareholders and the public its competency in not only supply chain management but also operational risk management. Ericsson's handling demonstrates that an insufficient response to a disruption is costly and hazard insurance may only cover the immediate loss of inventory/physical assets and not total revenue loss or brand damage. As globalization enables the use of worldwide supply chains, disruptions are still possible due to such things as border issues, terrorists, natural disasters, or labor disputes. In fact, the cost of recovery in natural disasters has increased since the 1960s, with their cost having risen "by a factor of 10."[39] In effect, it is important for companies to consider the threats posed to supply chain disruption and their associated costs, in an operational risk frame.

A typical drop in the share price after negative supply news is about 8% in the first two days, which is particularly damaging relative to "a delay in the launch of a new product (which triggers an average fall of 5%), [or] untoward financial events (an average drop of 3–5%), or IT problems (2%)."[40] As Ericsson experienced, a new product delay may accompany supply chain disruption when global capacity for an input is scarce. The impact is not limited to the short term as "operating income, return on sales, and return on assets, are all significantly down in the first and second year after a disruption."[41]

To avoid these costs, companies must implement an operational risk design with standards for "strategy, processes, and values ... supported by technology," which provides the company with options to adapt and respond to supply chain problems.[42] Part of this flexibility may be addressing the issue of a lean supply chain. While less costly, a lean supply chain creates risk through a complete reliance on a sole provider.

---

[39] Eglin, R. (2003). "Can Suppliers Bring Down Your Firm," *Sunday Times*, November 23.

[40,41] "A Survey of Logistics: When the Chain Breaks," *The Economist*, June 17, 2006.

[42] Mukherjee, A. S. (2009). "The Fire That Changed an Industry: A Case Study on Thriving in a Networked World," in *The Spider's Strategy: Creating Networks to Avert Crisis, Create Change, and Really Get Ahead*. Upper Saddle River, NJ: FTPress.

Thus, companies need to consider the tradeoffs in their risk management strategy between holding inventories or using multiple supply sources and avoiding disruption. However, a completely risk-averse strategy in a supply chain may result in a company carrying too much inventory or spreading suppliers over such a large geographic range–an approach that is prohibitively costly and which smaller firms might not afford. Thus, companies must tailor fit a strategy that balances costs with risk-management practices to avoid the large direct and indirect costs of a disruption.

Recovery Efforts Are Critical to Preventing Persistent Risks

The fire in New Mexico was a costly setback for Ericsson that helped end its independent mobile phone production. It revealed that the company's mismanagement of its cell phone brand extended to its operational risk practices because it failed to recognize how such supply chain disruptions impacted the bottom line. In contrast, Nokia's awareness of the importance of getting products to shelves, including its acute monitoring of input supply, helped the company contain the fire.

After the fire, Nokia was not immune from falling sales and a sinking share price in November of 2002 that was "less than a third of what it was at its peak in June 2000."[43] However, it performed better than its competitors due to the preparation of management in weathering the overall market changes and applying the same logistical and risk management acumen that managed the fire. As the bubble's repercussions subsided, Nokia still occupied strong market share over its nearest competitor. It also continued receiving numerous accolades, including a signal distinction as "Europe's biggest corporate success story of the last decade," according to the *Financial Times* in 2004.[44] Nokia's next big challenge in the second decade of the twenty-first century will be facing competition from Apple and potentially, Google — a new test for the old-pros in Finland.

For Nokia, the risk was managed, minimized, and even became an opportunity to seek competitive advantage. The risk event ended and was finite.

---

[43]Brown-Humes, C., R. Budden, and A. Gowers (2002) "Nokia Forecasts Rise in Handset Market," *Financial Times*, November 18, 17.
[44]Brown-Humes, C. (2004). "Vote Ollila," *Financial Times,* January 9.

For Ericsson, the risk persisted and drastically impacted its strategy and overall fate. The treatment of information by these firms and the processes for risk identification and risk response set the stage for the final outcomes.

Case Review

This case highlights many aspects of risk and the impact of the treatment of information on how risk is manifested at the firm. The case is also an excellent example of the perils of single supplier operations and how this led the electronics industry to a mode of operations that encourages multiple sourcing.

Ultimately, we see that actions by Nokia to remedy the risk posed by the disturbance in supply allowed it to maintain operations and gain market share at the expense of Ericsson. This is classic. Risk management is manifested as a competitive advantage. Let us consider the key activities that contributed to Nokia's advantage in handling of this risk. Figure 4.1 outlines these.

The Nokia Reaction

- On March 20, 2000 Nokia detects that shipments from Philips have slowed (within 3 days of fire!)
- Philips case placed on "special watch list"
- Daily calls to Philips
- Nokia quickly determined that loss of chips could impact over 5% of company sales
- Nokia offers to send "help"
  - Initially declined
  - Nokia presses for CEO level meetings
  - Nokia scans international market for chip supply (and buys what was available)
  - Nokia and Philips operate closely ("as one") to remedy Nokia's issues

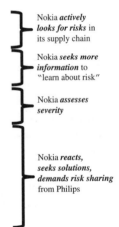

Nokia *actively looks for risks* in its supply chain

Nokia *seeks more information* to "learn about risk"

Nokia *assesses severity*

Nokia *reacts, seeks solutions, demands risk sharing* from Philips

Figure 4.1.   Nokia's response to the supply issue.

Timeline Corporate Activity/Capability

In contrast, Ericsson executives didn't even know about the fire until early April, by which time Nokia had already secured its supply of chips. Ericsson scrambled to locate new sources for the chips because it had previously streamlined its supply chain by making Philips the sole provider. This search delayed the debut of its much-anticipated T36, the first mobile phone to feature Bluetooth technology, by six months and proved a fatal blow to Ericsson's independent production of mobile phones. When it finally announced the loss of the chips to the market in April, shares fell by more than 11%. By April 2001 Ericsson had launched a 50-50 venture with Sony for producing cell phones, and by 2010 it was a much smaller company, having dropped to 82,500 employees from 100,000 in 2000.

Consider the impact to Ericsson. Ultimately, Ericsson lost market share and its ability to launch a new phone. This is an example of how operational risk can be persistent and pose great contagion to the firm. For Nokia, the adept handling, rapid response, and quick assessment of the impact to the firm's profit function allowed it to contain the risk. Contagion did not happen at Nokia and the supply chain disruption was manifested as a minor (and finite) operational loss.

In the two figures (Figures 4.2 and 4.3), we see that the mapping of risks realized by Nokia and Ericsson led to different levels of contagion and persistence. Nokia was able to block contagion of the operational risk and end the impact of the supply chain shock (preventing persistence).

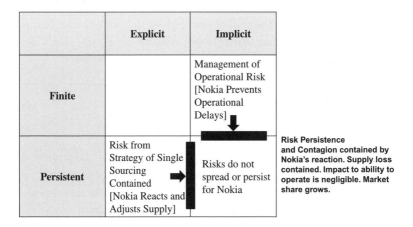

	Explicit	Implicit	
Finite		Management of Operational Risk [Nokia Prevents Operational Delays]	
Persistent	Risk from Strategy of Single Sourcing Contained [Nokia Reacts and Adjusts Supply]	Risks do not spread or persist for Nokia	**Risk Persistence and Contagion contained by Nokia's reaction. Supply loss contained. Impact to ability to operate is negligible. Market share grows.**

Figure 4.2.   Nokia's actions prevent persistence and contagion in risk.

	Explicit	Implicit
Finite		Management of Operational Risk
Persistent	Risk from Strategy of Single Sourcing	Risks realized include inability to operate for prolong time and miss of next generation technology

Risk Persistence occurs as small perturbation in Ericsson's supply chain prevents product launch and results in large market share loss.

Risk Contagion occurs as strategy to rely on a single supplier is not revisited. Ericsson, effectively, exits market.

Figure 4.3.   Ericsson's risks lead to persistence and contagion.

For Ericsson, the lack of both risk metrics and an understanding of the impact of the loss to the enterprise left them unprepared to take action. The mapping of Ericsson's operational risk shows the presence of both contagion and persistence. The seemingly small delay in shipping led to an inability to sell in a key market segment and proved to be a material enterprise loss.

Operational risk, especially in complex systems, poses a unique danger. Given the complexity of systems and reliance on outsourcers and automation, operational risks can trigger additional risks, growing in contagion. The inflexibility of such systems is also an issue as impacts can linger for long periods of time after the risk event. This is the unfortunate feature of persistence. Examine complex operational systems, especially global supply chains, for risk events that can cause contagion and persistence.

Risk Management Lessons

Proactive information gathering

Nokia's proactive approach to measuring disturbances in the supply chain provided it an opportunity to identify an anomaly worthy of further examination. This is akin to a Knightian uncertainty being unraveled and discerned for measurement. For Ericsson, the supply chain perturbation remained an uncertainty. The activity of proactively gathering information, searching for information on the unknown is also a corporate discipline. In many industries, it might be considered due diligence, confirmation, or even be considered an audit activity. The ability of a firm to seek such new information and then relate that information to critical processes and the overall profit function is what allows risk to be contained.

Measuring risk requires information and an ability to acquire it when it is not known. This suggests 1) investments in information systems, 2) data collection and creation, 3) development of risk metrics, and 4) authority of individuals to respond to information when it becomes available. These key components are beyond the science or mathematics of risk, but are tied to the execution of risk management in practice.

Investments in information systems

It is difficult to consider risk-relevant information unless it is organized and related to previous observations. Although many software vendors sell solutions for doing this, the reason for having information available and organized is to search for patterns and to understand when and if key indicators have changed. Identification of anomalies in key risk indicators is important in predicting what will likely happen next. Organizing the data and relating it to your firm's operations and profit may indeed require a large Enterprise Resource Planning (ERP) installation or a simple spreadsheet. The solution is driven by scale and complexity, the capability of having data accessible and related permits the understanding of risk.

Take inventory of the information that your firm has. Is it accessible? Can you answer how key risk indicators have changed over the last year or 5 years? Why have these changes occurred? Focus on the functionality to make such information accessible to management when developing an information system.

Data collection and creation

In order to seek competitive advantages, firms must constantly be looking for new and relevant measurements to identify risks internally and externally. In the case of Nokia, they had developed a rather advanced measure of supply chain perturbations and integrated that successfully with the communication tools of the firm. Ultimately, this served as an advantage. In the Financial Crisis of 2008, various credit card lenders mined credit card transactional information for signs that a customer had lost employment or income. Examples such as changes in shopping behavior and types of stores frequented (from premium to discount) did prove valuable in identifying accounts subject to new credit risk. In such an example, the credit card lenders created new data through metrics (before and after). Credit card lenders could have waited for credit bureau information to report changes in customer risk, but at that point, the information is available across lenders and the advantage is lost. Thus, it is insufficient to rely on market available data solely for risk decisions. Creation of new risk data provides a competitive advantage that is worthy of exertion in the marketplace, not different than competitive advantages in operating costs or labor.

In Apgar's *Risk Intelligence*, he suggests that competitive risk information is in fact the basis for competitive advantage. The most extreme example, perhaps, is to know the price (or likely price) of a stock tomorrow.[45] Removing this competitive advantage is the basis for insider trading laws. However, the advantage of information on a firm's ability to operate is equally valuable and rooted deeply in capital decisions. Creating incentives and a culture that stimulates the nearly scientific-like pursuit of new data is critical.

Although it is hard to drive a culture of cultivating great data in and of itself, it is easier to drive a team to use data to make recommendations to management. In doing so, the team will realize that data is needed to support claims and evaluations. Look at the funding and project approval processes in your firm. Consider how risk and risk information are considered as appropriations are made. Require that projects fairly and adequately present data on risk in order to gain funding. Also require an update on how key risk indicators have changed. It will drive the measurement of risk and creation of new risk variables in the enterprise.

Development of risk metrics

The discipline of proactive information gathering as part of risk management is tied to 1) developing policies for reporting risk and information and 2) using metrics to report risk. John Hunkin, Chairman and Chief Executive Officer, Canadian Imperial Bank of Commerce (CIBC), stated it very well when he said: "To manage risks facing an institution, we must have a clearly defined set of risk policies and the ability to measure risk."

---

[45] Apgar, D. (2006). *Risk Intelligence: Learning to Manage What We Don't Know.* Boston, MA: Harvard Business School Press.

Related to the ability to create new data is the ability to relate that data to the firm. More specifically, developing risk metrics allow management and all levels of the team to understand how risks have changed. Risk metrics also allow management to assess the value and improvement of investments in the mitigation of risks that are unattractive. In the example of Nokia and Ericsson, it is stunning that Ericsson dismissed delays in shipments from suppliers "as typical" or "normal." Although delays may happen frequently, the delays are potentially different in nature. This is an important differentiation. A delay due to a missed freight connection is different than a delay due to a shipment never happening. These have different natures and impacts to the firm. Unraveling this uncertainty, as Knight would guide us, leads us to the underlying risk. Building on the example of delayed shipments, Ericsson might have considered a new shipment verification process (at some cost). Various metrics might be appropriate such as number of shipment delays per month and duration of delays. All such metrics become valuable in measuring the risk of shipment delays and the investment of any process to improve performance.

In general, such risk metrics should be developed with a firm's specific operations in mind. Ultimately, these risk metrics should be suggestive of action on the part of management, meaning that the measures should be customized and proprietary. Such metrics can be developed even without an insider's perspective. As an example, I can recall a Morningstar analyst report that looked at the Starbucks Corporation's growth potential in the US. In a very thorough and clever manner, the analyst related the number of coffee outlets of competitors (e.g., Dunkin Donuts, McDonald's, etc.) and the number of Starbucks outlets per urban area to the population of working adults. This analysis was done before the Starbucks reduced the number of retail outlets in many US markets, providing a powerful foreshadowing or what ultimately unfolded. It showed clearly the over investment (and risk) in specific markets and the opportunity (under investment) in others. In this manner, the risk posed by Starbucks stock was being related to specific risk metrics, namely the stores and competitor stores per capita in specific cities. The example is powerful, in that risk metrics need not be complex or esoteric. The best are transparent and understandable by all in the business. The risk metrics should relate to the profit function of the firm. The use of charge-offs (dollars lost per dollars lent) in the credit card industry is simple and direct and allow for clear mapping of risks to the profit function of the firm. The airline industry, like many mature industries, has similar metrics. The metric of revenue passenger miles and aircraft yield speak directly to the risks posed by an airline's operating model and its performance.

It is important to note that it is not critical, at least initially, to have thresholds for risk metrics. For a firm that is developing risk metrics for the first time, assigning severity (acceptable versus intolerable) is not necessary. Directionally, the risk metrics should speak clearly. Increases in credit card charge-offs are dangerous to banks, but up to what level and under what economic conditions? The answers to such questions require the relation of data in time and across different conditions (economic, market, etc.). The value of risk metrics is that over time, such thresholds can be established and management can drive operations to meet specific risk metric goals.

Once the enterprise is focused on collecting relevant data for the purposes of project approval and tracking, the next step to developing risk metrics will be natural. Track the metrics in your organization. Consider both internal and external risk measures. Require that risk measures be reported on a regular basis. Ask why changes have occurred and seek explanations for unexpected changes. The discovery process is sure to provide new insights on risk drivers for the enterprise.

Authority of individuals to respond to information

In developing a winning risk management strategy, it is necessary that the entire team understand the importance of information and of communicating that information. In many ways, the Nokia-Ericsson case highlights the difference in how these two firms permitted decision-making. Nokia encouraged and facilitated dedicated SWAT teams to break through issues. Ericsson did not have the same dedication to risk management or flexibility in deploying human resources. The case notes that the call from Philips was handled by a staff technician which suggests that either the technician's interest or ability to influence management was low. That is not entirely or wholly the technician's fault. Communication happens between two parties. Was management receptive? If not, shouldn't management entrust its team to execute decisions? This of course requires a trust by management and follow-though by the team. Both are made easier when information is shared and made available across the enterprise. Setting the culture for this behavior is critical. The classic example comes from Hewlett Packard, where Mr. Packard had an "open door policy" for employees to bring concerns, information, and ideas. So true was this open door policy that the bright Californian sun bleached the whole wall of redwood cabinets, sparing those covered by the open door. The actual door and cabinets can be seen during a tour of HP headquarters.

In our world of mass centralization of processes and information, it is important to remember that information is not gathered at the nexus of the firm, but rather at its periphery. Decisions might be made at the nexus, but are executed at the touch points with suppliers and customers. So much information can be lost as it moves from the source to the headquarters and back to the operational interface. When data cannot be easily centralized, an approach that is worth considering is to entrust teams with a risk and information minded process for analyzing results. Consider the direction of J.W. Marriott, owner and founder of Marriott Hotels when he directed hotel managers to vary the price of rooms by the number of cars in the hotel parking lot and the competitor's parking lot. That is a rather unusual approach to pricing, but one that led to the practice of yield management which is the modern day approach to making pricing decisions in the hotel industry. It uses real-time information on market price and inventory levels to set prices and optimize profit. Yield management is now commonplace in the entire hotel industry. In today's focus on system integration, it would be tempting to wait until a complete and centralized process could handle everything. Such is the promise of many enterprise-wide communication and data systems. However, the value is not strictly in the system but rather in how teams can access and deploy the information. The execution can be easier if management has set the right tone and has made the right information available.

Examine in your enterprise how your teams can leverage information to make risk based decisions. Does that information need to come from a centralized process? If so, make it easy to use and accessible. Make reporting information from the periphery of the enterprise to the nexus easy and affirm the role of information providers, even when the information is disconfirming of expectations. If the information does not need to come from a centralized process or doing so is difficult, provide the support and culture that drives decisions from risk-based information.

Measurement of the competitive landscape

The Nokia-Ericsson case always reminds that for a winner there is a loser. In the case of Nokia, it was able to press forward with launching a new phone, while its major competitor was hampered by operational risks, coming from the Philips plant fire and ensuing delays. In this manner, gaining the upside associated with taking risks requires information on how risks are being manifested in the marketplace by competitors, not just about how your own firm is handling risk. Remember the best time for a price discount is when your competitor can least accept it. The benefit, clearly, is the condition left after the competitor realizes the uneven risk.

This has profound implications for an organization and impacts strategy and tactical operations. Although most people would see risk management as an internally focused function, we cannot lose sight of the need to relate the company's fate and advantage to the competitive landscape and marketplace. This requires measurement of competitors and the marketplace in general by developing risk-based metrics that measure the state of the marketplace and providing management the opportunity to understand how the competitor has changed due to industry-specific risks. When considering the Nokia-Ericsson case, I wonder if the Nokia engineers on site at the Albuquerque plant after the fire reported the lack of presence of Ericsson engineers or the lack of shipments to Ericsson. Such information is powerful on a competitor. Reporting that kind of information is a critical capability so that it can be leveraged for the purpose of gaining value. Simply put, information on competitors provides additional confidence that specific competitor risks are reduced and that upside risk or opportunity may be available.

Acquiring information on competitors has some legal limitation. However, competitors make a great deal of information available publicly. Consider examination of financial fillings and press releases of competitors. You may wish to look at job postings to determine needs (and weaknesses) on the part of competitors. Your customer, who may also be a customer of your competitor, can often offer great information about how the competitor is doing. Gather that information, track it, and aggregate it. Identifying your competitor's key risks will reveal where to move to next and provide guidance on operational strategies for gaining marketing.

Identification of alternatives

So much has been written about how risk management must measure the downside and loss impact to firms. Indeed, that function is critical, but if that is the sole purpose of the risk management office in a firm, it serves as little more than a calculator, exercising some calculus for the purpose of enumeration. The management of risk is of course dynamic and subject to changing needs. The nature of risk and its uncertainty suggest that those closest to studying risk have powerful lens on how risk can be altered for the best. As firms look to risk management professionals for expertise, it is important that that function of risk management also includes the cultivation of alternatives to assist the firm, especially in the midst of a crisis. In the Nokia-Ericsson case, the authority entrusted by Nokia's CEO to his team to make executive decisions and work on alternatives was key. For many organizations, the problem of a supplier not meeting service level requirements is viewed as one with simple legal remedy. Nokia recognized the value of the supplier to the firm's profit function and worked on an engineering solution. In this manner, the alternative identified changes the risk to Nokia. The ability to prevent a persistent risk and reduce its contagion to other forms of risk is a key benefit in the cultivation of alternatives. The development of solutions is paramount to the management of risks.

Building a risk management functionality in your team should include the ability and authority to propose alternatives and the capability of integrating such alternatives into business operations. Risk management teams should not be constructed purely from financial and audit teams. Inclusion of front-line and technical talent will prove useful in managing risks. Additionally, risk management is not a process reserved for senior managers or a select few. Make risk and its appreciation for preventing unexpected events a key focus for all members of the team.

For many large organizations, the development of risk professionals is done through a rotation program, whereby experts from lines of business rotate into a centralized risk management team and then leave to a new business line some time later. In such a dynamic organizational deployment, informal "alumni" or risk managers in nearly every business line are available, providing another level or access to information when needed. In such an approach, the risk management process at the firms evolves to include resident knowledge and specific technical knowledge that is relevant in measuring risk at the enterprise.

Focus on preventing persistence and contagion in risk

For Nokia and Ericsson, the risk source was essentially the same, a shock to the supply of a critical and irreplaceable component to their product. For Ericsson, the manifestation of the risk was persistent over a long period of time. Not only did the shortage of memory chips linger, the inability to make new products also impacted its ability to go to market with new phones. Ultimately, the risks weighed on market share and firm value and resulted in Ericsson merging with Sony. The risk from the supply shortage showed contagion and persistence at Ericsson, both dangerous features in operational risks. Ericsson, for many reasons, did not or could not control the persistent nature of the risk or its contagion.

Nokia, through its focused approach at understanding the risk and unraveling the uncertainty associated with it, prevented such risk from spreading to other aspects of its business, thereby limiting the exposure to a rather small, finite (and hardly significant) event. In this manner, both persistence and contagion of the risk were controlled. This was only possible because Nokia took action, action driven by risk metrics. Tactically, this was done by deploying a large team to overcome the "bottlenecks" in supply. The deployment of teams to tackle live crises is expensive. This cost is more like an investment against allowing a contagion to take root.

As Nokia scoured the international market for memory chips, it recognized that there were indeed few options. In securing essentially the entire international supply, Nokia surely made the calculated decision that buying inventory of memory chips was not only a good use of capital, but it would prevent the persistent nature of supply shocks in its business model. The purchasing of the memory chips also created an offensive or competitive advantage relative to Ericsson. In reality, managing an operational risk to a finite level versus allowing it to play out under market conditions, where contagion and persistence become issues, becomes advantage. The following schematic in Figure 4.4 highlights how operational risk impacts firms. It often appears as a shock and managing it to prevent contagion and persistence can result in a competitive advantage.

As your firm examines operational risk, consider a process to deploy resources to ensure the risk is prevented from becoming persistent and causing contagion. This requires communication and involvement across business functions and business lines. The ability and flexibility to hold impromptu meetings and to specialize resources are critical. This requires flexibility on the part of the enterprise. Communication of information is also necessary in providing direction to the business lines impacted. Removing the stigma from an operational loss or perceived failure in one business line is key, because that will allow learning to occur so that the operational

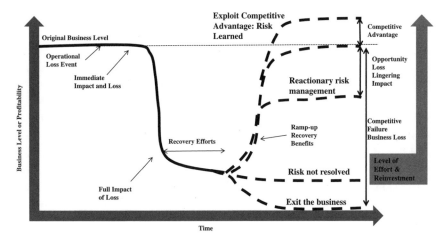

Figure 4.4.   Schematic on impact of operational risk through persistence and contagion.[46]

risk is not repeated or spread to another business line, or cause a new problem at the firm.

Protection of the firm's profits

The actions of Ericsson and Nokia are not only strikingly different; the fates of the firms are also strikingly different. One leaves the case thinking that Nokia had in place better risk metrics for its suppliers and perhaps a better communication system for such risk information, but ultimately, what is the benefit of risk management and its affiliated processes? It is to maintain and grow the firm! In this regard, protection of profits is the goal. Nokia succeeded and Ericsson failed. In examining the actions of Nokia, it was clear that early in their supply chain crisis, they recognized the potential impact of the disruption not just in terms of supply but of profits. For Ericsson, the same revelation and understanding were not in place. Protection of a firm's profit is, of course, tied to maintaining its market value, especially for a publicly held firm. The ability to protect profits is also tied to understanding the impact of any and all small deviations to the business model. Again, it is highly tied to seeking risk data. But more

---

[46]Sheffi, Y. (2007). "Building a Resilient Organization," *The Bridge*, 37(1), 30–36.

powerfully, protection of profits is tied to understanding early enough how an event or risk can impact profits. Building a corporate capability to assess the impact to firm profits is critical.

A friend of mine, who serves as a risk manager in a large financial services firm, summed up nicely what a risk manager does by saying: "A risk manager reminds the CEO during good times that success is due to his actions. In bad times, the risk manager convinces that CEO that things would be much worse without him."

Firms reward those who "create" profits. Shouldn't they also reward those who prevent losses to profits? In many ways that value to the firm is the same, although one might argue that the relationship is not linear. Protection of profits and efforts to do so are best examined with marketplace and competitor results. Examine how your firm performed relative to the market place and relative to your competitors. Did you have the same risks? Were you at a greater disadvantage? State your expectations for the firm's performance in light of the risks and consider the impact to protect profits. Reward protection of profits along with the creation of profits in the firm, as it will set the correct incentives for the team to consider risks in decisions.

Failures in risk management result in the transfer of assets between firms

The fallout of the Nokia-Ericsson case shows the dangerous persistent and implicit nature of many forms of operational risk. Although we can count many ways in which Ericsson failed to measure, report, and act on the risk, the largest tragedy for Ericsson is that it lost 3% of the world's cell phone market share to Nokia, during a fierce fight for dominance. Reclaiming such market share is difficult to do quickly and, of course, comes at great cost. The winning party, in this case Nokia, gains market share, an enormous asset, yet has paid nothing to Ericsson or its shareholders. Indeed, the shares and value of Ericsson plummet in response. Assets are transferred below par, simply due to the manifestation of the risks! In the case of Ericsson, there may be some argument that Philips owes them some remedy. However, even if a service level agreement were in place to protect Ericsson, no service level agreement could protect Ericsson from the contagion that prevented it from launching a new generation of phones, falling behind a major competitor, and losing a large piece of the world market share. None of that can be insured. Philips could likely argue that its operational risk (fire) was an act of God or was caused by *force majeure*, changing its obligation to its customers in many legal ways. It is an uncomfortable reminder that operational risk has peculiar properties. Its impact on the profit function of the firm is potentially catastrophic and may be persistent and non-negotiable (unlike same credit and market risks).

The transfer of market assets due to risks being differentially manifested in firms is seen many industries. Consider the concrete industry. CEMEX, the large Mexican-owned concrete supplier has made a name by entering markets at low prices and driving smaller competitors out of business. In the aftermath of a competitor shutting down, it is often CEMEX that buys the idle concrete plant.[47] In doing so, CEMEX acquires a plant at a bargain, prevents the entry of a competitor and lays claims to both physical assets (the plant) and marketplace assets (market share and pricing power) without paying a fair price. In fact, the fair price might be an unsolicited take-over offer that considers the competitor's market share before any price war. Similar examples exist in nearly every industry. The danger and opportunity are the same.

The opportunity, of course, is to better position your firm in terms of risk so that you may be in a position to claim or purchase competitors' assets at a discount. Tracking the competitive landscape through risk metrics is key. Taking action that accentuates the difference in how risk is manifested at your firm and your competitor is important. Knowing that your competitor is vulnerable and that you are stronger (and having information on this) allows one to win with risk.

Taking action on this information is the next step. Provide your firm the flexibility to acquire assets. Ensure that you have access to credit and capital to purchase assets during your competitor's demise. Consider short-term strategies that make operating more difficult for your competitor. Maybe a price cut, volume discount, change in tariff policy, or even a new product launch will provide your competitor with that difficulty needed to give up assets.

Case Questions

1. List what steps Nokia took that were correct and affirming of its position.

---

[47] Harvard Business School Cemex Cases 308-022, 308-023.

2. List what steps Ericsson should have taken. What did Ericsson fail to do?
3. Did Philips do anything wrong? Legally, ethically? Should they have communicated more strongly with Ericsson? Should they have split the supply of memory chips with Ericsson?
4. Is the fate of Ericsson the fault of a low-level technician taking the call from Philips?
5. What communication processes would you have put in place to prevent the loss of such critical information?
6. How would you seek information on critical and single source suppliers? Be specific.
7. Develop a list of risk metrics that you consider appropriate for managing a supplier.

Chapter 5

Reliance on Technology Increases Operational Risk — Often It Is Not Obvious

It is not because things are difficult that we dare not venture. It's because we dare not venture that they are difficult.
— Lucius Annaeus Seneca, Roman Philosopher
and Statesman

The dominance of the Information Age has changed many business models forever, altering how risk is manifested and even the risks that are faced. The role of information and digital transformation has many benefits to businesses and customers, but in this fast-paced movement to become efficient and digitally wise, operationally, businesses have often overlooked the risk impacts that technology can pose. Risk can become amplified and highly nuanced. Let us consider a case that highlights these complexities.

In November 2005, several local banks in Louisiana began noticing fraudulent charges on their customers' credit card accounts occurring from as far away as Mexico and southern California. In one instance in January 2006, the thieves spent nearly \$5,600 in just four days.[48] Across the Gulf of Mexico in Florida, thieves with more expensive tastes spent nearly \$8 million on high-end goods using gift cards purchased with stolen credit cards. While not clear at the time, both incidents were the result of the largest theft of customer data known thus far that compromised nearly 46 million credit card accounts belonging to TJX Companies' customers.

---

[48]Pereira, J. (2007). "Breaking the Code: How Credit-Card Data Went out Wireless Door — In Biggest Known Theft, Retailer's Weak Security Lost Millions of Numbers," *Wall Street Journal*, May 4, A1.

The scope of the crime was truly international, with fraud related to the stolen accounts appearing in more than a dozen countries.

Banks, who were forced to issue new cards, and credit card companies, who were required to reimburse fraudulent charges, turned their sights on TJX for compensation and an explanation. The company divulged that the hackers had been able to tap into their wireless payments system, which TJX had delayed upgrading after concluding that the risks of a breach were low and the costs of an upgrade were high. With hindsight being 20/20, the cost associated with this theft of customer data may have reached $1 billion.

TJX Companies — Background

TJX Companies, based in Framingham, Massachusetts, is the parent company of more than 2,600 discount fashion and home accessories stores in the US, Canada, and Europe. In the US, TJX runs T.J. Maxx, HomeGoods, and Marshalls. In Canada, it operates Winners, HomeSense, and Marshalls. In Europe, a subsidiary oversees T.K. Maxx and HomeSense. The majority of TJX's operations were part of a parent retail conglomerate, Zayre, whose first store opened in the US in 1956. In 1988, the Zayre chain of stores went bankrupt and a competing chain bought the Zayre stores and name. The remaining operation rebranded itself the TJX Companies and successfully expanded across the US. In their 2009 fiscal year, the company had net sales of $20.3 billion — up nearly 17% since 2006.

A Routine Audit Reveals a Hack

In the fall of 2006, TJX performed a series of audits on its wireless security system, the first of which revealed the company was in violation of Visa and MasterCard's Payment Card Industry Data Security Standards (PCI DSS). The auditor cited the "outmoded WEP encryption and missing software patches and firewalls," as not in compliance with the credit card companies' security standards for its merchants' payments systems.[49] A subsequent audit in December revealed peculiarities in the card data, prompting TJX

---

[49]Pereira, J. (2007). "Breaking the Code: How Credit-Card Data Went out Wireless Door — In Biggest Known Theft, Retailer's Weak Security Lost Millions of Numbers," *Wall Street Journal*, May 4, A1.

to alert the US Secret Service.[50] The Justice Department and the Royal Canadian Mounted Police also joined the investigation as it became clear the system was compromised.

Initial reviews suggested that system infiltration occurred starting mid-2005, but data revealed that the hackers had access to data as far back as 2003 from TJX operations in the US and Canada. At the request of the investigation team, TJX delayed announcement of the hack until January 2007, at which time they admitted that nearly 46 million accounts were impacted by the security breach.

Hackers Use "War Driving" to Strike TJX

The first major breach into TJX's system occurred in the summer of 2005 via a hacking method known as "war driving." Hackers involved in war driving would drive around retail centers scouting for stores that had permeable networks. Should a permeable network be detected, using a laptop, antennae, and mobile wireless connection, hackers would try to break into a company's system. They successfully infiltrated the Marshalls network, where they eventually established a connection with the main TJX server in Framingham and uploaded a sniffer program. This sniffer software was able to extract "data like credit card numbers from the network traffic."[51] About the same time, Sports Authority, OfficeMax, DSW, and Barnes & Noble, also experienced breaches because of war driving.

The criminals involved in war driving were no ordinary hackers — they were part of a large and sophisticated international network that bought and sold pilfered card information on the Internet. With direct access to the server, the hackers were able to download the server's card data into their own personal folders. After obtaining the data, the gang would then load blank cards from China with the numbers and then charge online buyers anywhere from $10 to more than $100 per card. Buyers could then withdraw money from ATMs or purchase merchandise they could later sell. The hacking exercise was not for sport, but for exploitation. The victim

---

[50]In the US, financial fraud falls under the Secret Service's mandate "for maintaining the integrity of the nation's financial infrastructure and payment systems." Available at http://www.secretservice.gov/criminal.shtml.

[51]Stone, B. (2008). "A Global Trail That Revealed a Cyber-Ring," *New York Times*, August 12, A1.

would ultimately be TJX. However, this embedded risk could have been avoided.

In Operational Risk, Details Are Critical

For TJX, two deficiencies in their security system became apparent: 1) the company had not updated its wireless system, and 2) the company continued to transmit and store data in an outdated approach. Both of these matters were in breach of their contracts with the credit card companies.

First, TJX neglected to migrate to Wifi Protected Access (WPA) wireless networks from the dated Wired Equivalent Privacy (WEP) system — the original mainstream wireless system. WPA became the standard soon after "security experts showed that hackers equipped with off-the-shelf tools could easily break" WEP's defenses in 2001.[52] Executives knew that WPA was a more superior system and that continued use of WEP posed a risk. In an email exchange dated 2005, the Chief Information Officer thought the company could "defer some spending from FY '07's budget by removing the money from the WPA upgrade," if everyone agreed the risks were small.[53] A different employee responded: "It must be a risk we are willing to take for the sake of saving money and hoping we do not get compromised."[54]

In February, Visa disclosed: "TJX was storing card number, expiration date, and card verification value codes, all of which are prohibited by PCI," and despite annual reports suggesting otherwise.[55] The storage of the data was likely the result of old software made unsafe by the fact that the hackers had access to all of the data in an unencrypted form, which also violated PCI DSS.[56]

TJX accepted an operational risk, assuming that its system would not be compromised. Although their assessment that the probability of a hack

---

[52]Arar, Y. (2003). *Better 802.11 Security*. Available at http://www.pcworld.com/article/111330/better_80211_security.html.

[53,54]Goodison, D. (2007). "TJX E-Mails Tell the Tale; Execs Knew of Info Security," *Boston Herald*, November 28, 23.

[55]Greenemeier, L. (2007). "Data Theft, Pushback, and the TJX Effect — Details of the Largest Customer Data Heist in US History Are Beginning to Emerge," *Information Week*, August 13, 36.

[56]Berg, G. G., M. S. Freeman, and K. N. Schneider (2008). "Analyzing the TJ Maxx Data Security Fiasco: Lessons for Auditors," *The CPA Journal*, August 1, 78(8).

might be quite small, they also implicitly assumed that the firm could detect or react to such a hack before much damage was experienced. This was incorrect. The movement to digital and electronic platforms has increased the severity of operational risk. When things go wrong, the damages can and do have greater severity. It is a reminder that operational risks are more quantum in nature than incremental.

Catching the "SoupNazi"

In the summer of 2007, investigators received a break in the case when officials gained access to a suspect's hard drive in Turkey. Experts were able to match the sniffer program on the drive as the same one used in the TJX case. They then analyzed messages between the suspect and his affiliates in the US, linking the crime to a well-known hacker whose username referenced a "Seinfeld" character. The Secret Service knew the username well.

In 2004, the Secret Service completed a major investigation into Operation Firewall, a case involving a global network of criminals charged with credit card fraud. They arrested more than twenty people, including one of the leaders of the cyber gang, Albert Gonzalez. He escaped prosecution after agreeing to become an informant. His criminal activities continued however, as he masterminded the TJX hack. In March 2010, he received concurrent sentences of 20 years for his crimes, including the TJX breach and participation in other breaches at Dave & Buster's, Hannaford Bros, Office Max, and elsewhere.

Operational Risk Leaves Unclear Liability

Following TJX's announcement of the data breach, investigators notified those impacted, and the affected parties sought to recuperate costs. However, lawsuits for such data breaches were legally complicated because as of 2010, no all-encompassing data security legislation existed at the Federal level concerning identity theft and fraud, apart from limiting consumers' financial liability. Laws concerning breach notification exist in some 40 states, but as of April 2010, only three states — Washington, Nevada, and Minnesota — had legislation holding retailers liable for data breaches stemming from PCI DSS compliance violations.

National legislation on the issue does not exist because legislators and industry analysts predict a race to the bottom should it occur; companies would treat any legislation as a baseline for action.[57] Moreover, policies are at the mercy of legislative cycles and are slow to change, suggesting government is unable to update legislation as quickly as the technology evolves. Furthermore, free marketers argue that companies that fail to enact proper standards suffer on the bottom line — a more impactful deterrent than from potential legal repercussions. In the case of TJX, the benefit of reduced expenses on security systems was the "gain" for accepting the operational risk of a permeable security system.

In many ways, the investment in security systems is competitive. Consider the example of a neighborhood where neighbors are investing in security protection technology. Those with less technology and protection are viewed as more attractive by the thieves. Homes with less protection are burglarized more. There ensues an unattractive economic game to constantly outdo your neighbor in protection, so that your home is not the most vulnerable to attack. In the context of electronic hacking, the sophistication and surveillance by hackers result in deliberate attacks. The reality is that operational risk via attacks is increased when protections are disproportionately less than others in the market. TJX learned that lesson all too well.

Operational Exposures Have High Leverage — The Cost of a Breach

In 2009, the total average cost of a breach for merchants was $6.75 million or $204 per compromised record.[58] For TJX, the total charge may be more than $1 billion over five years, after "costs for consultants, security upgrades, attorney fees, and added marketing."[59] Any further lawsuit settlements would be an additional burden. TJX has not released an official figure related to the data breach, but it settled several lawsuits:

1. $40.9 million to Visa Inc. and Fifth Third Bancorp
2. $24 million to MasterCard International

---

[57] "Retailer TJX Suffers Data Breach; PCI Compliance Unknown," *Warren's Washington Internet Daily*, January 19, 2007, 8(12).
[58] Ponemon Institute, *Ponemon Study Shows the Cost of a Data Breach Continues to Increase.* Available at http://www.ponemon.org/news-2/23.
[59] Pereira, J. (2007). "Breaking the Code: How Credit-Card Data Went out Wireless Door — In Biggest Known Theft, Retailer's Weak Security Lost Millions of Numbers," *Wall Street Journal*, May 4, A1.

3. $9.7 million in a settlement with 41 US states
4. $525,000 to four banks in Massachusetts

While the Federal Trade Commission (FTC) could not exact a fine, it settled with the company after charging it with engaging "in practices that, taken together, failed to provide reasonable and appropriate security for sensitive consumer information."[60] Every other year for the next 20 years, TJX will be subject to a FTC review by an independent third-party auditor, who will ensure the company is establishing and maintaining, "a comprehensive security program reasonably designed to protect the security, confidentiality, and integrity of personal information it collects from or about consumers."[61]

Industry Movements to Reduce Operational Risks — Standards in Security

In December 2004, American Express, Discover Financial Services, JCB International, MasterCard Worldwide, and Visa Inc. aligned their individual data security requirements with the Payment Card Industry Data Security Standard (PCI DSS). There are twelve major requirements within PCI DSS that regulate over 200 elements of a firm's security network and payments processing system. Compliance to the PCI DSS is legally binding via the "merchant agreement" between a retailer and their card company.

Card brands monitor merchants' compliance to the PCI DSS, the stringency of which depends upon the merchant's transaction volume. At the uppermost level, merchants must field an annual on-site review from an auditor and must perform quarterly systems scans using commercial software. The PCI Council regulates the list of auditors and software. Some card brands have offered incentives for compliance: Visa levies fines on merchants that are not compliant while offering financial bonuses to others who are on track towards compliance through its PCI Compliance Acceleration Program. One year after the TJX attack, PCI compliance among merchants

---

[60,61]Federal Trade Commission, Agency Announces Settlement of Separate Actions Against Retailer TJX, and Data Brokers Reed Elsevier and Seisint for Failing to Provide Adequate Security for Consumers' Data. Available at http://www.ftc.gov/opa/2008/03/datasec.shtm.

that processed more than 6 million card transactions was 40%.[62] In 2009, Visa listed compliancy among the same merchant level at 96%.[63]

The PCI DSS has been criticized by the retail lobby which believes that the standard is "a tool to shift risk off the banks' and credit card companies' balance sheets and place it on others."[64] Merchants further assert that in total, the cost of compliance is much larger than investments by credit card companies to employ better card technology.[65] In 2009, most merchants spent approximately $5 million each on PCI compliance.[66] Critics also cite the fact that compliance costs are uncertain, since new standards are emerging to reflect new technology or threats. In fact, the current standard has been revised four times in four years, and another release was in the works in October 2010.

Despite the criticism of PCI DSS by the retail lobby, individual retailers' commitment to PCI DSS compliance can still impact the reduction of credit fraud. In 2009, the Ponemon Institute conducted a survey of 517 security practitioners who are actively engaged in their companies' compliance efforts. The Ponemon Institute is a non-profit organization "dedicated to privacy, data protection and information security policy."[67]

The survey illustrates that merchants were not as committed managing data security and had a jaded perception of PCI DSS[68]:

1. 71% did not think their firm handles "data security as a strategic initiative," and only

---

[62]Vijayan, J. (2007). "Breaches Pushing Retailers to Adopt PCI," *Computer World*, August 6, 32.

[63]Visa, Inc., *Compliance Validation Details for Merchants*. Available at http://usa.visa.com/merchants/risk_management/cisp_merchants.html.

[64]Condon, S. (2009). "Retailers: Credit Card Data Inadequately Protected," *CNET News.com*, March 31.

[65] "Security Expert Believes Banks, not Merchants, Should 'Own up' to Responsibility to Protect Data," *Cardline*, January 19, 2007, 7(3).

[66]Ponemon Institute, *2009 PCI DSS Compliance Survey*. Available at http://www.ponemon.org/local/upload/fckjail/generalcontent/18/file/PCI%20DSS%20-Survey%20Key%20Findings%20FINAL4.pdf.

[67]Ponemon Institute, *Why We Are Unique*. Available at http://www.ponemon.org/about-ponemon.

[68]Ponemon Institute, *2009 PCI DSS Compliance Survey*. Available at http://www.ponemon.org/local/upload/fckjail/generalcontent/18/file/PCI%20DSS%20Survey%20Key%20Findings%20FINAL4.pdf.

2. 52% saw their organization actively managing "privacy and data protection risks."
3. 56% did not think PCI DSS compliance "improves their organization's data security posture."
4. 55% thought their CEO lacks "strong support for PCI DSS compliance efforts."
5. 60% did not think their organization has "sufficient resources to achieve compliance with PCI DSS."

First, it is apparent that data security is not a priority for firms despite the frequency of data breaches (79% of respondents reported a least one data breach).[69] Furthermore, PCI DSS is not seen as a wholly credible system for improving a company's security architecture, one which management does not strongly support and which is prohibitively expensive. It is unclear, however, whether a firm's position on data security may influence its perceptions of PCI DSS and any compliance requirement. Regardless, sentiments about data security and PCI DSS suggest that there is limited awareness on the risks that PCI DSS is attempting to eliminate, and that such attitudes might not prevent another TJX breach.

Market Inefficiencies in the Payments System

The inadequacy of the status quo in curtailing credit card fraud helps drive calls for a larger role by the government in the payment system. Other interested parties, especially economists, believe there is a role for regulation because of market failures such as asymmetric information and externalities that exist in the system. Moreover, government has an interest in the public continuing to benefit from an efficient and credible payments system, which would suffer should fraud escalate and Americans eschew electronic payment.[70]

However, for the firms dealing with the operational risk that comes from electronic fraud, there is little hope that the liability and exposure will be reduced. It will likely remain that firms taking possession of electronic

---

[69]Ponemon Institute, *2009 PCI DSS Compliance Survey*. Available at http://www.ponemon.org/local/upload/fckjail/generalcontent/18/file/PCI%20DSS%20Survey%20Key%20Findings%20FINAL4.pdf.
[70]Shreft, S. L. (2007). "Risks of Identity Theft: Can the Market Protect the Payment System?" *Economic Review*, Federal Reserve Bank of Kansas City, 4th Quarter, 26.

payment information will be responsible for the operational risk of handling that information. The increase in scale of businesses suggests that a breach or fraud case can easily impact many thousands if not millions of customers. The implication is that governmental regulation cannot ever remedy or reduce this exposure. It remains a responsibility for each firm to address.

Asymmetric Information Impacts Risk Choices

Asymmetric information exists between the customer and the merchant about the merchant's payment security apparatus. Merchants that invest in better security systems could charge a higher price for their goods, ideally. Yet sadly, customers do not typically differentiate sellers based on security practices, and thus, merchants are not inclined to invest in better security systems.[71] This problem is exacerbated by the fact that customers have little to lose, apart from the cost of their time spent resolving the fraud, and thus, customers have little incentive to demand information about their merchant's security system.[72] The market does not demand information or make available information that rewards those firms for adhering to higher standards in security processes. More specifically this means that the operational costs of increased security are not realized incrementally in each transaction, but are realized in quantum shifts and loss events, like the one experienced by TJX.

The asymmetric distribution of risk information poses another problem for the likes of TJX. In typical risk management frameworks, one would look at the operational risk that TJX faces from payment processing and suggest a risk transfer strategy, namely because the firm is not specialized in managing such risk. This risk transfer might traditionally come in the form of an insurance policy. However, the lack of specific operational information to the insurer makes pricing and acceptance of such a risk by the insurer nearly impossible. As firms have a larger and larger electronic and e-commerce presence, there will be a need to gain competencies in these

---

[71]Shreft, S. L. (2007). "Risks of Identity Theft: Can the Market Protect the Payment System?" *Economic Review*, Federal Reserve Bank of Kansas City, 4th Quarter, 26.

[72]An individual that is the victim of identity theft will spend, on average, 21 hours resolving the issue. Available at https://www.javelinstrategy.com/uploads/files/1004.R_2010IdentityFraudSurveyConsumer.pdf.

realms and adhere to best practice standards, as options for risk transferring will be strictly limited, due to asymmetric distribution of risk information.

The Cost Externalities Can Be Hard to Recover

Second, the full cost of credit fraud is not visible or passed onto the impacted customer directly. For example, even if buyers did differentiate between retailers, they will not consider the costs of finding, prosecuting, and jailing fraudsters, because all taxpayers share this bill. Other parties to the payment network (internet retailers, banks, merchants, processors, etc.) will pay the full costs for good security practices "but only receive part of the benefit from it."[73] As a result, one link in the chain forces costs on the rest of the network when a breach occurs. For example, banks were not able to recuperate the costs of reissuing customer cards following the breach at BJ's Wholesale Club because in that case, there was no previous contractual obligation regarding data security.[74]

In many ways, the legal examples of precedence, standards for due diligence, and even definitions of negligence in the digital and electronic space are evolving. Parties to such transactions can and do see real costs (losses) but may not have easy avenues for recovery. This requires that firms price such risk into the "cost of doing business." Operational losses in data systems become embedded risks that cannot be removed easily from the business.

TJX in the Wake of the Hack

A year after the announcement of the hack, year on year TJX sales from the first-quarter in 2008 rose 6% and net income fell less than 2% — even after the large settlement payouts.[75] As of 2009, TJX continued to benefit from customers seeking deep discounts — it projected a 5% retail space

---

[73]Shreft, S. L. (2007). "Risks of Identity Theft: Can the Market Protect the Payment System?" *Economic Review*, Federal Reserve Bank of Kansas City, 4th Quarter, 25.

[74]Sullivan, R. (2007). "Risk Management and Nonbank Participation in the US Retail Payments System," *Economic Review*, Federal Reserve Bank of Kansas City, 2nd Quarter, 28.

[75]Greenemeier, L. (2007). "Data Theft, Pushback, and the TJX Effect," *Information Week*, August 13, 36.

expansion in 2010 and 6% in 2011, and net sales were up 7% in 2009.[76] While TJX's bottom line did suffer from the breach, it is unclear whether the data breach affected sales. One perspective is that customers place a lower priority on data security versus getting a discount in hard times. Another perspective might be to consider if sales would have been greater in the absence of the data breach. In the final analysis, TJX must wrangle with this idea in considering the final hit to its bottom line.

Consumers and experts would think a company that suffered such a public and expensive data breach would immediately implement a rigorous data security environment. That may not be the case for TJX. In May 2008, information about the company's lax network security appeared on an Internet forum. Specifically, a blogger revealed that employees could use blank passwords on the servers, and being that the server was always in administrator mode, "made it easy for hackers — or store employees — to have escalated privileges on the system once they entered it."[77] The employee alleges he brought the security problems to the attention of his store manager before he chose to blog about it. TJX fired the employee and did not comment on the matter publicly.

The Growing Cyber Threat

Using a secure and sophisticated computerized payment system has become more important and necessary because of growing cyber threats. In February 2010, Director of National Intelligence Dennis Blair told Congress "malicious cyber activity is growing at an unprecedented rate."[78] While Blair's primary concern is protection of US government information, the rising sophistication of international cyber criminals and their operations is apparent.

Not only should nations take heed of cyber attacks, but large organizations and enterprises are, and will continue to be, targets for hacking. The operational risk posed by hacking is an embedded risk that is difficult to remove from the operation of the business. The key for firms is to contain such risk from growing in scale and persistence as seen at TJX.

---

[76]Holmes, E. (2010). "TJX's Profit Rises 58%," *Wall Street Journal*, February 24.
[77]Zetter, K. (2009). "4 Years After TJX Hack, Payment Industry Sets Security Standards," *WIRED*, July 17.
[78]Gjelten, T. (2010). "Cyber Insecurity: US Struggles to Confront Threat," *National Public Radio*, April 6.

Case Review

This case study provides an important wake-up call to companies on many fronts. At the core, this case is about the company that accepts an embedded risk, an operational risk of transmitting sensitive customer information. Their business model does not show specialization in technology management or even operational risk management. Surprisingly, TJX recognized this risk, yet dismissed the investment to mitigate it. This becomes the trap for many firms. When dealing with risks outside of their specialization, there is a temptation to not take the risk seriously. Risks posed by technology are especially dangerous, and this case highlights the reality that because of the interconnectedness of technology with centralized operations, the exposure is more highly leveraged than before. Consider a thief who wanted to steal from a retailer's till at a network-level, before the advent of wireless transmission. It would more or less require stealing from every store. The exposure for theft was limited to one store at a time. With technology and the fact that such sensitive information is not physical but digital and centralized, the risk is now magnified in terms of exposure.

For TJX Companies, this operational risk comes with the cost of doing business. Such is the case with many operational risks that are driven by process and system failures. TJX Companies failed to recognize that this risk, although low by their estimates, was of a large and likely unacceptable exposure. That is to say, the risk moved from being finite to persistent (impacting customers over many years). Moreover, it impacted a larger scope than originally anticipated. Figure 5.1 below captures this growth in

	Explicit	Implicit	Risk Persistence and scale of impacts increase. Embedded risk of handling payments results in major liability rooted in decision on security standards.
Finite		Management of Operational Risk in Payments Systems	
Persistent		Risks spread in persistence and in magnitude	

Figure 5.1. TJX neglect leads to persistence.

the operational risk over time. By not following industry standards or even having an outside examination, the payment risks grew and were undetected, leading to a larger, persistent exposure over time.

Examine how your enterprise relies on automated and electronic systems. If these systems touch customers or transmit sensitive information, take heed of the industry standards and remain aware of changes in technology that can render your position vulnerable to attack.

Risk Management Lessons

There are some best practices that are worthy of consideration in review of this case.

Operational risk and embedded risk require attention to detail

The old adage that "the devil is in the details" applies to technology. We have all experienced a glitch on a computer or printer, only to realize that the inability to print or operate the computer was controlled by one setting or driver, or some seemingly inconsequential detail. The same is true for information and technology systems at the enterprise scale. In your business, invest in talent and expertise that can adequately examine details, their impact to operations and the embedded operational risks that are unacceptable to the firm. This investment in talent and expertise is especially necessary in technology, as technology does and will continue to change at a rapid pace, and because the knowledge needed to assess risk in technological operations is indeed quite advanced and otherwise not self evident.

The movement to greater reliance on data systems and the development of processes that rely on automated data feeds suggests management needs to fully consider the operational risk surrounding this new reality. This requires a level of measurement of systems and proactive detection of anomalies to answer if the details are different and appear suspicious. The irony is that electronic systems came to the world of business with the promise that cost savings would be realized. Indeed, great operational savings have been realized and great increases in productivity have been seen. However, in many ways, the costs are moved from transactional costs in operations to larger operational risk losses with great scale. This type of operational risk is best contained by developing a deep understanding of the processes at work in the operation.

Technology has made operational risk highly levered

The benefits of digital operations and information movement and storage are countless. However the dangers change the exposure from an incremental loss to a quantum or shock loss. Beyond the lessons in the TJX case, we can also look the failures of JetBlue Airways in 2007 and RIM's Blackberry over the last few years, where technological failures prevented JetBlue from operating it entire fleet, and RIM lost service to millions of customers on multiple occasions. The failures stemmed from seemingly small and modest system or process errors. However, the impacts were felt by many customers over a protracted period of time. This again serves as an example of how a technological risk in operations can persist and even cause contagion and impact to the brand and reputation.

Many of us can recall the danger or losing a prized electronic file or photo. In the paper world, this was resolved by careful organization and labeling (likely a lost skill by many). But now that files are digital, there is hardly one among us that has not experienced some catastrophic and complete loss of data, made possible by the reality that failure mechanisms impact all of the data. Technology, in this regard, poses a dangerous operational risk that is embedded in many business processes and made more severe due to its exposure to centralized systems. When such risks turn to reality, they are often manifested as a complete and sudden shock, and massive in exposure. Although the likelihood of events may be low, the exposure and severity of loss would be high. It suggests that reasonable caution is appropriate when dealing with technology risks.

Employees are your greatest asset . . . and risk

During an interview, the owner and founder or the SAS Institute, Jim Goodnight, was quoted as saying, "my greatest asset is the employees."[79] There are countless executives who would share the same sentiment. However, the examples of operational risk from rogue employees at Barings (1995) and

---

[79] "SAS: The Royal Treatment," *CBS 60 Minutes*, October 13, 2002.

Société Générale (2008) and elsewhere show that employees with access to nuisance knowledge about the firm and its customers are a huge risk. Nearly every bank in the world has considered procedures to limit who can access customer information, and some have even limited the functionality of thumb drives and other devices that would make removal of customer data easy. It is unfortunate that the risks of a few require such special consideration, but consider the failures of Arthur Andersen, Barings, UBS, and Olympus to name a few.

The major takeaway for management is to know your employees. Know their actions and access. In many businesses, keystrokes are monitored, and in others, physical location is tracked. Of course, the most clever of the motivated will likely still find a way around these. But removing attractive targets (through safeguarding) and building teams that are less motivated in this regard are important actions that business managers can take to reduce losses from rogue employees.

Recognize your competencies and seek an outside partner to transfer those operational risks

For the shareholders in TJX Companies, what is most frustrating is that these losses did not come from a weak business model, capital structure, or even a poor product. The losses, as we have said, were embedded in the operations, outside the core competency of the firm. One cannot doubt that TJX has excellent skills in retail, site location, and store management. However, it does not appear to be an organization on the leading edge of data transmission capabilities. Indeed, this reality likely came into consideration when the hackers identified vulnerable targets.

Accepting operational risks, embedded in business processes, can offer limited upside, so look for business partners that specialize in such operations. Moreover, consider business transactions that transfer some or all of the risk. Few retailers actually make their own physical cash deliveries due to the risk, employing the likes of Brinks to securely process the delivery. Isn't it ironic that retailers would not look for similar experts in the transmission of electronic funds? So be honest in what your team and organization can do best and partner when needed even if it may cost more incrementally.

Look beyond laws for the best solution to dealing with operational risks in technology

The pace of technological development, especially coming out of the Internet age, has brought business new capabilities and benefits in terms of data accessibility and information on employees and customers. The governments of the world have been slow to provide guidance on what is legal in terms of technology. Although firms may not find themselves outside of legal compliance in regards to technological operations, public sentiment towards this potential risk to employees and customers has increased. It is important for management to set a clear and safe direction in regard to the use of technology. At the time of this writing, I know of many large multi-national companies that cannot verify the safety of the popular smart phones on their internal email systems. They have elected to prevent the use of such smart phones. The outcry from the employees is loud, of course. Yet, many other companies, facing the same risk, elect to move forward. Of course the risk at a bank might be heightened due to the presence of sensitive customer data, but the failure mechanism is similar. Be willing to set the direction for your firm and answer to a higher authority than simply the law.

Case Questions

1. As a customer, how would you react to learning that your information was compromised by a store or service provider? What restitution would you expect? Would you shop with them again, if they apologized?
2. Did the TJX team exercise sufficient care in protecting its payment transmissions?
3. How would you advise a company to manage customer data?
4. What principles would you put in place for ensuring that your team acts "above the law" in regards to customer data security?
5. In our new age of information sharing and accessibility, what level or protection is reasonable to expect?
6. Courts have struggled with assigning damages in cases of customer data breach. Should customers be compensated or paid for breaches? What there are no observed financial losses for the customer?

Chapter 6
Dealing With Contagion
and Persistence in Risks

The pessimist sees difficulty in every opportunity. The optimist
sees the opportunity in every difficulty.
> — *Winston Churchill, British Prime Minister*
> *and Nobel Laureate*

On the morning of March 26, 2007, Conseco executives, including CEO
C. James Prieur, were in for a rude awakening. On the front page of the
New York Times was the story of an elderly woman who had faithfully set
aside money for years for a Conseco long-term care (LTC) policy. By her
early 80s, the woman had developed diabetes and hypertension, and subsequently suffered from dementia. According to the article, Conseco had
denied payout claims on her LTC policy even though she was a likely can-
didate for coverage. The cost of her care eventually forced her family to sell
their business and take on care for the woman until her recent death. The
family eventually pursued litigation. Conseco executives were frustrated by
the article's vague assertions about Conseco's complaint statistics and its
disorderly filing system. Furthermore, the journalist backed-up his story
using depositions from potentially unfavorable sources such as a former
employee, a former insurance insider, and an insurance claims attorney.
Executives needed to address what went wrong and take another look at
the long-term care business.

The Rise and Fall of Conseco

In 1979, Stephen Hilbert and David Deeds founded an insurance business
that after a series of acquisitions in the early 1980s evolved as Conseco, Inc.
Conseco and its subsidiaries started-off selling various insurance policies and
annuities, and went public in 1985. Hilbert became President and CEO after

Deeds left in the 1980s. In 1996, the stock price was 9,000% of its 1985 value and Hilbert's annual salary was in the tens of millions of dollars.[80]

By 1998, Conseco had acquired 19 total companies in just 16 years, "usually with its own shares rather than cash."[81] Part of these acquisitions included American Travellers, Transport Holdings Inc., and Washington National Insurance Co. in the mid 1990s, from which Conseco gained its long-term care insurance business. A subsequent acquisition of a mobile-home lender for $6.4 billion in stock put millions in bad loans on Conseco's balance sheet. Two years after the acquisition, Conseco's share price dropped more than 90%, and each quarter, the company sustained losses as it tried to shore up its debt.[82] In 2000, the board replaced Hilbert with former General Electric executive Gary Wendt, but the change came too late as unsustainable debt forced Conseco to file for bankruptcy in 2002.

In 2003, the company emerged from bankruptcy and downsized to focus on insurance via its three main brands, Banker's Life, Conseco Insurance Group, and Colonial Penn. However, not all went according to plan. First, Wendt resigned in 2002, and the next CEO left two years later. The succeeding CEO lasted only two years before C. James Prieur took the helm as CEO in mid-2006. Although Conseco and the new CEO ended 2006 on a positive note of $96.5 million in net income, the long-term care business was suffering losses from "a combination of higher than expected incurred claims and lower than expected reserve releases for policy terminations."[83] The company would have to raise premiums to ensure solvency in the long-term care segment.

Embedded Risks in the Long-Term Care Industry

Companies sold long-term care (LTC) insurance, as early as the 1960s, and by 2007, there were six to seven million policies outstanding. Annually, Americans spend approximately $135 billion (8.5% of total health

---

[80]Hallinan, J. T. and M. Pacelle (2003) "Turn of Fortune: In Collection Battle, Conseco Ex-CEO Is Fighting Back," *Wall Street Journal*, December 5, A1.

[81] "Sub-prime Lenders — Trailer Trashed." *The Economist*, April 11, 1998.

[82]Hallinan, J. T. and M. Pacelle (2006). "Turn of Fortune: In Collection Battle, Conseco Ex-CEO Is Fighting Back," *The Wall Street Journal*, December 5, A1.

[83] "Conseco's Third-Quarter Net Income Drops 43.1 Percent on Long-Term Care Policies in Run-off," *Best's Insurance News*, November 2, 2006.

expenditures), "or roughly 1.2% of GDP," on LTC, excluding donated care.[84] LTC consists of full or part-time assisted care for people that can neither perform at least two of the basic activities of daily living such as eating, bathing and walking, nor are capable of self-care. Benefits usually commence following a brief elimination period, although companies offer a wide range of insurance options that may decrease the elimination period or protect against inflation. Sales agents earn hefty fees for selling a policy, garnering between 30 to 65% of the first year's premium and around 4% of the premiums for subsequent periods.[85] The average first year premium in 2007 was $1,950 and the average buyer was 58 years old.[86] Typical LTC policies cost approximately $3,500 per year in the current market for someone at age 65, with the average policyholder needing the benefit around age 80.

Embedded Risks Challenge Insurers — Industry Supply Decreases

Despite the lucrative commissions in the industry, the number of insurers offering LTC policies waned from 143 in 1990 to around 80 in the mid-2000s, with many major sellers such as CNA Financial Corp. and TIAA-CREF exiting the market.[87] This exodus occurred because across the industry, long-term care companies started to realize that earlier pricing for LTC premiums proved financially unsound and became problematic as customers defied actuarial calculations. LTC purchasers were living longer, the rates of Alzheimer's, Parkinson's and diabetes were increasing, and yet lapse rates for canceling insurance were lower than lapse rates used for standard life insurance. This paradox challenged the industry's expectations for pricing LTC products. In standard life insurance, one measures life expectancy and lapse rates. Customers that lapse or do not pay, offering significant profits to the product. Due to increased health care and emergency care,

---

[84]Hagen, S. (2004). "Financing Long-Term Care for the Elderly," April, Congressional Budget Office, Washington, DC. Available at http://www.cbo.gov/doc. cfm?index=5400&type=0.

[85]Levitz, J. and K. Greene (2008). "States Draw Fire for Pitching Citizens on Private Long-Term Care Insurance," *Wall Street Journal*, February 26, A1.

[86]McQueen, M. P. (2008), "Insurer Casts-off Long-Term Care Policies," *Wall Street Journal*, December 3, D1.

[87]Zawacki, T. P. (2004). "Basic, Complex Flaws Block LTC Expansion," *SNL Insurance Daily*, September 10.

people were living longer and experiencing periods of intensive care before death. Additionally, people saw immense value in LTC and did not lapse in payments as seen in life insurance. The previous actuarial assumptions in the risk profiling for LTC were wrong. The norms had changed.

Aside from errors in actuarial calculations, costs for typical health care also rose exponentially as companies paid out $34,000 annually for assisted living facilities or $75,000 for full-time care, on average.[88] Moreover, competition and short-term gain drove insurers to set initial premiums too low, and they soon realized they needed to raise premiums frequently for financially viability. As increases to premiums require regulatory approval, insurers often received little support from regulators on this matter. Furthermore, the forecasting of other economic variables that affect the cost of LTC provision and reserve calculation was a complex prospect.

Economic variables relating to LTC premiums include interest rate (the duration of LTC liabilities is extremely long when the policies are written), morbidity (the incidence rate of claims), persistency (if you have higher lapse rates, profitability goes up), longevity (the reverse of mortality), and medical inflation (while most policies now have a maximum pay/day, that had not always been the case; at times, medical inflation has been seen to increase at twice the rate of inflation). Virtually every variable went against industry predictions in the last two decades. Part of this was simply a mistake on the part of industry actuaries, which is unsurprising given the relative "newness" of the product. While the life insurance industry has centuries of data about mortality, and can offer estimates with a high degree of confidence, no such longitudinal data existed for the LTC product (and experience would vary from country to country because of different societal safety nets).

Mistaken assumptions on persistency proved significant. The industry assumed that LTC policies would realize the same 4% lapse rate as life insurance policies. The actual rate was 1% or lower, as policyholders were intent on keeping coverage and accepted rate increases. It became clear policyholders valued LTC more than other forms of insurance.

At the time several large players remained in the game aside from Conseco, including Genworth, John Hancock, and MetLife. These providers belonged into one of two camps: 1) those with controlled distribution — Bankers and MetLife, and 2) those who sold through

---

[88]Genworth Financial 2009 Cost of Care Survey, April 2009.

independent agents — Conseco, Hancock, and Genworth. The companies with independent agents (Camp 2) were conscious of price increases because of the fear that independent agents might sell existing customers a new policy from a competing insurer. Typically, when insurers with independent agents introduce increases in LTC premiums, independent agents try to shift healthy customers to lower cost policies, as customers that are not as healthy cannot easily find new insurance and prefer to hold their existing policy in spite of price increases. The net result is a block of vintage policies that has higher morbidity (or incidence rate). Risk managers often call this selection bias. It is an unfortunate reality of insurance and also appears in lending. Those most in need of a loan are the least attractive customers.

For a long time, Conseco was the only insurer increasing LTC rate premiums. Other insurers such as Genworth and Hancock competed on the promise to never increase LTC premiums. In the last couple of years, almost all competitors have dramatically raised their LTC premiums as they saw the economic realities of the product turn against them.

Health Costs Increase — Industry Demand Increases

Insurance companies have had mixed interest in long-term care insurance. With approximately 7 million LTC policies outstanding and a rapidly aging US population, insurance companies should expect a lucrative market. Yet, growth has often been in the low single digits each year. This is attributable to the government's participation in this space and continued confusion by consumers over their LTC entitlements. The government-sponsored LTC provision in the United States is only available to the poor, and the total maximum amount of insurance is insufficient ($200/day for 3 years or about $219,000) given today's cost expectations. Thus, the real market for a private, LTC product exists for middle income and older Americans who own some assets and do not qualify for Medicaid. This reality limits economies of scale on this LTC insurance product, which causes insurers to price premiums above a competitive market equilibrium. One study points to Medicaid as the reason 66 to 90% of the population does not buy comprehensive LTC insurance, despite the fact that Medicaid only covers 60% of an average person's expenditures and is limited to the poor.[89] Even if insurers

---

[89]Brown, J. R. and A. Finkelstein (2004). "The Interaction of Public and Private Insurance: Medicaid and the Long-Term Care Insurance Market." Working Paper no. 10989, NBER, Cambridge, MA.

resolve supply-side issues, low and high-income individuals might continue to view LTC insurance as too costly an expense. Furthermore, only 20% of the American public knows that Medicare does not provide indefinite LTC coverage, causing many consumers to forego this type of insurance on an incorrect assumption of full coverage.[90]

Further complicating the sustainability of LTC businesses is that as premiums have risen, sales of private LTC insurance have fallen: "annual sales fell to fewer than 300,000 policies in 2006 and 2007, from 580,000 in 2002."[91] Yet, demand is increasing as baby-boomers age — around "two-thirds of people that reach the age of 65 will require some form of LTC before they die."[92] Other trends such as more women in the work force and smaller families would assume greater demand on LTC insurance because of the scarcity of familial care givers.

However, a fall in sales might ultimately be a result of market contraction and the rise in premiums. Consumers have good reason to question whether their LTC insurer will remain in business to pay their LTC claims over the life of the policy. As premiums trend higher, consumers may wonder whether such insurance will remain affordable over the life of their policy. Should premiums become unaffordable and consumers be forced to cancel their policy, they may only recover a small portion of their already paid-in premiums.

Industry Regulation Poses Constant Risks

Insurance companies, including LTC insurance, are regulated at the state level, with little regulation existing at the federal level. Insurers must thus gain states' approval on premium increases. States also act as insurers for the insurers, with twenty-three states guaranteeing "long-term-care insurance policies up to $100,000, six covering policies to at least $500,000 and the rest covering up to a limit of $300,000."[93]

---

[90]Mulvey, J. (2009). "Factors Affecting the Demand for Long-Term Care Insurance: Issues for Congress," May 27, Congressional Research Service, R40601. Available at http://assets.opencrs.com/rpts/R40601_20090527.pdf.

[91]"The Drawing Board," *Best's Review*, February 1, 2010.

[92]Mulvey, J. (2009). "Factors Affecting the Demand for Long-Term Care Insurance: Issues for Congress," May 27, Congressional Research Service, R40601. Available at http:// assets. opencrs.com/rpts/R40601_20090527.pdf.

[93]McQueen, M. P. (2008). "Insurer Casts-off Long-Term Care Policies," *Wall Street Journal*, December 3, D1.

Many of the state laws on LTC insurance stem from the National Association of Insurance Commissioners (NAIC). The NAIC is a non-profit organization that brings together industry professionals to discuss emerging issues in the insurance industry, and among other responsibilities, set standards to be used in its evolving Long-Term Care Insurance Model Act. This model works to protect consumers and promote fair competitive practices through ten-year rate history disclosures, actuarial certifications for rate increases, or options to purchase a non-forfeiture benefit. Given the early pricing mistakes experienced by LTC insurers, the NAIC suggested implementing an initial minimum loss ratio of 58%, meaning 58% of the original premium must be set aside for claims payment. Any premium increase would then need to meet a 58% ratio. This proposal deters companies from pricing new policies artificially low for competitive gain, only to raise premiums significantly later. While no state has uniformly adopted the Long-Term Care Insurance Model Act as legislation, all states have enacted at least some of the proposals.

The LTC insurance product is renewable annually, yet insurers cannot cancel an individual policyholder's coverage unless he/she lapses on the premium. Underwriting is conducted at the point the LTC product is sold, and any changes to the premiums have to occur on the entire block without changing policy attributes. The only accepted basis for changing the price is a deteriorating loss ratio, the ratio of claims payments to premium. Such price changes are contingent on the state regulator's approval.

Insurers requesting a premium rate increase on a block of LTC policies would have to demonstrate how the loss ratio deteriorated through claims/premiums (losses due to declining interest rates are not recoverable). Given that LTC insurance is regulated at the state level, some state regulators would approve premium increases while others might not. In the case of Conseco, its blocks were much older than typical blocks in the rest of the industry and covered policyholders 65 years old and older. As a result, the claims ratio was much worse, providing regulators with a reasonable justification for a premium rate increase.

Conseco's LTC Business — Background

In spite of the state of its LTC policies, Conseco had a harder time than the typical insurer at obtaining rate increases because of the company's colorful history. In the late 1990's, former CEO Hilbert was the best paid American CEO and his personal life became front-page news. Conseco was also developing a reputation for corporate greed and mismanagement where previous management and directors borrowed $400 million for their own personal accounts, to be guaranteed by Conseco for the purposes of buying stock. The reputational risks associated with past CEO activities remained with Conseco for many years and made rate increase requests a challenging experience.

Nevertheless, rate increases did occur and they became the biggest reason for customer complaints. A close second on the list was poor policy administration and slow resolution time to consumer questions. In many cases, the company acknowledged that the processing of claims and the handling of policy changes were too slow.

Conseco had two major blocks of LTC policies: the Conseco Senior Health Insurance (CSHI) block and the Bankers Life block, which Conseco still owns. There was a huge difference between the two blocks: the Bankers block consisted of a series of evolving generations of policies that were generally homogeneous in features and risk level. The CSHI block, by contrast, had very different provisions depending upon the company that had written the business, and so the claims adjudication for the old CSHI block became an administrative challenge for Conseco. Policy terms varied significantly by policy and required intense work owing to poor back-office systems. Essentially, someone would have to pull the original policyholder file and read the provisions of the policy. This was in contrast to Bankers Life policies, in which the provisions were largely similar, and variations of policies numbered in the low hundreds.

The Risk Unfolds — Crisis Occurs

The top brass discussed the *New York Times* article and recognized that it created a distorted view of the current situation at Conseco. While complaint levels were higher than other companies, complaints mainly focused on payout timeliness and frustration with premium increases — not necessarily claims denial. In fact, Conseco officials knew the denial rate in 2006 was less than 2%.[94] Executives were aware that timeliness had been an issue since Conseco emerged from bankruptcy and was updating its computer systems. Embedded risks from operational processes are commonplace and

---

[94]Wall, J. K. (2007). "Long-Term Care a Long-Term Problem for Conseco," *Indianapolis Business Journal*, 28(14).

can be magnified, as was the case at Conseco. Although the technical glitches were minor and could be remedied, these became front and center for the media and served as a claim against Conseco.

A legislative onslaught soon resulted with five senators, including Senators Hillary Clinton and Barack Obama, sending letters to the head of the Government Accountability Office (GAO) calling for an investigation. Hearings in the House were subsequently scheduled. The situation soon was a public relations problem for Conseco and of concern were shareholders' and investors' perceptions. Not only did it have to handle the immediate situation but Conseco also needed to address the viability of its LTC segment.

Containing Risk and Preventing Contagion: Conseco Settles With States on Penalties

In May of 2008, Conseco settled with 39 states following an investigation into how its subsidiaries, Bankers Life. and Conseco Senior Health Insurance, handled payout claims on long-term care policies. On-site examinations revealed problems were primarily because of claim payment delays as a function of outdated technology, rather than claim denials. Regulators also found that Bankers Life needed to bring its training and marketing/sales programs into compliance.

States split a $2.3 million penalty while Conseco was obliged to review denied or partially denied claims that occurred from 2005–2007 and set aside $4 million in remediation should harmed policyholders be found. Conseco also agreed to invest $26 million to upgrade its computer and claims processing systems. States would be allowed to collect an additional $10 million if Conseco did not comply with these mandates within a two and half year period.

Following a careful review of operational risk concerning LTC and potential insolvency, Prieur decided in August 2008 to close Conseco's largest LTC unit. The new plan would create a non-profit trust for 160,000 policyholders of the CSHI block. Health professionals and former regulators would run the new Senior Health Insurance Co. of Pennsylvania (SHIP), which would operate with an aim to remain solvent and not-for-profit. The trust would have approximately $3 billion in assets, and Conseco planned to add an additional $175 million. Despite these funds, "SHIP may require a combination of rate increases, reduced benefits and policyholder forfeitures to maintain adequate long-term capitalization." By spinning off CSHI to a trust (where the trustees were C. Everett Koop, a former Surgeon General, two retired insurance regulators, and the then-current head of the American Society of Actuaries), the business could more easily obtain justifiable rate increases.

One year later, SHIP settled a small lawsuit with California for $500,000. There, regulators alleged the company had engaged in wrongful denial and burden some administrative practices. In addition to the half million-dollar penalty, the trust would "retroactively pay certain policyholder claims back to January 1, 2004, along with interest at an annual 10% rate."

The Current State of Long-Term Care Insurance

The LTC industry has continued to decline because of poor market conditions, regulatory delays in permitting premium rate increases, and government provisions in the LTC space. Demand for private insurance has also continued to fall despite the increase in demand for LTC. Other major players, like Allianz, recognized the adverse market conditions and followed Conseco in exiting the market. In the second quarter of 2010, John Hancock (Manulife) announced it would take a $700 million after-tax charge for their LTC business, having researched the economics and acknowledging what they probably should have recognized a long time ago. Their share price dropped dramatically over the summer.

A large industry setback came around that time, in March 2010, when President Barack Obama signed into law the health care reform bill. Part of the legislation included a provision for a private-public LTC insurance program through the CLASS Act. Working adults could now voluntary contribute to a government-administered LTC insurance program via payroll taxes that offered coverage of $50 per day following a five-year vesting-period. Numerous groups found fault with the program's bottom line and its impact on private insurers, including the non-partisan Congressional Budget Office.

By 2010 positive forecasts resulted from "Conseco's improved risk-adjusted capital levels and financial flexibility," a recapitalization plan that the company concluded at the end of 2009. This had produced strong results for 2009, and Conseco ended the year with nearly $85.7 million in net income. With the marked increase in the fortunes of the company, executives sought one further change — soon Conseco Inc. would become CNO Financial Group Inc.

Case Review

There are many aspects of risk management at work with Conseco, as it related to the LTC care business. First, the actuarial calculations for estimating risk (mathematically speaking) proved incorrect owing to erroneous assumptions about the customer response, market conditions and health care costs. This is an industry risk, one that persists since the risks are held for a long period of time and explicit in the decision to enter the LTC business.

The technology problems that resulted in delays and denials of coverage are clear operational risks, embedded in the requirement of servicing insurance policies. By Conseco's own admission, the patchwork of outdated systems acquired through many mergers had grown unmanageable. This embedded risk which impacted customers ultimately caused contagion, resulting in a reputational risk event that was manifested in a front page *New York Times* article.

James Prieur had a difficult situation on his hands. Perhaps the easiest matter is settling with the impacted family and doing the right thing legally and ethically. However, the media, regulators, and other constituents were not satisfied by such remedies. Jim found himself with many constituents looking for answers and information. Here is a partial list of their concerns:

1. **Employees**: Is the article true? Did Conseco try to cheat it customers?
2. **Bondholders and Investors**: Are you able to survive this? Will I get paid?
3. **Independent Agents**: How can I sell a Conseco product with so much negative attention on the product?
4. **Customers**: Is my policy safe?
5. **Regulators**: Where do we begin?

Prieur began by calling his employees together to reiterate Conseco's commitment to customers. He shared information that countered the claims in the newspaper piece and left the all-hands meeting to a standing ovation.

Next, he needed to calm the bondholders and investors. It would take some time to do this. They wanted clarity that the ensuing penalty would not damage Conseco. Without a healthy set of investors and bondholders, it would be difficult to carry forward. It was clear to Prieur that negative press impacted the company's reputation. There was little that he could say in detail to independent agents and customers that was believable in the face of the newspaper piece. He did reiterate his position, but it was time for action.

In a move unprecedented in the industry, Prieur wrote to all state regulators demanding a review of Conseco's processes and procedures. He was aware that a penalty was likely. He also knew there were operational issues, but not nearly as bad as some claimed. The moved changed the conversation with the regulators. As opposed to a punitive tone, the regulators were now forced to search and find the problems. In the end, the fees paid by Conseco were relatively minor. The promises to add new computer systems and processes were easy to accept. These investments were needed and planned anyway. Prieur's willingness to confront the risk and expose his firm to examination altered the likely path with regulators.

The risks facing the LTC business at Conseco were many. First, the actuarial risks were incorrectly estimated. This resulted in risk growing over time and showing persistence. Conseco could not back out of policies once those were written, meaning that it faced a long-term liability that was not properly estimated (See Figure 6.1 above). To be fair to Conseco, the insurance industry mostly missed this too. However, Conseco experienced operational risk, stemming from IT systems and processes that were slow and resulted in delays in the approval of customer claims. The fix was clear; it required investment to remedy the operations. However, as this operational risk impacted customers, it eventually spiraled into a public relations crisis and major reputational risk. The operational risk had spread and caused contagion by leading to new and great levels of risk. Prieur was able to contain much of the risk and direct the

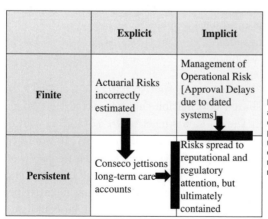

Figure 6.1.   Conseco overcomes risk to contain persistence and contagion.

regulatory investigation to the underlining operational risks. Still, it is safe to say that without the operational risks and the impact to customers, the events would likely have not included a *New York Times* front-page article.

Still, there was the problem of the damaged brand. At the end of it all, Prieur recognized that the Conseco name had seen too many difficult days. The move to rebrand to CNO was an affirmative effort to communicate a new beginning for everyone, employees, investors, agents, and customers. The Conseco brand had too much persistent risk.

Risk Management Lessons

Firms can be attractive targets for regulation

The insurance industry is regulated to protect customers and investors alike. However, regulatory scrutiny is subject to the winds of political opportunity. Recognize when you are an attractive target. A firm's previous actions can position it as a target. Success and size are unfortunate reasons for being a target. Consider the new scrutiny and attention (especially to its labor policies and pricing policies) that Apple has seen as it has moved from a quirky computer company to the world's most valuable brand. In the case of Conseco, it took a disparaging article to suggest that Conseco mistreated elderly people and reneged on its promises. This controversial assertion by the media signaled alarm and brought attention to the matter very quickly. The role of a victim or victimized class amplifies the attractiveness of regulation and the penalty that is likely to ensue. The fact that the charge involved a perceived vulnerable party and protected class made Conseco a great target for further regulation. Any effort to lambast the media and submit a rebuttal to such a claim would have been an exercise in futility. The media and regulators, alike, love to see a big, bad company brought down. In your business, ensure that vulnerabilities to regulation are addressed. Conseco failed when the embedded risk of delayed claims became problematic and ultimately impacted a vulnerable customer. This risk caused contagion and exposed the firm to additional regulatory scrutiny. Look for embedded risks that might be at work in your firm.

Also recognize how victims, especially socially-perceived protected classes, can be impacted by your firm's operations. Once a victim is identified and seen as vulnerable due to your firm actions, the recovery is more expensive. Containing the impact to victims is critical.

Recognize and remedy wrongs quickly — move on and focus on the long-term goals

For Conseco, it was clear that the impacted family needed to be compensated. A protracted lawsuit would only add fuel to the fire. However, resolving the risks facing Conseco would not be accomplished by words and arguments with regulators. It was important to move on to action. Conseco needed to resolve the regulation, and in asking for regulatory review could it clear its name and carry on with its business.

In your business, examine the long-term goals. Look for how you can most quickly get back on track when side lined by a risk. Waiting for legal remedy or waiting for time to past will only allow the risk to persist and cause additional contagion. Move to close the risk quickly and address the root cause right away.

Risk management and recovery from a crisis requires attention to all constituents

It is easy in a crisis to think only about the damages to the firm or the impact to the stock price. Don't forget that you have many employees who have trusted the company to offer employment and stability. Risks to the firm often cause flight of talent. The firm's ability to recover when talent is leaving is reduced. Think of your employees first. In building a recovery plan, be sure that the risks manifested to all constituent groups are addressed. Investors will want to know how you will recover. It is important that you can provide a realistic approach to investors and creditors on the plan for recovery. The loss of talent is in many ways a death spiral. As a firm loses people, it often loses is best employees first, and the market's perception of the company becomes reinforced.

A brand is a promise

All products and services are delivered with some level of guarantee, implicitly or explicitly. Your customer expects some level of quality and assurance, even if it is not formally stated or offered. For a highly regarded brand, this promise provides an opportunity to sell products for a higher margin than otherwise. Attacks and damages to the brand impair this most valuable of assets. Protecting your brand from contagion is critical. In hindsight, the actions of previous Conseco management and the cumbersome IT processes were sources of great risk that had spread to contaminate the Conseco brand. Prieur resolved that the damages to the brand's reputation ultimately required investment in a new brand. That can be an expensive proposition. Consider your firm's brand and how it might be put at risk from persistent and contagious risks. Ensure that the team you have in place recognizes the value and importance of protecting the firm's promise to customers. Provide your team the authority to take action at the periphery to limit risks so that they do not spread.

A company's brand is also the most fundamental asset of the firm. It is the recognition, promise, and license to operate. It embodies the past and the future for the firm. Containing the contagion and persistence of risk, especially operational risks, is ultimately about protecting the firm and its ability to operate in the future. Negative impacts to the firm's brand are the greatest attack to its ability to operate successfully in the future and emphasis in containing such risks should be paramount.

Manage your regulator

All businesses have a license to operate. It may be a formal license as in insurance and banking and involve a relationship with regulators, or it might simply be that your business is not deemed of sufficient interest to merit formal inquiry by regulators. Recognize that your regulator has an agenda. It may be that regulator has sincere motivations to protect the common interest. It may also be that your regulator has political motives or other agendas. Manage your regulator and the process. Do not let it overtake you. I have heard from many executives at banks, where regulation is commonplace, that regulators with other agendas are not uncommon. Train your staff to professionally interact with regulators, monitor what they do, and what information they access. It is not only legal but also appropriate. When being unfairly treated, be willing to take your case to a higher authority. In the case of a large enterprise, this may require intervention by political forces.

Take charge of how you are viewed by constituents and recognize that regulation can be an infinite risk with persistent impacts to the firm.

Case Questions

1. Consider your message to major constituents in the case. Examine the importance of calming employees and investors first.
2. Consider the role of a vulnerable party in the article. How does this alter Conseco's actions to refute the claims?

3. Would you have offered a rebuttal to the newspaper article?

4. Consider your message to the US senators seeking an explanation for this grave newspaper story. Would you send a public relations specialist or respond as the CEO?

5. Knowing the troubled history of the Conseco brand, do you agree with Prieur's decision to rebrand the firm? What are the risks and benefits of doing so?

6. Consider the impact of risk contagion at Conseco. Was this crisis avoidable?

7. Consider the facts about the LTC industry. What does this say about the cost of health care, especially as provided by social systems?

Chapter 7

Risk Management as a Corporate Competency

Take calculated risks. That is quite different from being rash.
     — *General George S. Patton, US General in World*
                                            War I and II

Jamie Dimon, CEO of JPMorgan Chase & Co. (JPMorgan) was celebrating his 52nd birthday on Thursday, March 13, 2008, when his cell phone rang. Bear Stearn's CEO Alan Schwartz was on the phone to ask for an emergency overnight loan. Bear Stearns did not have enough cash to open for business the next day, and Dimon was Schwartz's last hope. Dimon left his party, called his team in, and went to work with Bear Stearns executives and federal officials to determine a solution. The initial result: JPMorgan would borrow from the Fed's discount window to provide an emergency loan to Bear Stearns. Investors remained uncertain of Bear Stearns and its stock tumbled 47% to $30 on Friday. Over the weekend, talks shifted to JPMorgan acquiring Bear Stearns before bankruptcy became a foregone conclusion. By Sunday, officials reached a deal: JPMorgan would buy Bear Stearns for the rock bottom price of $2/share and would have access to a credit line of $30 billion from the federal government.

Even though he was a fairly new CEO at the time this event transpired, Dimon had been in the financial arena for decades. He was known for playing it safe, and during his first two years as CEO, "many analysts lost interest in JPMorgan," because while a "skilled cost-cutter, Dimon lacked the imagination to grow the business from within."[95] Critics pointed to JPMorgan's profits in 2006 that were below those of its competitors, which

---

[95] McDonald, D. (2008). "The Heist," *New York Magazine*, March 24.

put it at a disadvantage to expand without excess cash.[96] Two years later, an entirely different story would be told as many Wall Street execs saw their balance sheets crumble, offering the unimaginative but well-capitalized CEO access to unprecedented growth opportunities.

JPMorgan Chase & Co. — Background

The JPMorgan Chase & Co. of today is the conglomeration of more than a thousand financial institutions, the earliest of which Aaron Burr founded in 1799 (the Bank of the Manhattan Co). Aaron Burr was an early American political leader who served as vice president under Thomas Jefferson from 1801 to 1805. However, he is infamously known for killing the first Treasury Secretary, Alexander Hamilton, in a duel in 1804. The bank persisted despite the scandal and later evolved into the Chase Manhattan Bank. Chase and several other larger cross-country institutions, (Bank One, Manufacturers Hanover Trust Co., Chemical Bank, First National Bank of Chicago and National Bank of Detroit) eventually merged into the current brand. Owing to the geographic reach of these banks and their founding institutions, JPMorgan can claim it helped finance important American projects such as the railroads, the Erie Canal, and the Statue of Liberty. Moreover, in the 1990s, a JPMorgan team originated and sold the first credit derivative products, including the credit default swap.[97]

Some of the biggest mergers in the company's history occurred after the 1990s, when JPMorgan & Co. and The Chase Manhattan Corp. joined in 2000, and in 2004, when JPMorgan Chase & Co. merged with Bank One Corp. (the sixth largest bank in America). This latter merger allowed JPMorgan Chase to absorb Bank One's strong retail outlets and credit card presence in the Midwest and Southwest, which created "the second-largest financial conglomerate [by assets], just behind Citigroup, with $1.1 trillion in assets."[98] In 2008, JPMorgan Chase & Co. bought the Bear Stearns Companies and Washington Mutual, Inc., to become the largest bank in America

---

[96] "JPMorgan: Dimon Effect Paying Off," *Crain's New York Business*, October 2, 2006, 1.

[97] Lanchester, J. (2009). "Outsmarted: High Finance vs. Human Nature," *The New Yorker*, June 1.

[98] Lim, P. J. (2004). "Banking Bonanza: JPMorgan and Bank One to Merge," *US News and World Report*, January 18.

by market capitalization.[99] Investment Banking, Asset Management, Treasury Services, Securities Services, the Private Banking and Client divisions, and the Equity divisions all fall under the JPMorgan brand. Chase is the face of the company's consumer and commercial banking services.

Jamie Dimon: Cost-Cutter Extraordinaire

Jamie Dimon is a second generation American who followed his family's footsteps into America's financial services industry. After his grandparents emigrated from Greece to New York, his grandfather became a stockbroker and subsequently, so did his father. Dimon spent his childhood in the boroughs of New York before his father's success allowed the family to move into more luxurious surroundings on Park Avenue.

He studied Psychology and Economics at Tufts University; and during a summer job he met his future mentor and business colleague Sandy Weill, then president of the second largest securities brokerage firm. Weill was a family friend who had previously worked with Jamie's father on the deal that formed the large brokerage. After graduation in 1978, Dimon worked in consulting for two years before returning to earn a Master's degree in Business Administration at Harvard Business School. After Harvard, Weill, then the president of American Express (AmEx), convinced Dimon to ignore lucrative offers from other financial firms and to come work for him. In 1986, Weill and Dimon both quit AmEx after Weill butted heads with the Chairman, and the duo turned their attention to running a struggling subprime lender in Baltimore, Commercial Credit.

In Baltimore, Weill and Dimon perfected the art of "rolling up" companies or "buy[ing] them for not much money, kick[ing] them into shape, mak[ing] a lot of money, and mov[ing] on to the next one."[100] Over time, Commercial Credit became a multi-faceted financial services firm that added Travelers Insurance, Salomon Brothers Inc., and Smith Barney to the fold. In 1998, their work and financial acumen paid off when they completed an $80 billion merger with Citicorp that created "the world's biggest

---

[99]Mildenberg, D. (2008). *JPMorgan Chase's Market Value Tops Bank of America.* Available at http://www.bloomberg.com/apps/news?pid=20601087&sid=aIIE-BDZG3kFU&refer=home.

[100]Guerrera, F. (2010). "DimonDays," *Financial Times*, February 25, 2010.

financial services firm."[101] John S. Reed, chief executive of Citicorp, and Weill would serve as co-chairmen and co-CEOs while Dimon would serve as president.

Several months later, the storied partnership ended when Weill and Reed fired Dimon. Myriad reasons caused the separation, including professional tensions between executives of the newly merged company, Dimon's ambitions, and that fact that Dimon had not promoted Weill's daughter. Following a two-year hiatus from finance, Dimon returned in 2000 as Chairman and CEO of Bank One, the fifth-largest US bank by assets out of Chicago. Dimon went to work with his no nonsense approach, "pushing out top managers, slashing costs by $1.5 billion, and transforming a $511 million loss in 2000 into a $3.5 billion annual profit three years later."[102] His success helped bring about the Bank One merger with JPMorgan Chase in 2004, where he assumed the role of President and COO. Dimon packed up his family and headed back east to the Big Apple. In 2005, Dimon became CEO of JPMorgan Chase & Co.

Risk Management as a Corporate Focus

In his partnership with Weill, Dimon paid close attention to the numbers and operations, having honed his skills and business acumen across many acquisitions to ensure each venture's success. He succeeded in this role, in part, because he had a personality that eschewed paternalism, politics, and general niceties in the business world. He was also obsessed with creating a "fortress balance sheet." Upon leading JPMorgan, he began "methodically increasing its profits, adding to credit reserves, and expanding market share in a number of different businesses."[103] These attributes, in combination with a strong team, allowed him to create and lead a superb risk management operation at JPMorgan that was able to avoid most of the financial pitfalls of the subprime mortgage crisis.

When he ascended to CEO at JPMorgan, Dimon established monthly, all-day operating-committee meetings. In these meetings, top brass would scrutinize executive management reports and their key performance

---

[101] Kassenaar, L. and E. Hester (2008) "The House of Dimon," *Bloomberg Markets*, June.

[102] Kadlec, D. (2004). "Jamie Dimon: JPMorgan Chase," *Time*, December 17.

[103] McDonald, D. (2008). "The Heist," *New York Magazine*, March 24.

indicators (KPIs) to share information and ensure that no product or service was subsidized.[104] Should the information reflect too risky of a strategy, the team sold or closed the product or service. Indeed, "the team's ultimate strength was its willingness to shun products its competitors craved, even if that meant sacrificing short-term profits."[105] PowerPoints were rare at these meetings because Dimon demanded the details, specifically risk metrics and trends in risk metrics. In one instance in 2006, Dimon uncovered expenses for 50,000 phone lines that were not in use and immediately had them removed.[106]

Building the Team for Risk Management

Surrounding him at these meetings was a "mix of longtime loyalists, JPMorgan veterans, and outside hires."[107] They were not there because of their pedigrees but rather, because they were outstanding performers that knew the nuts and bolts of their divisions and could handle constant scrutiny. Dimon also sought those who embraced informal discussions of what could go wrong, or what was going wrong and were not afraid to voice dissenting opinions.[108] Spurning "yes" men for a team of independent thinkers would prove incredibly advantageous for JPMorgan when arcane financial products like Structured Investment Vehicles (SIVs) became popular with the industry and even with Dimon.

A Healthy Skepticism

Part of Dimon's active risk management strategy also included product diversification and "a healthy skepticism of mathematical-risk models and metrics."[109] This skepticism proved timely during the rise of products such as residential-mortgage backed securities, which rating agencies evaluated

---

[104,105]Tully, S. (2008). "How JPMorgan Steered Clear of the Credit Crunch," *Fortune*, September 2.

[106]Barr, A. (2008). "Dimon Steers JPMorgan Through Financial Storm." Available at http://www.marketwatch.com/story/dimons-tactics-help-jp-morgan-benefit-from-crisis.

[107]Tully, S. (2008). "How JPMorgan Steered Clear of the Credit Crunch," *Fortune*, September 2.

[108]"A Matter of Principle," *The Economist*, February 13, 2010.

[109]"A Better Black-Swan Repellent," *The Economist*, February 13, 2010.

with flawed historical data. As it turned out, some models failed to account for the possibility of large numbers of subprime borrowers simultaneously defaulting, and emptying entire neighborhoods. As a result, Moody's default models initially predicted lenders could recoup 70% of the loan (as was historically true) although they later had to adjust that figure down to 40% in the fall of 2007.[110] Many firms had billions of dollars worth of write-downs on highly rated financial products that became worthless overnight.

Credit Markets Bring Innovation and New Risks

While Dimon did suffer several missteps during the credit crisis, he did mitigate the fallout at JPMorgan with a strong balance sheet, a dedicated team, and a willingness to engage in the direct management of the firm's risk operations. In combination, these forces shaped a risk strategy that scorned trendy products such as structured investment vehicles (SIVs) and collateralized debt obligations (CDOs), which Dimon's competitors were happily snapping up in the mid-2000s.

When Bank One merged with JPMorgan, Bank One had an $8 billion structured investment vehicle (SIV) that JPMorgan later sold in 2005. In testifying before the FDIC, Dimon said JPMorgan viewed SIVs "as arbitrage vehicles with plenty of risk but little business purpose."[111] Initially however, Dimon wanted to retain the SIV because it was popular with clients even though this contrasted with the opinions of his Investment Banking executives. They believed SIVs were too risky on the basis that the insurance backing SIVs — credit default swaps — was very expensive.[112] Dimon ultimately conceded that the risk outweighed the potential return and sold the SIV. Many banks that maintained SIVs into 2007 had to take on the SIVs' assets once short-term credit dried up, which were often toxic. By October 2008, the last SIV had liquidated.

Another popular financial product was the collateralized debt obligation (CDO), which allowed financial service firms to repackage their debt

---

[110]Tett, G. (2009). "How Greed Turned to Panic," *Financial Times*, May 9, 20.
[111]Federal Deposit Insurance Corporation, Testimony of Jamie Dimon, before the Financial Crisis Inquiry Commission, Jamie Dimon (Washington DC: January 13, 2010), 2. Available at http://www.fcic.gov/hearings/pdfs/2010-0113-Dimon.pdf.
[112]Tully, S. (2008). "How JPMorgan Steered Clear of the Credit Crunch," *Fortune*, September 2.

(mainly mortgages) and sell it in tranches based on different risk profiles. Dimon saw internal opportunities to securitize Chase Home Loans, and by early 2006, JPMorgan was "growing substantially in securitizing mortgages and dabbling in subprime CDOs." However, in October of 2006, the mortgage-servicing department detected increasing late payments on Chase subprime loans and more specifically non-Chase loans which were performing three times as worse as the Chase loans.[113] Questionable and potentially insufficient underwriting standards explained the disparity, which the division quickly shared with the rest of the JPMorgan team.

The investment banking executives also had misgivings about the costs of insurance backing CDOs versus their potential payoffs. Rating firms had labeled some CDOs as AAA (despite the fact that nearly all of it was from the equity tranche of a Mortgage Backed Security), creating a perspective that the risk of default on the debt was low. Firms packaging CDOs often ended up holding the AAA-rated tranche since "hedge funds, insurance companies, and other customers were clamoring for the high-yielding CDO paper."[114] Insurance payments on the CDOs, in combination with a suspicion of deteriorating, industry-wide underwriting standards for subprime loans, led Dimon to rid the firm of nearly all its CDOs.

However, the move was not an obvious one, especially when fees for securitizing CDOs were lucrative and the paper was rated AAA or 'safe'. As defaults rose though, it became clear that a AAA rating was of little assurance as entire CDOs collapsed. As of October 2008, Citigroup wrote down $34.1 billion in CDOs — the largest write-down for such instruments, followed by AIG at $33.2 billion and Merrill Lynch at $26.1 billion. As of mid January 2009, JPMorgan only had $1.3 billion in write-downs on its CDOs.[115]

The Bear Roars no More

Bear Stearns was the fourth-largest investment bank and securities brokerage in the US, and had been a Wall Street institution for eighty-five years. It had survived the Great Depression and the 1987 crash, and "until the

---

[113,114]Tully, S. (2008). "How JPMorgan Steered Clear of the Credit Crunch," *Fortune*, September 2.

[115]Benmelech, E. and J. Dlugosz (2009) "The Credit Rating Crisis," NBER Working Paper No. 15045, June. Available at http://www.nber.org/papers/w15045.

very end, the firm never had a losing quarter in its history."[116] However, by May 29, 2008, the subprime mortgage craze brought down this financial giant.

A series of events that began in the summer of 2007 tell the outward story of the collapse: First, two Bear Stearns hedge funds went bankrupt on bad CDOs in July 2007. Second, at the end of 2007, the company suffered massive write-downs and its first quarterly loss. In January 2008, the CEO resigned, and by March, rumors of a liquidity crisis panicked investors, who began pulling their money out of the firm. On March 14, 2008, as an emergency loan was no longer viable, Dimon and the Feds instead discussed how JPMorgan could buy the bank and avoid a Bear Stearns bankruptcy. Eventually, the Fed agreed to assume the risk on $29 billion of Bear's $30 billion portfolio, with JPMorgan assuming the first billion of any losses. Dimon upped the price per share to $10 to encourage Bear Stearns shareholders to approve passage of the sale. Just fourteen months earlier on January 17, 2007, Bear Stearns had traded at $171 per share.[117]

To JPMorgan, the Bear Stearns acquisition meant expansion in equities, energy and commodities trading, investment banking, and additional assets for the prime brokerage desk. Dimon was also keen on acquiring the "securities-clearing operations," and the impressive Bear Stearns building in downtown Manhattan worth around $1.2 billion.[118] Despite the windfall, Dimon acknowledged that he would not have completed the deal without the Fed's support on Bear Stearns' debt. This illustrates how far leveraged one of the most resilient and savvy Wall Street players had become.

The Largest Banking Failure in US History — Washington Mutual

Washington Mutual, a 119-year-old Seattle-based retail banking operation with $307 billion in assets, was drowning in $30 billion of bad loans in 2008. In part, this was the result of the business expanding to "cater to

---

[116]Cohan, W. D. (2009). "Inside the Bear Stearns Boiler Room," *Fortune*, March 4.

[117]Kassenaar, L. and E. Hester (2008). "The House of Dimon," *Bloomberg Markets*, June. Available at http://www.bloomberg.com/news/marketsmag/mm_0608_story1.html.

[118]McDonald, D. (2008). "The Heist," *New York Magazine*, March 24.

lower- and middle-class consumers," who were previously ignored by mainstream credit card and mortgage lenders.[119] While initially profitable, failures in the housing market resulted in mortgage delinquencies and large asset write-downs, accompanied by increased delinquencies in credit card payments.

In March 2008, Washington Mutual struck a deal with the TPG private equity firm for a $7 billion cash infusion that would give the troubled lender new credit and valuable time to sort out its balance sheet. TPG thought it could "stabilize the bank's wobbly capital base, suffer through more bad-loan exposure, and ride out the economic downturn."[120] With new capital, Washington Mutual was able to reject a takeover bid from JPMorgan at $8 per share — a fraction below the then-share price of $10.

Months later, on September 15, 2008, Lehman's bankruptcy announcement affected Washington Mutual depositors who subsequently initiated a bank run on Washington Mutual. Over the next ten days, depositors withdrew $16.7 billion or 9% of the bank's total deposits. This was following a summer in which customers had already taken out $5 billion as a result of the precarious conditions at the bank. Washington Mutual was nearly insolvent and regulators agreed to a takeover because the bank was in "an unsafe and unsound condition to transact business."[121] The federal government seized Washington Mutual and opened the bidding process for buyers. On September 25, 2008, Dimon paid the government $1.9 billion for the assets of the largest-ever failed bank thus far in US history.

Despite expected write-downs on some of Washington Mutual's assets, JPMorgan investors reacted positively to the news. The purchase added 2,239 banking branches to JPMorgan in strategic locations such as California, Oregon, Florida, and Washington. Chase had little presence in these states and Florida was particularly appealing for Chase's New York clientele that wintered down south. Moreover, JPMorgan added nearly $188 billion in deposits to its capital base. Finally, the government's seizure of the bank precluded JPMorgan from having to acquire Washington

---

[119]Dash, E. and A. R. Sorkin (2008). "Government Seizes Washington Mutual and Sells Some Assets," *New York Times*, September 25, A1.

[120]Lattman, P. (2008). "Washington Mutual Fall Crushes TPG," *Wall Street Journal*, September 27, B1.

[121]Sidel, R., D. Enrich, and D. Fitzpatrick (2008) "Washington Mutual Is Seized, Sold off to JPMorgan, in Largest Failure in US Banking History," *Wall Street Journal*, September 26, A1.

Mutual's entire balance sheet — meaning they could avoid the debt and leave Washington Mutual investors with next to nothing.

JPMorgan received $25 billion from the US Treasury's Troubled Asset Relief Program (TARP) in October of 2008. Dimon would later divulge that JPMorgan was sufficiently capitalized and sold the government preferred stock and warrants only "because it was in the country's best interests."[122] Less than a year later, JPMorgan was one of the first banks to repay the TARP money, along with Goldman Sachs and Morgan Stanley, in June of 2009. American taxpayers earned dividends on the preferred stock they held in the companies, receiving nearly $795 million from JPMorgan alone.[123] Citigroup and Bank of America (BoA) each needed nearly $20 billion more from the Treasury. BoA returned the funds in December of 2009, but as of March 2010, Citigroup had yet to return the full sum.

Risk Management Requires Discipline

While a strong risk management operation helped JPMorgan avoid the worst of the crisis, it was not immune to the subprime recession. Although Dimon normally kept a keen eye on his balance sheet, a late investment into a $2 billion CDO escaped his notice in 2007. The loss amounted to a $1 billion write-down and sent "Dimon on another manic crusade to tighten risk management."[124] Moreover, there were $500 million in losses stemming from the firm's late foray into JUMBO mortgages (mortgages above a government regulated limit), $3 billion in write offs on LBOs, and losses from the decline of its preferred stock in Fannie Mae and Freddie Mac.[125]

Another outstanding loss in 2010 occurred within the consumer lending division as borrowers continued to default on credit cards and mortgage loans. Specifically, "Chase Card Services... lost $2.23 billion in 2009 and is unlikely to turn a profit [in 2010] ... [while] Chase retail services eked out a $97 million profit for 2009, though it posted a $399 million loss in the fourth

---

[122]Sidel, R. (2009). "Profit Solid, JPMorgan Aims to Repay TARP Funds," *Wall Street Journal*, April 17, C1.

[123]Sorkin, A. R. (2009). *JPMorgan and 9 Other Banks Repay TARP Money.* Available at http://dealbook.blogs.nytimes.com/2009/06/17/jpmorgan-repays-treasury-as-tarp-exits-continue.

[124,125]Tully, S. (2008). "How JPMorgan Steered Clear of the Credit Crunch," *Fortune*, September 2.

quarter."[126] In early 2010, the bank set aside billions more in reserves for expected future losses in these divisions and moved to stem foreclosures by working with borrowers to modify their loan terms.

Winning With Risk Management — Superior Outcomes

In spite of the aforementioned setbacks, there is no question of JPMorgan's superior performance during the crisis relative to that of its main competitors.

In 2009, JPMorgan doubled its profits year over year to $11.7 billion, became the number one investment bank with respect to fees, expanded the reach of its retail banking empire, and employed 40,000-plus more employees than it did at the end of 2007.[127] On profits alone, its competitors fell short: In 2009, Wells Fargo reported net income of $8 billion, Bank of America came in at $6.3 billion, and Citigroup suffered a net loss of $1.6 billion. The accolades rolled in for Dimon, now the subject of numerous books, whose celebrity was bolstered by JPMorgan's stock that "rose more than 50% over 12 months," from February 2009 to February 2010.[128]

His success can be attributed to maintaining a powerful balance sheet as part of his larger commitment to being actively engaged in his company's risk management strategy. As a man once exiled to the financial wilderness and criticized for a lack of vision, Dimon's reputation now seems invincible in an industry that has felled giants.

Case Review

The US subprime crisis and related real estate boom produced many losers and a few winners. For those who went long on real estate, the news is not good. For those who went short on real estate, the benefits are clear. The reality of the market is that the decline in real estate prices impacted different parts of the country differently. There are fascinating economic lessons in this. How JPMorgan could have stayed clear or this ensuing maelstrom is

---

[126] "JPMorgan Chase Earns $11.7 Billion," *New York Times*, January 15, 2010, B1.

[127] Onarn, Y. (2010). "JPMorgan Tops Goldman in Investment Banking as Fees Swell 13%," *Business Week*, March 4.

[128] Guerrera, F. (2010). "Dimon Days," *Financial Times*, February 25.

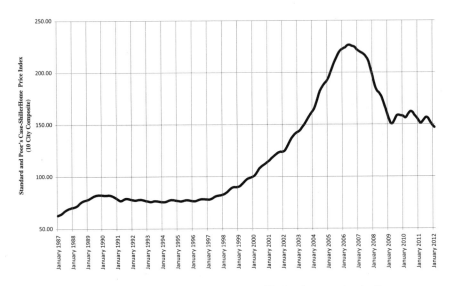

Figure 7.1.   Standard and Poor's Case-Shiller home price indices.

indeed owed to diligence in measurement and risk management. Figure 7.1 shows the Standard and Poor's Case-Shiller Home Price Index for multiple metropolitan regions provides a snapshot of the severity of the drop in housing prices and the rapid increase that we enjoyed beforehand.

This case highlights that even in an economic crisis, which impacts all market participants, there are opportunities to win with risk management. The healthy skepticism that Dimon maintained for new products and the non-transparent rating of mortgage-backed securities drove JPMorgan to measure and investigate the residential mortgage industry with great attention.

The conviction to forward a risk position even when the marketplace and competitors are taking the opposite position is powerful and rare. In an unwavering outlook on risk and complex financial instruments, JPMorgan stayed clear of the maelstrom that pulled so many banks into the subprime crisis.

The other important observation, similar to that which we saw with Nokia, is that diligence and preparation are rewarded after market shocks. The dramatic and rapid failure of Bear Stearns, and to some extent Washington Mutual, is unparalleled in the history of US banking. As JPMorgan was one of the only banks with a "fortress balance sheet," it was able to invest after the crisis.

With regard to active risk management, the actions taken by JPMorgan contained the credit risk to an absolute risk. In fact, the exposure to residential mortgages was reduced. This, as we saw, required the development of key risk measures and the conviction to exit the market. It allowed JPMorgan to reduce persistence in the risk. For competitors, the risks associated with residential mortgages lingered for many years and remain to this day. For many mortgage lenders, the precipitous downturn in the housing market and actions, or lack of actions that led to its demise, has become a point of concern for many constituents. Investors of nearly every bank have sued for lack of information and guidance in the housing market. Homeowners, municipalities, regulators, and secondary market bond buyers have also raised lawsuits to banks issuing mortgages. What began as a seemingly direct, explicit and finite risk, namely an absolute risk or issuing credit, has given rise through contagion to reputational and regulatory risks across the industry that has now persisted for many years after the initial real estate bubble burst. For the most part, JPMorgan was able to not only reduce its credit risk exposure, but prevent the major issues of both reputational and regulatory risks.

The study of JPMorgan in its deployment of risk metrics to prevent (or miss) the largest financial crisis in the last 80 years is valuable. JPMorgan recognized that residential mortgage risk, formerly a credit risk, is explicit in loans. Figure 7.2 demonstrates that through measurement, the finite and explicit risks of residential mortgages were more or less contained at

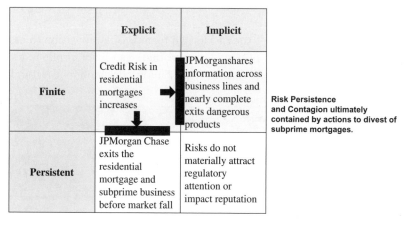

Figure 7.2.   JPMorgan thwarts risks from subprime crisis and contains persistence and contagion.

JPMorgan. The implicit risks are bets that the US real estate market will continue to be healthy. By tracking the loan performance on a leading indicator for risk, JPMorgan was able to test its assumptions about the implicit risk and exit the market before the market collapsed. With the ability to contain the exposure and take action, JPMorgan prevented the residential mortgage risk from causing significant regulatory or reputational harm that was otherwise felt by the likes of Bank of America, AIG, and Citi.

Winning with risk management allows and requires that firms take action on opportunity. JPMorgan could have remained on the sidelines, but seizing the opportunity to invest and buy assets below par enabled it to not only grow in size but fortify its strong position in the US banking industry.

Key Behaviors for JPMorgan

The case certainly celebrates the outcome of JPMorgan and the actions of its management. The efforts to exercise diligence and seek new information are key parts of a decision making process. However, the ability to seize the market opportunity and prepare for a market shock are tied to competencies in risk management. In summarizing these actions, it is valuable to consider key behaviors taken by JPMorgan, across its enterprise. These key behaviors are as follows and related to each other in Figure 7.3.

1. **Identify** — for JPMorgan, this involved identification of key risk indicators that would test its outlook on the market and the health of the mortgage industry in particular. Special attention to disconfirming information was critical.
2. **Assess and Analyze** — the JPMorgan team was in a position to assess and analyze the impact of new data and findings on the profit function of the bank. This requires an in depth knowledge and understanding

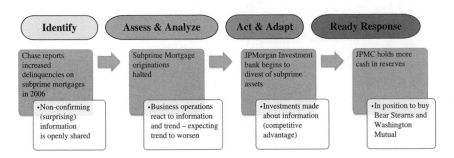

Figure 7.3. Key risk management behaviors at work at JPMorgan.

of how the investments of the firm are linked to profit. It also requires an understanding that specific risks can spread through contagion and develop into new and more troublesome risks. The ability to assess risks that can evolve and grow is also critical.

3. **Act and Adapt** — the actions of the leadership team provided the proactive preparation that allowed the bank to survive the Great Recession. By recognizing that the risk in previous investments had changed (based on new information), it was possible for the team to take action, sell specific assets and move away from the troublesome mortgage industry (before others saw it as troublesome).

4. **Ready Response** — preparing the firm for a crisis or shock is always harrowing. Believing that market or economic conditions could worsen requires preparation. However, knowing when such a shock might occur is nearly impossible. JPMorgan positioned itself to be short on the residential mortgage market and long on cash. In doing so, it was solvent and flexible, allowing for the market shock to pass and impact competitors. Opportunities to buy assets at discounted prices became available, which is common for winners for market shocks.

In Figure 7.4, the steps of this framework (Identify, Access and Analyze, Act and Adapt, and Ready the Response — IAAR) are related to the corporate capabilities that must be in place to execute these steps in the IAAR framework. Note the importance of the learning cycle in bringing newly discovered risk information, such as risk factors, to the assessment and analyze phase.

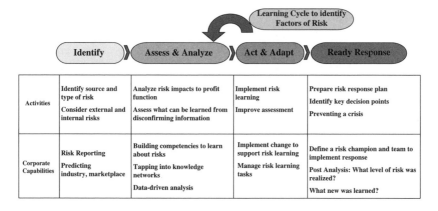

Figure 7.4.   The IAAR framework for enterprise risk management.

Consider the IAAR process in your enterprise and examine your enterprise's ability to conduct each step. Examine those external events or processes that are material to the firm and develop risk metrics in order to link the change in the market to the firm's profits. Many firms fail to link the functions in the IAAR framework, as the capabilities reside in different corporate functions. Linking these functions requires senior support for the risk function in the enterprise.

Risk Management Lessons

Scale risk management polices and measures across the enterprise

The attention to detail and the search for disconfirming information was not restricted to the retail banking operations at JPMorgan. Jamie Dimon ensured that risk management policies spanned across the enterprise. Information about the performance in the retail banking operation was used by the investment banking operation to make and divest of investments.

It is not natural for disconfirming information to flow easily through an enterprise or across business units. Elements of personal hubris and even positioning are sure to drive individuals and teams to hide or even disguise disconfirming information. Encouraging and requiring such information to come to light requires leadership to value data in the decision-making process. It is a powerful yet laborious approach. It paid off handsomely for JPMorgan.

In your organization, state clearly the market and economic outlooks for the business. Identify those investments that are most suspect and assumptions that are questionable. Determine where data is most limited and deploy teams to begin the measurement and tracking to remedy the void. Develop key risk indicators (KRIs) that are believed to serve as disconfirming (or confirming) signals of your hypothesis and outlook for market and economic conditions. And, finally, be willing to share the information across business lines and take action.

Develop a dynamic and investigative nature to your risk management

For many companies, risk management is part of a set of requirements. It might be akin to an audit function or linked to a procedural verification.

It might even look and feel like "checking a box." However, risk management, when practiced to its highest form, is not static and reporting in nature; it is dynamic and investigative. Risk management is ultimately about preparing the firm for what will (or might) happen next. The need to seek information on changes in the market place and complexities in business operations and projects is high. In the case of JPMorgan, the organization looked to the rise in the residential mortgage industry with skepticism and even disregarded the credit rating agency ratings of mortgage-backed securities. It is amazing that so many large banks failed so dramatically in the mortgage industry. The early warning signs were there to suggest some issues existed. However, the profits in the mortgage industry, previous to the downturn, were too tempting. For many banks, the disconfirming information was neither sought, nor considered for the sake of short-term profits.

In your organization, develop a risk team that has the ability and flexibility to investigate concerns as they arise. A static risk team will serve little more than to gather reported information. The risk management function should be able to create new information proactively. In addition, the team should focus on investigating key risks and assumptions implicit in the firm's strategy and investment portfolio.

Risk management is important during prosperous times

When speaking with firms that are building or strengthening a risk management function, it is common to find that the investment in risk management is during a financially or operationally difficult period. Although it is fine to invest in such times, the value that risk management can provide here is largely responsive. The example of JPMorgan shows that risk management, when practiced as a part of corporate strategy and during prosperous times, provides the proactive feature that allows firms to win with risk management. Measurement, tracking and investigation are needed as much before a crisis as during the crisis. That way, the firm is best positioned before a crisis or shock emerges.

I'll admit that it can be difficult to sell or even convince a team that risk management is critical during prosperous times, especially when the profits are rising. However, as we have seen, risk management is not about securing short-term profits. It is about protecting the firm in the long-term and ensuring that it can be prepared for the next shock to the market. Ask anyone who has lived in a climate with harsh weather. They will always tell you that preparation begins and happens before the storm. Ensure that your risk management team is looking out for the next storm, even if the weather is calm and enjoyable.

Develop an ability to question data — not to dismiss data

For many organizations, the process of making decisions is tied to the influence of key individuals. Perhaps the person with the most experience or best track record has greater credibility. There are reasons to grant such respect. However, opinions are just that. The function of investing as a firm requires information and data. JPMorgan demanded information, very detailed information on loan performance. The investigation of JPMorgan's originated versus third-party originated mortgages was not only important to understanding the performance of the market, but the performance of their own mortgage platform. It would have been easy for a team to assert that the Chase products were safer. In response, it is important to ask by how much? And why?

The ability to question data from the team must be done professionally so that it does not appear as an attack of the team. The culture for using detailed data and seeking new data is critical. When disconfirming information arrives, do not dismiss it, even it you believe it erroneous. Ask how it was developed, why the conclusions are such, how the data impacts the firm, and dispatch the team to provide explanations that make sense of the data.

Be willing to take bold decisions — but look to data for guidance

Dimon's commitment to looking at risk metrics and key risk indicators was impressive enough, but the conviction to take a contrarian position in the marketplace was even more so. While the large banks were raking in profits for mortgage-backed securities, JPMorgan was divesting of its mortgage-related holdings and even winding down mortgage originations. Indeed, JPMorgan refrained from such short-term profits. More short-term profits in 2006 and 2007 would surely have helped JPMorgan's stock price and quelled the concern that the firm was too conservative and not growing. Of course, it would have been difficult for Dimon to have announced publicly that he believed the mortgage industry unworthy of investment, while his competitors were feasting on one of the largest booms in the US real estate market. The ability to take action, lead with conviction and stay the course are indeed virtues of leadership that get tested under such conditions.

Examine the actions needed in your firm. Consider the impacted constituents. Ensure that employees understand and respect your approach and direction. Make clear to your board of directors that risk is part of your decision process. Educate board members and internal teams on the data and key risk indicators to build understanding and an appreciation for your contrarian stand. Invite new data and new perspectives too.

Case Questions

1. Comment on JPMorgan's outlook on the mortgage industry.
2. Why is developing key risk indicators so key in predicting shocks?
3. Was it fair for JPMorgan to buy Bear Stearns and Washington Mutual with Federal backing?
4. Consider the Case-Shiller House Price Indices. Examine the rise and fall of major metropolitan regions. Pick a few regions that interest you. Develop your explanation for the rise and fall. Note that some fall more than others. Why?
5. Consider how JPMorgan prevented an absolute risk (credit risk) from taking on contagion and persistence. What steps would you have put in place to manage such risks?
6. Should JPMorgan have shared its early insights on the demise of the housing market with other constituents, such as regulators, investors, buyers of mortgage-backed securities, etc.?

Chapter 8

Protecting the Enterprise From Itself — Learning From History, Again

A man who has never gone to school may steal a freight car; but if he has a university education, he may steal the whole railroad.
— Theodore Roosevelt, US President and Nobel Laureate

Nearly every banking risk manager studies the famous case of Nick Leeson and Barings bank. It is so important in modern-day risk management that one can indeed say that many of the provisions in Basel II's definition of operational risk were driven by the lessons learned from Barings bank and the actions of Nick Leeson and his complicit management.

Barings Bank, which has a long and storied history for taking "extraordinary risks", came to buy a brokerage house in Singapore. Its operations were not fully integrated with the headquarters in London. There were audit, reporting, and cash flow irregularities. Nick Leeson, a trader at the Singapore brokerage house, took large, long positions on the Japanese Nikkei market. The Kobe earthquake hit Japan in 1995, sending the Nikkei into a nosedive. Barings Bank was holding uncovered or "naked" positions. The bank was long the Nikkei market, and needed to come up with funds to cover its out-of-the-money long positions. The bank ultimately lost over one billion dollars and became illiquid. It was the largest bank failure caused not by market or credit holdings, but by a "rogue trader" and management's complicit tolerance of such behavior. Nick Leeson and many experts contend that the executives of Barings encouraged the dangerous risk taking at the Singapore brokerage house, as the investments were generating upwards of 10% of Barings pre-tax profits![129]

---

[129] IMD Cases on "Barings Collapse," Case #IMD001 and #IMD002 (1995).

When news of this became public, the banking world woke up to understand the importance of controls, governance, and checks and balances. Bank investors everywhere sought assurances that their banks would not be next. Meanwhile, regulators cracked down on irregular activity and hundreds of consultants and service providers developed products for measuring banking compliance.

So, it is surprising that such a dramatic and colorful lesson might need to be repeated. The following case of Société Générale demonstrates some key issues in risk. Often, the lessons are repeated because of human and corporate hubris, over-confidence or optimism bias in risk reporting, weak cultures for risk management and, of course, the temptation for taking unreasonable risks. Consider the following case and the parallels with the Barings case.

Société Générale — Background

On January 20, 2008, Maxime Kahn received a call from Société Générale's headquarters in the posh Parisian business district of La Defense. Kahn was an experienced options trader and was the head of Société Générale's European options operations. His superiors needed his assistance to help a client divest of large positions. Kahn retreated to a quiet office set up specifically for this task. He spent the next five days unwinding huge positions[130]: "€30 billion on the Euro Stoxx index, €18 billion on the German Dax, and €2 billion on the UK's FTSE." He would discover later that there was no client, and that the positions were those of a single trader in the firm, Jerome Kerviel. The losses on the positions would total around €5 billion and create a maelstrom for Société Générale's leadership and future earnings as well as the French banking industry. Chairman and Chief Executive Officer (CEO) Daniel Bouton and the head of investment banking, Jean-Pierre Mustier, offered their resignations upon announcing the scandal but the board quickly rejected these overtures. The survival of Société Générale was on the line, and the firm needed their experience, leadership and due diligence to guide the bank out of this unforeseen disaster.

---

[130]Bennhold, K. (2008). "Societe Generale Case Hears From Options Specialist," *New York Times*, October 16.

A French Institution

In 2008, Société Générale reached its one hundred and forty-fourth anniversary, marking its continued distinction as one of the oldest French banks. Its history was linked to the political and economic history of France itself: founded by a charter that Napoleon III authorized, nationalized in 1945 following the financial fallout of World War II, and returned to the private sector under the conservative era of Jacques Chirac in 1987. It was one of the largest French banks by market value, second only to that of another bank with a similarly long history in France: BNP (Banque Nationale de Paris) Paribas. At Société Générale's helm was CEO and Chairman Daniel Bouton, who had led the bank for nearly 15 years. As a graduate of top French universities, he had also held a series of impressive positions both within the financial and government sectors. Société Générale's head of the investment banking division, Jean-Pierre Mustier, and the Chief Financial Officer Frederic Oudea, also claimed impressive resumes and equally elite academic pedigrees.

Pioneering Efforts and a History of Taking Risks

In the 1980s, Société Générale became "a pioneer in the development of sophisticated equity derivatives," gaining international recognition and acclaim in the field.[131] Société Générale's success in the area of complicated financial modeling was a natural by product of its employees, mostly graduates from France's prestigious schools (École Polytechnique, École des Mines, and École Nationale d'Administration) with very technical backgrounds in physics or engineering. Société Générale's strategy was initially unorthodox but proved successful in the investment banking industry, as they targeted "stronger links with sophisticated buyers of structured investment products, such as Swiss banks and the client base of Lyxor, its high-end asset management unit."[132] They also seized new distribution opportunities for their products. Apart from its corporate and investment banking division, Société Générale's two other primary divisions were retail and financial services and global investment services.

[131,132]Hughes, C. (2008). "France's Derivatives Assembly Line," *Financial Times*, January 30.

The Fight for Independence — Taking More Risks

Société Générale survived a series of takeover wars that occurred in the French banking sector in 1999. Société Générale and another leading bank, Paribas, announced their intentions to merge. BNP reacted by launching a subsequent hostile takeover bid of both banks, securing majority control of Paribas's voting rights but less than one third of Société Générale's. Bouton fervently lobbied that BNP failed to secure effective control of Société Générale based on a 1966 law regarding takeovers. Authorities ultimately ceded to Bouton's appeal that Société Générale should remain independent, but approved BNP's acquisition of Paribas. Although Société Générale was able to dodge this takeover, this would not be the last time that Société Générale would encounter a similar threat.

Maintaining an independent bank for 144 years in the French financial environment was not an easy feat. Unlike other countries, French are "peculiarly hostile to the forces of capitalism that have made their economy world's sixth largest and their companies global leaders."[133] A 2006 survey reflected this disdain for capitalism that was in contrast to the American and British perspective: "Only 36% agreed that the free market was the best system available, compared with 71% of Americans and 66% of the British."[134] Even France's President Nicolas Sarkozy, who campaigned and won on a relatively conservative economic reform platform that included fewer taxes, utilized the Davos economic conference in 2010 to criticize inequity, financial speculation, and call for global regulation of markets and firms.[135]

The Fall of 2007

In the fall of 2007, the shouts against capitalism began to echo as global markets started to feel the downturn caused by defaults in the subprime mortgages in the US housing market. Société Générale's share price began a steady decline into December as the company divulged debt positions backed by these same mortgages. Other financial giants slowly revealed similar positions, and compromised balance sheets began to proliferate.

---

[133] "Biting the Hand That Feeds It," *The Economist*, January 31, 2008.
[134] "France Faces the Future," *The Economist*, March 30, 2006.
[135] "Davos 2010: Sarkozy Calls for Revamp of Capitalism," *BBC News*, January 27, 2010.

Several French firms, including Société Générale, followed the lead of US financial firms and announced an investment fund of €1 billion in highly rated asset-backed securities "aimed at bailing out small to midsize asset managers in case of a liquidity shortage," to guard against potential fire sale of the assets.[136]

In early November 2007, Société Générale announced write-downs of €404 million in assets and reduced quarterly profits — the first in a series of negative announcements that the firm released on the effects of the subprime crisis. One month later, as short-term financing became increasingly scarce, Société Générale announced it would need to cover its structured investment vehicle (SIV), which put on its balance sheet $4.3 billion worth of questionable assets from an off-the-books fund. Despite damaging reports from its investment department, Société Générale's retail sectors continued to be profitable and expand in developing markets.

Black Monday for Société Générale — Risks Are Realized

As 2007 ended, global markets continued on a downward spiral. The "Black Monday" of January 21, 2008 was a sign that it was not over yet. Massive sell-offs began early in Asian markets, driven by announcements of German write-downs and fear of a US recession, which quickly spread to Europe (the US was on holiday). From January 17 until January 23, the CAC-40 lost 10%, the DAX lost 13% and the NIKKEI 225 was down 7%. On Tuesday, Federal Reserve Chairman Ben Bernanke slashed the federal funds rate 0.75-percentage points, hoping that he could keep credit flowing and mitigate fallout in the US. American President George W. Bush and the American Congress also announced development of an economic stimulus package that would include tax breaks for businesses and individuals as well as an extension of unemployment benefits.

Meanwhile, across the Atlantic, from January 17 to January 23, Société Générale's share price dropped 15% on the Paris exchange. On January 24, leadership made a surprise announcement that it would suspend shares trading and then disclosed a larger than anticipated asset write-down of €2.05 billion.[137] That however, was not the worst news. Most devastating,

---

[136]Parasie, N. (2007). *French Banks Reportedly Setting up Conduit to Help Asset Managers*. Available at http://www.marketwatch.com/story/french-banks-reportedly-setting-up-conduit-to-help-asset-managers.

was the admission of nearly €5 billion in losses linked to the newly exposed positions of a single trader, Jerome Kerviel.

Jerome Kerviel — Corporate Culprit

Jerome Kerviel's origins were modest: he was born in 1977 to a lower middle class family from a small town in northwest France. His educational achievements were equally modest, having attained finance and graduate business degrees from less prestigious schools than those of his colleagues at Société Générale. Yet he received his break while in graduate school through an internship at BNP Paribas's back room or "The Mine." Upon graduation in 2000, Société Générale offered him a permanent position in "The Mine." By 2004, Kerviel moved up to junior trader at the bank's "Delta One" unit, having benefitted from a company initiative to promote back room personnel, and by 2007, was earning a modest salary of €100,000, with potential for a performance bonus. Kerviel's career progression was a great accomplishment, and yet he was not regarded highly as other traders at Société Générale.

"The Mine" vs. "Delta One" — Organizational Implications

At Société Générale, "The Mine" and "Delta One" served very different purposes. In "The Mine," employees were a part of the general operational control apparatus, monitoring and processing transactions. As a result, employees had access to and knowledge of the many different levels of Société Générale's myriad accounting systems. Kerviel's first job in the back office entailed reconciling the events on the trading floor with computer records. This was followed by acting as a communication liaison between trading desks and risk-management divisions.

Back office employees were often new graduates from less prestigious universities, as opposed to their trader colleagues who had earned degrees from the top tier schools. This organizational structure created an interesting dynamic between the younger monitors and the traders they were supposed to monitor. Politically, it was often difficult for back office operations

---

[137]Gauthier-Villars, D, C Mollenkamp and A MacDonald (2008). "French Bank Rocked by Rogue Trader," *Wall Street Journal*, January 25.

to resolve questionable trades or reconcile numbers, as some traders did not take seriously back office concerns over their actions.

Delta One is a unit found in many investment banks that conducts program trading on exchange traded funds (ETFs), swaps, and indices among other things. Traders in the Société Générale outfit primarily bet on European stock indices such as the Euro Stoxx 50, Germany's DAX Index, and France's CAC-40, creating arbitrages between long and short positions on futures contracts. The hedging nature of the operation results in small profit margins but these operations scale up the size of the investments and hence profits. Banks can also earn interest on the initial margins investors put up at the outset of the trade. In general, these Delta One divisions were viewed as a low-risk operation because of the expectation that all traders would net their positions at the end of the day.

Going Big, Taking Bigger Risks

Beginning in 2005, Kerviel began placing large bets that index futures would continue to rise and purposely failed to net those positions. He covered his tracks with a web of fake trades, creating counterfeit hedges, or using "time-dependent securities such as warrants for counter parties (because warrants were not confirmed by the back office until a few days before they expired)."[138] He also buried some trades in colleagues' accounts, after gaining knowledge of their passwords and logins. Furthermore, he capitalized on his knowledge of back office internal controls and kept up friendships with the staff, allowing him to manipulate records and remain up-to-date on the latest monitoring procedures. Shortcomings in the accounting system were also fortuitous for Kerviel. "Positions are often hedged using bespoke derivatives contracts that can take weeks to be formalized, leaving the bank exposed and with a huge backlog of unsettled trades."[139] As a result, Kerviel had a convenient excuse available whenever questions arose about his positions.

Since he was not hedging, his trades would pay out large gains should the indices rise or fall according to his real position. At one point, his scheme resulted in approximately €1.4 billion or more profit in the fourth quarter of

---

[138,139]Hollinger, P. (2008). "Hard Hitting Lagarde Points up SocGen's Lack of Control," *Financial Times*, February 5.

2007.[140] Throughout this time, he rarely took a day off and always worked well into the night.

The Beginning of the End

His positions unraveled as indices around the world began a steady decline in the fall of 2007. The bank conducted audits in preparation for its annual report due out in February of 2008. Managers from all departments sent their figures to measure Société Générale's capital to assets ratio. The auditing team found inconsistencies, which they slowly pegged to one trader. On January 18, managers discovered a trade whereby Kerviel "changed a tactic he had been using to conceal his trades and...took a position that prompted a possible margin call."[141] Without telling French or American authorities of the discovery, Société Générale unraveled the trades just as markets suffered rapid losses.

Despite the magnitude of Kerviel's positions, Société Générale's actions did not account for more than 8% of the daily volume.[142] Once they had closed the books on his trades, Société Générale announced the losses and their indictment of him as a stand alone actor. French authorities subsequently arrested Kerviel, but soon released him to conduct a wider investigation into the allegations against him; prosecutors had no clear charge against a "rogue financial trader."

The Risk Becomes Real

Kerviel created severe problems for Société Générale's leadership and balance sheet that called into question its historic reputation and more importantly, its ability to manage risk. New funds were critical to the survival of the 144-year old institution but it needed to consider carefully how to raise the funds. This was a difficult prospect in an environment where most financial firms were on life support amidst growing malaise towards the banking sector. Leadership set to work on the numbers while investigations

---

[140]Clark, N. (2010). "Rogue Trader at Societe Generale Gets 3 Years," *New York Times*, October 5.
[141]Gauthier-Villars, D., C. Mollenkamp and A. MacDonald (2008). "French Bank Rocked by Rogue Trader," *Wall Street Journal*, January 25.
[142]Hollinger, P. (2008). "Hard Hitting Lagarde Points up SocGen's Lack of Control," *Financial Times*, February 5.

began into how Société Générale failed for two years to recognize a trader's extraordinary series of actions that cost the firm billions.

Damage Control — Too Little, Too Late

On January 28, trading of Société Générale resumed and the stock price continued to hemorrhage, falling 7.4%. New capital was critical, and Société Générale was able to secure a rights issue underwritten by JPMorgan Chase & Co. and Morgan Stanley. The shares would be sold at a discount of 30 to 40% of the current price, "diluting earnings" and prompting Citigroup to shift its outlook on the stock "from medium risk buy to a high-risk sell." Société Générale considered tapping sovereign-wealth funds as these were a popular outlet for cash-strapped firms, but "there wasn't time to negotiate such a deal, and bankers believed that French President Nicolas Sarkozy might object."[143] Société Générale would wait for its 2007 final earnings report and for its investigation into Kerviel's actions to conclude before asking shareholders for nearly €5.5 billion.[144]

Insiders at Société Générale had other matters to worry about besides a crack in its reputation. They hoped that a successful capital infusion would signal confidence in its leaders and ward off a potential takeover. With French officials like Sarkozy disparaging bank executives in public, and the continuing fall of Société Générale's share price (it had already fallen 30 per cent in one year), the moment was a ripe for a takeover. BNP Paribas and Crédit Agricole were likely bidders, and should they take interest, foreign suitors would soon follow, even though foreign control of an entrenched French institution would have been unacceptable to the French government. Serious offers were unlikely until officials revealed the entire story behind the scandal. By February 1, 2008, the stock price had lost a third of its value from the previous year.

Risk Revelations and Regulation

In the aftermath of the scandal, the French Finance Ministry and other financial institutions presented reports which detailed the shortcomings of

---

[143] Gauthier-Villars, D., C. Mollenkamp and A. MacDonald (2008). "French Bank Rocked by Rogue Trader," *Wall Street Journal*, January 25.
[144] "After JK," *The Economist*, May 29, 2008.

Société Générale and its monitoring staff of more than 2,000 personnel. Finance Minister Christine Lagarde criticized Société Générale's career development program that promoted employees from the monitoring side of the business to its trading desk, the poor computer security, the failure to inform the government of the scandal, and the failure to notice atypical employee behavior.[145] Going forward, Lagarde recommended a fine larger than €5 million for Société Générale, the maximum fine the banking commission could impose at the time. She reasoned that a higher fine would prevent future cases of moral hazard in operational risk management. Finally, Lagarde also chastised the bank for ignoring two memos sent to Société Générale's Daniel Bouton from her commission, "setting out areas where controls needed to be reinforced after several inspections." There was unanimous agreement that to prevent future Société Générales, there needed to be greater expansion of regulatory authority over financial firms and their products.

Industry Perspective — Unacceptable Operational Risk

The Committee of European Banking Supervisors also produced a report after polling affiliated members on their views about the scandal. Interestingly enough, the report stressed that while banks cannot eliminate the possibility of rogue trading, good risk management can mitigate the scope of the damage. Surveyed banks detailed five categories in which Société Générale needed to improve their risk management practices based on publicly available information about the scandal:

1) Segregate "duties between front...and back offices."
2) Implement an IT system with a strong security focus.
3) Create quality "business/management practices": ensuring employees take holiday, confirming the "process of OTC transactions with clients/counterparties and pending counter party certification," and reconciling "daily cash flows."
4) Create a better internal controls system that monitors the holistic position of an individual trader (e.g., cash flows, amended trades, volume traded).

---

[145]Hollinger, P. (2008). "Hard Hitting Lagarde Points up SocGen's Lack of Control," *Financial Times*, February 5.

5) Implement better processes/standards in place for resolving alerts, warnings and suspicious behavior.

The Basel Accords — Going Against Best Practices

All of these suggestions reflect well-known principles of the Basel Accords, which promote a strong operational risk management environment. The Basel Accords are a series of guiding principles for creating laws and regulations that work to standardize international banking using best practices. Many of the leading global economies have membership on the Basel Committee, which periodically updates its recommendations. In its February 2003 publication on operational risk, Basel members outlined that any effective environment will have "clear strategies and oversight by the board of directors and senior management, a strong operational risk culture and internal control culture (including, among other things, clear lines of responsibility and segregation of duties), effective internal reporting, and contingency planning." Ten principles more fully explain their suggestions which Société Générale execs had chosen to disregard in taking on big risks.

Kerviel's Side of the Story — It Involved Many

Subsequent interviews with Kerviel paint a picture of events that was unflattering to Kerviel and Société Générale and confirmed Société Générale's lax risk management system. He first acknowledged there was some opportunity for personal gain from his trades; at the end of 2007, Société Générale approved a €300,000 bonus for him. Next, he repeatedly claimed his superiors knew about his transactions and purposefully ignored alerts about his trades, implicitly encouraging him so long as he was making money.[146] He based this claim on the fact that his trades generated such large profits initially, which was highly uncharacteristic of an operation like Delta One. He also said that he had only requested four days off in 2007, which should have signaled he did not want anyone looking through his books.[147] Finally, Kerviel described an incident that was particularly indicative of poor oversight at Société Générale: for several months after a manager had resigned,

---

[146,147]Matlack, C. (2008). "Jerome Kerviel — In His Own Words," *Business Week*, January 30.

Kerviel signed off on his own trades. Manager or not, Jerome Kerviel was able to act freely on his own ambitions within Delta One.

Kerviel's direct supervisor, Eric Cordelle, was a typical Société Générale climber: a graduate of a prestigious school with work experience in a foreign Société Générale office, and a quick rise to a management position without any specific trading experience.[148] Cordelle received more than 60 alerts that specifically questioned Kerviel's trading pattern.[149] The back room issued many of the internal alerts while external alerts came from Eurex (the world's largest futures and options exchange), which sent several inquiries to Société Générale over a two-year period. These alerts were in addition to the usual daily reports they sent to firms about the net exposure of traders and trading departments, as well as margin data on specific traders. In one specific instance, they flagged a trade in October 2007 that was more than $1.5 billion; "the entire Delta One desk was not supposed to trade more than $190 million in a day."[150]

Each time Cordelle or other bank managers questioned Kerviel about an alert, he would claim that the numbers were a mistake, backing up his excuses with phony emails or quickly adjusting his computer records before subsequently re-entering his fake trades.[151] He achieved all of this for quite some time, despite the incredible magnitudes of some of his margin calls — upwards of €2.5 billion. Despite the entirety of these claims, Cordelle attested that at no time did he suspect anything nefarious from his trader. Société Générale eventually fired Cordelle and Martial Rouyère, head of the Delta One trading desk, along with five other supervisors and colleagues.

The Fight for Independence, Part Deux

In the months following the scandal, takeover fears went unrealized as many firms dealt with their own balance sheet issues. One by one, Deutsche Bank, Santander, Intesa Sanpaolo, Crédit Agricole, and UniCredit took themselves out of the takeover race; BNP Paribas remained uncommitted. Société Générale, along side Crédit Agricole, UBS, CitiGroup, and Barclays

---

[148,149,150]Matlack, C. (2008). "Why Conspire When Nobody's Looking?" *Business Week*, March 14.

[151]Matlack, C (2008). "Jerome Kerviel — In His Own Words," *Business Week*, January 30.

approached the Financial Guaranty Insurance Company (FGIC) on a potential plan "to commute, or unwind, their credit-default swaps," that they had entered into with "FGIC and other bond insurers to guarantee their portfolios of collateralized-debt obligations."[152] Société Générale also announced that it had a loss of €3.35 billion in the fourth quarter of 2007, well below the previous year's fourth quarter profit of €1.18 billion. The 2007 fiscal year was profitable at €947 million, but this was 82% lower than the profit earned in 2006.

The Recovery Trust

The bank issued rights to increase equity and stabilize its balance sheet. It was also an opportunity to rebuild trust with investors and the banking community. The rights issue was an incredible success for Société Générale, confirming investor confidence in the bank's leadership and strategy. While the board requested only €5.5 billion in new capital, investors purchased more than €10 billion worth of new shares. Société Générale investors could "buy one newly issued share at €47.50 for every four shares held... a 39% discount to the market price."[153] Mr. Bouton, in a show of support for his bank and its future bought €1.5 million worth of more shares (although not all of his fellow board members were as outwardly supportive).

Despite the successful rights issue, the stock fell 25% from the beginning of February 2008 until mid-April of the same year — not unlike other banks at the time. In March, BNP Paribas officially announced it would not bid on Société Générale, which left new leadership free to devote their entire attention to the ongoing crisis and "plot a course back to health."[154] This included Daniel Bouton stepping down as CEO, and CFO Frederic Oudea assuming the post. The resignation was symbolic in nature as Bouton would remain Chairman.

---

[152] *Wall Street Journal*, February 7, 2008.

[153] Viscusi, G. and A. S. Chassany (2008). *SocieteGenerale Plans Offer to Raise EU 5.5 Billion*. Available at http://www.bloomberg.com/apps/news?pid=newsarchive&sid=aY1ywT_wCWUM&refer=home.

[154] Guernigou, Y. L. and S. Kar-Gupta (2008). *BNP Paribas Says Will not Bid for SocGen*. Available at http://in.reuters.com/article/2008/03/19/us-socgen-bnpparibas-idINL1267801220080319.

As CEO, Mr. Oudea continued to execute Mr. Bouton's plan of "investing excess cash flow from the company's domestic and investment-banking operations into expanding its international retail, asset-management and consumer-credit activities," primarily in developing countries. While the credit crisis caused havoc in asset management and the investment banking divisions, profit remained strong in international retail. In May 2008, Jean-Pierre Mustier announced former Bear Stearns executive Michel Peretie would replace him as head of Investment Banking and he would move to head the bank's asset management division. Investors reacted positively and Société Générale's share price rose. Peretie pursued a path of constrained investing policies while the company implemented €100 million worth of new monitoring and technology reform.

One further job change also took place: Kerviel found work in an IT consultancy that specialized in "network installation and security." However, he would eventually stand charges of forgery, abuse of trust, and hacking in June of 2010. In 2012, an appellate court upheld Kerviel's initial conviction of 5 years in prison with 2 years suspended and payback of all the losses incurred (about €4.9 billion).

The French Restoration and Regulatory Power — Increased Regulatory Risks

After the investigations were completed, Société Générale paid a €4 million fine. While Lagarde did not see a much higher fine than this for this abuse, she did increase her office's regulatory power: a new French pay czar, a hefty one-time bonus tax on financial service employees in 2009, and tougher regulation against credit-rating agencies. Moreover, she continues to call for greater regulation of sovereign credit default swaps, capital requirements, and hedge funds.

At Société Générale, losses plagued the company and its reputation and forced them to take a €1.7 billion loan from the French government in December of 2008. In light of the turmoil in the financial markets, the French government pumped more than €10 billion into the country's six largest banks. Société Générale also benefited from the US government bailout of American International Group (AIG), whose bailout funds totaled $185 billion as of February 2010. With the bailout money, AIG settled an $11 billion debt with Société Générale and several other debts owed to Barclays, Deutsche Bank and UBS.

Troubles continued in Société Générale's asset management division, and in January of 2009, the bank sold most of this division to Crédit

Agricole for €732 million. Industry consolidation was perceived to generate savings of over €100 million and would become the fourth largest firm of its kind in Europe. This sale helped Société Générale net positive fourth quarter earnings for 2009 of €221 million.

More Resignations — More Risks, More Involved

In April of 2009, 59-year-old Daniel Bouton resigned, citing that continued criticism of him was hurting Société Générale's employee morale and the company's reputation. Without the scandal, the company would have allowed him to stay in the role of Chairman until 70. Frederic Oudea, who became CEO following the scandal, assumed the role of Chairman while retaining his position as CEO.

A final blow to Société Générale's reputation, but perhaps not the last of the credit crisis, occurred late in 2009. Jean Paul Mustier, the former head of the investment-banking division and new head of the asset management division, resigned over allegations of insider trading. Officials launched an investigation of the sale of nearly half of his Société Générale shares in August of 2007, a short time before the various write-down announcements occurred. He was already planning to leave but wisely decided on an early exit. He had joined Société Générale as a graduate fresh from the École Polytechnique and the École des Mines, and had spent nearly 22 years with the firm.

Case Review

In examining the issues facing Société Générale, the parallels with the famous Barings case are almost too similar. First, the actions of a single individual are presumed to be the cause of the loss and failure. Although it may be true that Jerome placed the trades at Société Générale, his excessive trading volume was reported by the Eurex[155] on many occasions to Société Générale headquarters as an indication that something was awry. The warnings were disregarded. It is evidence that such rogue traders or failed employees do not act alone, but rather act within a culture and risk management system that is complicit, tolerant, and perhaps even accepting of the dangerous actions. It is clear that in the case of Société Générale,

---

[155]Hollinger, P. (2008). "Hard Hitting Lagarde Points up SocGen's Lack of Control," *Financial Times*, February 5, 2008.

the size of trades had become too large and dangerous. The trades were not covered, exposing Société Générale to large losses if the market moved against them. It was akin to gambling at the highest stakes. But why do organizations do this? Why are risk lessons repeated? There are some key factors related to risk and its treatment in organizations that can provide us guidance.

Cultural Hubris — is the arrogance or belief that an organization is different. It is immune to the realities of the market and assumes better performance because of its history, stature, fame, and people. Although hard to define clearly, we have all encountered cultural hubris when hearing, "It could never happen here." That admission sets the tone that disconfirming information is ignored or not even considered. Cultural hubris is an ever-present risk for business because it may be reinforced by corporate success. The management must work to ensure that actions follow policy and strategic outlook, and that they remain data driven as well.

Optimism Bias — is a structural problem in how we perceive risk and our ability to project such possibilities. When risks have not been observed, our ability to estimate them is impaired. We underestimate risks that we have not ourselves seen realized. Most traders working in banking during the Great Recession were too young to have worked during the recessions of the 1980s and 1990s in the US. In a similar manner Kerviel did not work during the Barings failure and did not have the perspective on how firms might suffer catastrophic trading losses. He surely believed that such things would not happen at Société Générale. Not only was Société Générale different, the risk was unknown or at least unseen, making it harder to contemplate. Organizations are faced with this constantly and must work to overcome the optimism bias. Consider your role as a business manager, where subordinates present ideas for investments. How often do your subordinates retract the proposals for investment and consider the investments too risky? Likely, very infrequently. That is the danger. That is the manifestation of optimism bias.

Cultures for Risk Management — are built up over time and are the product of the firm's history and path. By considering the history of Société Générale, we get a clear sense that its pioneering advances in the 1980s and its scrappy fight to remain independent during a recent takeover event left it with not only a sense that it was special, but that risk taking was part of its virtues. One wonders if risk was even considered by Société Générale during Kerviel's investment spree.

Moral Hazard — is the predicament that an agent (e.g. employee) encounters when he or she is motivated to behave in a way that runs counter to the wishes of the principal (e.g., firm). In general, moral hazard increases when there are 1) motivated agents and 2) attractive targets. Kerviel's background and standing in the bank provides some color on why he might be considered a motivated agent. Psychologists can speak more directly to personality traits and experiences that motivate people to do harm, but it is clear that social pressures, personal debts, a drive for social acceptance and wealth are known drivers. Management may not be able to control motivated agents, but as part of hiring processes and team selection, it is important to consider factors that reduce the likelihood of a motivated agent working at the firm. Attractive targets, in the context of actions at Société Générale, include the easy accessibility of trading funds or the ability to act out of formal authority. It is the responsibility of management to reduce attractive targets so that motivated agents find it more difficult to gain access to assets.

For financial firms like Société Générale, the risk posed by rogue employees is considered an operational risk, under the Basel Accord banking measures. In part, it is recognition that not only did a person(s) fail, but so did a system and process for prevention and detection. That system includes the human element and the process the oversight of management. In nonfinancial firms, there is less guidance or regulation in the prevention and detection of rogue employees and less industry focus on the issue. The failure of processes to contain or prevent rogue employees is also considered an operational risk. There is an expectation in the banking industry that such risk is contained through specific policies and detection or measurement. The absence of such policy and measurement allows both the risk to dangerously grow and for exposure to increase without management detection. The impact to Société Générale is that it is now linked along the same lines as Barings, and its ability to control operational risk will forever be questioned.

This has long-term impact in attracting business, responding to regulation, and taking a leading position in the marketplace. Société Générale will wear this scarlet letter for a long time. It is an example of how an operational risk, once realized at a large enough level can have near infinite impacts to the enterprise.

	Explicit	Implicit
Finite		Management of Operational Risk: Controls and Supervision
Persistent	Risk from Industry	Risks realized include industry scrutiny, regulation, and reduce competitive footing

Risk Persistence: Events of a few lead to large scale and prolonged effects

Risk Contagion: SocGen losses beyond trades

Figure 8.1. Société Générale experienced operational losses that lead to reduced reputation and increased regulatory scrutiny.

Figure 8.1 shows how the operational risk exposed Société Générale to persistent risks from investor and regulator scrutiny.

In addition to serving as a reminder on why risk lessons are repeated, the case also suggests some best practices. Namely, it appears that Société Générale had insufficient checks and controls in place to monitor the activity of a rogue employee. It would be expected that audit functions, trading platforms, and risk policies would have also raised red flags. By the sheer size of the cash movements, the Société Générale's Treasury function must have realized something was amiss. It is with this perspective that many look at the Société Générale case and claim that the management was complicit, tolerant, or encouraging of the activity in question.

Risk Management Lessons

Develop a risk management culture that has multiple layers of safeguards in place

The case highlights how such spectacular activity could be missed. It is similar to how Ericsson missed the supply deviations and the large banks missed the subprime crisis. It is important to have many layers of safeguards. Risk information does not have to be actively reported. It can be passively detected. The availability of IT systems to track deviations and disconfirming information is more powerful than ever. Follow-up when alerts are made. Look and ask for detailed explanation on what happened and why. If the explanation does not hold water, consider a team member change. Moving people in the organization not only spreads knowledge in the firm, it provides a set of fresh eyes for new investigation and inquiry. It can be the most useful safeguard of any.

In placing multiple safeguards, management sends signals and expresses standards. Such signals and standards for the acceptable treatment of risk information and the attitude towards risks are fundamental in the creation of a culture for risk management. Lax attitudes, indirect reporting, and blind-eye turning are also signals and set a different standard for the treatment of risk information.

Recognize moral hazards and motivated agents take steps to minimize these

It is difficult and demoralizing to imagine all the ways your employees can compromise the enterprise, but at some level it is necessary. Putting procedures and policies in place that prevent access and or limit the size of transactions by employees is a start. It also requires cultivating a culture that does not tolerate deviant behavior and openly questions disconfirming information. In the case of Société Générale, the operational risk of not protecting its assets from a motivated agent ultimately caused great loss and harm to the bank's brand.

Moral hazards and motivated agents often have accomplices. The complexity of the events at Société Générale suggests a dependence on many people in many functions. A key to managing risk in such a system is to alter the human system. Changes to reporting structures, rotational assignments, and movement of executives and associates across business lines bring new eyes and new questions. It is difficult for motivated agents to operate with success when the flux of associates brings new inquiry and discovery. Consider movement of talent not just for the purposes of developing a cross-trained workforce, but for the purpose of reducing risk in the human system.

Work to overcome optimism bias in your team

It can be challenging to question a team's rosy outlook without insulting them or reducing their spirit. As a result, ask that your team deliver recommendations using real data and that risk metrics be considered in any project or investment decisions. Lead by example and respond to only those projects that have a body of data and sufficient clarity in information to make a risk-informed decision. It will set a tone for expectations going forward. Lastly, consider the backgrounds, experiences, and perspectives of team members when forming teams. Look for diversity in experiences to counter the dangers of optimism bias. Allow and expect teams to report disconfirming information alongside proposals.

Learn from previous risk lessons — remind your team

Lessons from history are great teachers. A failure at a competitor firm is the best. It provides a learning opportunity without the capital costs. Identify risk lessons, both internal and external. Use this not to vilify employees, but to demonstrate the impact to the bottom line and the need to drive improvements in operations, reporting, and the understanding of risk. You will likely find that your team will have many great ideas on how processes can be improved and risks reduced when the stigma of mistakes is removed. Remind your team of risks that impacted your organization, industry, or market. Be on the lookout for data that is foretelling of such risks.

Verify results

Most companies of a significant size employ an audit team to verify results, performance, and even compliance with processes. In general, the audit function is most heavily applied in the finance and accounting function as well as in vendor management. Consider audits of internal processes and procedures. Develop an immense focus on data, its collection and use in decision-making. Audit functions in the enterprise are not traditionally audited. Look to HR processes and procedures to provide a measure of motivated agents. Audit safeguard procedures and the follow-up to alerts to determine if sufficient action was taken in regard to disconfirming information. And follow-up with the audit, requiring changes and verifying that the changes were made.

Case Questions

1. What processes and procedures would you put in place to reduce the possibility of a rogue employee?

2. Comment on the dangers of optimism bias. How might you formulate a team to reduce the impact of optimism bias?

3. A culture for risk management can be difficult to develop. How would you consider driving needed change in your organization's culture? What messages would you offer, and what policies would you forward to improve the culture for risk management?

4. Kerviel was known to work late and over the weekend, and not take vacation. These are, at least in the banking industry, known signs that an employee might be operating outside of policies or might be motivated to act toward a moral hazard. Develop a list of behaviors that might be considered key risk indicators for your company or industry.

5. Kerviel has been prosecuted under French law. It appears that he did steal a colleague's passwords in order to falsify a trade. Under French law, compromising someone's password is an offense. Surprisingly, there are few other laws in place to prevent or penalize a rogue employee's actions. Consider how legal authorities might actually alter this.

6. In the wake of the real estate crisis in the US, it has become clear that appraisers, loan officers, and loan brokers likely falsified information or took other action to circumvent the loan underwriting processes in the name of short-term profits. Compare and contrast a loan broker's actions in falsifying loan information with the actions taken by Kerviel.

Chapter 9
Forming an Organization That Competes on Risk: Organizational Implications

Be wary of the man who urges an action in which he himself incurs no risk.

— Lucius Annaeus Seneca, Roman philosopher
and Statesman

In managing risk and reward, firms often link the compensation paid to its employees with the firm's financial performance. This is often done through bonus and termed, "firm performance compensation." As rational as this may seem, the linkage is still incomplete in connecting the underlying risk decisions made by the employees (on behalf of the firm) to the impact felt by the firm (and not the employees). Frank Knight raises this question nicely in his famous thesis:

> The great complexity and difficulty in the analysis of business uncertainty and of profit as the remuneration connected with meeting it arises from this peculiar distribution of responsibility in the organization. There is an apparent separation of the functions of making decisions and taking the "risk" of error in decisions. The separation appears quite sharp in the case of the hired manager, as in a corporation, where the man who makes decisions receives a fixed salary, taking no "risk," and those who take the risk and receive profits — the stockholders — make no decisions, exercise no control.[156]

The question of aligning risk and risk taking is relevant in today's contemporary times. In the wake of the Great Recession, governments in the US and Europe called for executive compensation to be tied to long-term

---

[156]Knight, F. H. (1921). *Risk, Uncertainty, and Profit*. New York: Houghton Mifflin.

performance of the firm. In particular, the compensation of banking executives was called into question, given the risks that banks posed to the economic system and the requirement that all other industries have a safe and reliable banking system.

Recognized in this is the fact that an executive can and does make decisions that impact the firm beyond his or her tenure. This is, of course, the persistence of risk, inherent in many business decisions. Imagine a CEO being told that his or her performance-based compensation will be paid out over the next 10 years. Critics of legislation on risk and performance-based compensation argue that issuance of stock grants and options achieves this alignment. However, with CEO tenures at 4–5 years, one cannot expect that long-term risks are sufficiently factored in CEO decisions.

So, back to the simple proposal, requiring that CEOs' performance-based compensation be paid over a 10-year period, let's say. What would this do? Of course, it would make the CEO not only concerned about investment and risk impacts over a longer term horizon, but it would make him or her extremely vested in cultivating, grooming and mentoring the next CEO. There would be economic interest in succession planning. Communication of strategies from CEO to ensuing CEO would likely be smoother. CEOs would work as a continuum, building on each other's work, looking to safely grow the enterprise, avoiding shocks and catastrophes along the way.

This model seems foreign, almost impossible in the business world that we know. CEOs are brought in to provide new direction and leadership. The phrase stewardship, although appropriate for the role of a CEO, seems to rarely come up in what a CEO must do.

But there are places where such a business alignment of risks and compensations are aligned. Consider the world of family businesses, where ownership passes to heirs. The goal of the family enterprise is not necessarily maximum profits in the short-term but rather strength and survival over the long-term. To many family business owners, their approach to investment and risk, and their sense of responsibility to the firm are strikingly different from an executive at publicly-traded company. First, there are no buy out contracts, severance agreements and little to no prospect of "looking over the fence for a better deal." Family business owners view themselves as stewards of the enterprise in a position to develop and protect assets for their heirs and jobs for their employees. They are literally shareholders and executives combined. The perspective on risk is entirely different. The reward model is entirely different, and we can likely benefit significantly by having more of these aspects in the business world.

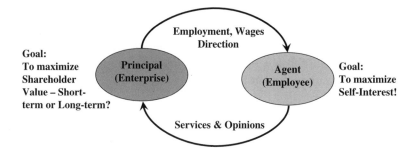

Figure 9.1. Principal agent problem.

This is not to say that employees or executives of a publicly-traded firm do not care. It is that risks and rewards are not entirely aligned. The problem is omnipresent. The situation does not require that the employee or executive have malicious intent. In fact, even with the greatest intent for the firm, we see that the alignment is the problem. At the core of this lack of alignment, and to Dr. Knight's point, is the classic principal-agent problem.

Figure 9.1 above highlights the alignment between a principal and an agent. The principal may be a bank or any enterprise. The goal of the principal is to prosper over a long period of time, although shareholders may place pressure on the firm to return short-term profits in the near term. The enterprise employs agents or employees for the purpose of running the enterprise. These agents are tasked with providing services and opinions that are material to risk-based decisions being considered by the enterprise. The agent has many short-term obligations in life, such as a family, mortgage, etc. The agent's goal is generally (although not entirely) to maximize short-term utility (salary, work-life balance, etc.). The employee, however, can often consider alternative jobs if the return for his or her work is unattractive. This essentially means that employees can short the employer. This prospect is of course in misalignment with the enterprise (employer), which remains long in its assets and investments. Such a prospect applies to a rational, ethical employee who may not be moved by temptations to act against the enterprise, but rather is simply acting in his or her best interests. The agent's contract of services does not directly link him or her to the long-term, persistent exposure to risk that the enterprise must take. If one considers a motivated agent willing to act maliciously or fraudulently against the enterprise, then the problem becomes amplified. In fact, the employee may actually take actions that are against the best interest of the enterprise in order to maximize his or her own self-interest. The most obvious examples include executives selling company shares before negative announcements (illegal as it is, the SEC catches executives doing this every year). The temptation for self reward at the expense of the firm is just too tempting for many.

The unfortunate news is that the solution to resolving this risk is difficult to develop. Perhaps a family business comes closest to providing a solution. Even private equity firms struggle, as the executive may jump ship for a different firm or industry.

As shareholders in firms, we are left with little assurance that an executive's compensation model is aligned with the risk he or she is authorized to take. Might the executive be exposing the firm to long-term risk, or ignoring contagion in risk that could be manifested in the future? Investors might look to regulators and the SEC to regulate and report on such moral hazard. However, The FDIC Subgroup on Moral Hazard (1999) said "The moral hazard issue may be addressed by ensuring good corporate governance and management of individual institutions, promoting market discipline...and regulatory discipline..." But according to Gary Stern (1999), President of the Federal Reserve Bank of Minneapolis, "The ability of regulators to contain moral hazard directly is limited..."

Shareholders cannot expect regulation to control the issues of moral hazard. Indeed, the government is not immune from moral hazard either. Boards of Directors of firms must recognize that the problem of moral hazard is most severe amongst those employees and executives with authority. Developing cultural norms for reporting and reacting to curious behaviors is critical. The propensity to react to a moral hazard is also related to the character of the individual, suggesting that those in the greatest positions of authority should be evaluated in all spheres of decision-making, not simply decision-making in business.

Chapter 10
Developing a Culture for Sound Risk Management

I am always doing that which I can not do, in order that I may learn how to do it.

— *Pablo Picasso, Spanish Artist*

On April 2, 2010, President Barack Obama lifted a 26-year ban on oil drilling in parts of America's eastern coastline and the eastern half of the Gulf of Mexico. He spoke of America's need for domestic energy sources to feed a growing economy. Part of his rationale was the low risk of an environmental downside for such a move: "It turns out . . . oil rigs today generally don't cause spills." [157]

Three weeks later on April 20, 2010 chaos erupted at the Deepwater Horizon oil rig in the Gulf of Mexico, as a fireball consumed the structure and pipes began spewing British Petroleum's (BP) oil off the coast of Louisiana. Eleven men lost their lives and for 45 days, the well spewed more than 200 million gallons of oil into the Gulf of Mexico. The record books took a new entry for worst oil spill in the history of the US and oil exploration. Congressional hearings, the Attorneys' General office, and journalists reviewed BP's safety practices. Their subsequent reports reveal a company that had been gambling on risk and beating the odds for nearly a decade. On April 20, the odds finally caught up with BP.

As we will see, numerous warning signs were either disregarded or missed. BP was under pressure to grow its business. The operational risk of oil spells reputational and regulatory risks. It would ultimately pay record fines and begin exiting many US businesses. Let's look at how the history of BP helped shape the firm, and how the events of 2010 impacted BP.

---

[157]President Barack Obama, April 2, 2010.

British Petroleum and Its Beginning

At the beginning of the 20th century, Iran (Persia at the time) was rich in untapped oil and gas reserves. British investments in oil exploration resulted in some of the first productive wells of the Anglo–Persian Oil Company, which was partly owned by the British government. At mid-century, company officials changed the company name to British Petroleum (BP), and developed a reputation for supporting political figures who were accommodating to the company's objectives in oil exploration. By the end of the 1970s, British Petroleum retreated entirely from Iran and much of the Middle East, having been "curtailed by the nationalization schemes of Arab states — in 1975, it transported 140 million tons of oil from the region, but only 500,000 in 1983."[158] BP subsequently embarked on a successful global expansion, including in North America, eventually divesting itself of public ownership during Prime Minister's Margaret Thatcher's era of privatization, which was heralded at the time. In order to be a world leader in oil exploration and production, BP would need to look to unconventional reserves — reserves with more operational risk.

John Browne, a former managing director, was picked in 1995 to lead the new British Petroleum into the twenty-first century. At the time, the company was nowhere near the revenues of oil giants like Shell or Exxon, and Browne sought growth by merging with Amoco, Arco, Castrol and Aral. Along these significant acquisitions, Browne made BP the first major energy company to acknowledge evidence in support of "global warming." This supported his company's subsequent investments into alternative fuels, bringing about a new and more apropos slogan of "Beyond Petroleum," part of a $200 million rebranding campaign that also changed the company name to BP.[159]

Internally, Browne took an eagle eye to the bottom line, a move to shake up a company where "bureaucracy ruled and operating costs were sky-high (BP's profit per employee was half that of Exxon)."[160] This brought about outsourcing, lay-offs, general cost-cutting, and an aversion to increases in operating expenses. He also pursued lucrative but risky opportunities to help the bottom line, resulting in "bold deals in politically volatile areas

---

[158]Tharoor, I. (2010). "A Brief History of BP," *Time Magazine*, June 2.
[159,160]Elkind, P., D. Whitford and D. Burke (2011). "BP: An Accident Waiting to Happen," *Fortune*, January 24.

such as Angola and Azerbaijan, and pushed oil exploration technology to the limit in the remotest reaches of Alaska and the deepest waters of the Gulf of Mexico."[161]

Profits climbed and Browne was praised for transforming a "sleepy second-tier European oil company into one of the biggest oil majors."[162] This professional success came to an unanticipated end in 2007, when Browne's professional conduct regarding personal relationships became the subject of court proceedings. While he was exonerated on charges of improper conduct, he had made false statements in court over the course of the ordeal.

Browne resigned and a fast-rising geologist named Tony Hayward became the new CEO. In the previous 11 years, Hayward had held such prestigious positions as treasurer and CEO of exploration and production. Hayward echoed Browne's earlier pledge to maintain a strict bottom line, since BP's "profitability [still] lagged far behind that of Royal Dutch Shell."[163] His other focus was on safety, championing a safety campaign known as the Operating Management System (OMS), "the foundation for a responsible and high-performing BP. It had two purposes: to further reduce... risks in our operating activities and to continuously improve the quality of those operating activities."[164] A leadership program, Operations Academy, was created to support this mission, where senior managers would learn "the skills to lead and sustain change in identifying and managing risk, both equally vital to achieving operational excellence."[165] A new commitment to safety and mitigating operational risk seemed apparent in the new leader.

Risk Brewing and Early Warning Signs

Hayward's safety campaign was, in part, an effort to reduce the number of accidents, both deadly and otherwise that occurred with alarming frequency

---

[161]Lyall, S. (2010). "In BP's Record, a History of Boldness and Costly Blunders," *New York Times*, July 12.

[162]Cowell, A. (2007). "John Browne Steps Down Abruptly From BP," *New York Times*, May 1.

[163]Crooks, E. (2009). "Back to Petroleum," *Financial Times*, July 7.

[164]BP, *Operating Management System*. Available at http://www.bp.com/sectiongenericarticle.do?categoryId=9032650&contentId=7059902.

[165]Kolmar, P. (2007). "A Standard of Excellence," *The BP Magazine*, Issue 4.

under John Browne. Yet, following each incident, BP's management failed to improve company safety efforts despite news of horrific and deadly accidents and millions in fines. Critics saw a company that was "operating at the margins of safety," with a corporate culture that had normalized red flags.[166]

It is helpful to consider a timeline of events, especially focused on BP operations in the US. Note the increase in accidents and the increasing severity of results from these accidents.

2003: A 50-50 venture with Russian authorities in Siberia representing "one-quarter of BP's global oil reserves," almost fell apart in 2008.[167] Government forces sought power concessions and "BP was forced to hand over operational control of the venture to its Russian partners, although it continues to reap vast profits from it."[168]

2004: A major explosion occurs at BP Texas City; no fatalities occurred.

2004: A worker falls to his death inside a tank at BP Texas City.

2004: Two workers are killed during a steam release at BP Texas City.

2004: A worker falls through a rotted railing at the refinery water plant in Whiting, Indiana and dies.

2005: A maintenance worker is found dead inside a tank in BP's Cherry Point refinery in Washington.[169]

2005: 15 people die at the Texas City refinery and 180 others are injured from a chemical explosion. The refinery "had long neglected maintenance and safety upgrades," and "chemical releases and minor fires were routine."[170] Several workers involved had been put in half-day shifts for more than a month.[171]

---

[166]Hoffman, C. (2010). "Investigative Report: How the BP Oil Rig Blowout Happened," *Popular Mechanics*, September 2.

[167,168]Lyall, S. (2010). "In BP's Record, a History of Boldness and Costly Blunders," *New York Times*, July 12.

[169]Olsen, L. (2004). "BP Leads Nation in Refinery Fatalities," *Houston Chronicle*, May 15.

[170]Elkind, P., D. Whitford and D. Burke (2011). "BP: An Accident Waiting to Happen," *Fortune*, January 24.

[171]Lyall, S. (2010). "In BP's Record, a History of Boldness and Costly Blunders," *New York Times*, July 12.

2005: Hurricane Dennis blows through the Gulf, and Thunder Horse, BP's new $1 billion platform, almost sinks. Inspectors find two separate causes: A valve installed backward had caused the vessel to flood during the hurricane and a welding job was so bad it "left underwater pipelines brittle and full of cracks."[172]

2006: An oil leak occurs on Alaska's North Slope. Corrosion in BP's Prudhoe Bay pipelines results in a leak and nearly 267,000 gallons of oil generate the worst oil spill on record there. The famous Alaska pipeline had endured many earthquakes and outlived its expected useful life. This failure was in part due to deferred maintenance by the operator, BP.

June 2007 to February 2010: BP's refineries in Texas City, Texas, and Toledo, Ohio, account for 829 of 851 industry-wide safety violations that the Occupational Safety and Health Administration (OSHA) calls "willful." OSHA suggests there is "plain indifference to . . . employee safety and health."[173] The rest of the industry totals 32.

2008: BP partners with China in Iraq and draws industry fire. Iraq had offered oil companies $2 a barrel to help it increase domestic production and others companies were incensed at the low price. The CEO of a rival firm called Hayward and asked: "Tony, have you gone mad?"[174]

While the totality of these events is independently troubling, it remains staggering when compared to other competitors' safety statistics: 10 times as many people have died in BP refineries as in those owned by Exxon over the past decade (Shell was the closest at half of BP's fatality total).[175] Moreover, the fines and payouts on totality of the incidents were not insubstantial and should have offered incentives for progress on new safety campaigns:

> *BP ultimately paid $373 million "in a combined settlement to resolve criminal and civil charges stemming from the pipeline leaks, the Texas City explosion, and unrelated charges of manipulating*

---

[172]Lyall, S. (2010). "In BP's Record, a History of Boldness and Costly Blunders," *New York Times*, July 12.

[173]Hoffman, C. (2010). "Investigative Report: How the BP Oil Rig Blowout Happened," *Popular Mechanics*, September 2.

[174]Lyall, S. (2010). "In BP's Record, a History of Boldness and Costly Blunders," *New York Times*, July 12.

[175]Olsen, L. (2004). "BP Leads Nation in Refinery Fatalities," *Houston Chronicle*, May 15.

*the propane market. The company pleaded guilty to a felony and
a misdemeanor, signed a deferred-adjudication agreement, and
agreed to three years of probation. It would pay another $2.1 billion
to resolve 4,000 Texas City personal-injury suits.*"[176]

Such settlements were astounding, and shareholders pressed BP to
resolve these issues. Concerns naturally arose over the ineffectiveness of
Hayward's OMS strategy. Critics of the plan suggested it did not go far
enough in creating a holistic focus on safety, nor did it offer "effective
procedures for guiding decisions during operations."[177] Rather, the plan
focused on individuals' safety, illustrated signs on company property that
reminded workers not "to walk and carry hot coffee at the same time, to
stick to marked walkways in parking lots and to grasp banisters while climb-
ing the stairs."[178] In 2007, two years following Texas City explosion, the
US Chemical Safety Board confirmed these shortcomings in its final report
on the matter, blaming "organizational and safety deficiencies at all levels of the BP Corporation" and spending cuts that ignored the potential
impact on safety.[179] The report detailed that BP's 25% cut to fixed costs in
1999 impacted operator training, and they were less prepared in general to
handle abnormal situations. Little changed at BP in the subsequent three
years following the report.

The Explosion in the Gulf

As mentioned, oil companies were seeking major finds and one solution was
deep water drilling, made possible by technological innovations that could
locate and extract the oil. While expensive (around $100 million per well
upfront), the payoffs were huge, and the Gulf of Mexico was an attractive
area due to its low political risk, "low taxes, and minimal regulation, as
well as nearby refineries and an insatiable market."[180]

[176,177]Elkind, P., D. Whitford and D. Burke (2011). "BP: An Accident Waiting
to Happen," *Fortune*, January 24.
[178]Lyall, S. (2010). "In BP's Record, a History of Boldness and Costly Blunders,"
New York Times, July 12.
[179]US Chemical Safety Board, "Investigation Details: BP America Refinery
Explosion," March 20, 2007. Available at http://www.csb.gov/newsroom/detail.
aspx?nid=205.
[180]Elkind, P., D. Whitford and D. Burke (2011). "BP: An Accident Waiting to
Happen," *Fortune*, January 24.

In February 2010, BP contracted the Deepwater Horizon rig to commence exploratory digging on its Macondo well in the Gulf of Mexico. The owner of the nine-year-old Deepwater Horizon rig was Transocean, a leading offshore drilling contractor, while the well-cementer was Halliburton, a large oilfield services company. As digging commenced, the total operation was costing BP more than $1 million a day.[181] In April of 2010, executives were not pleased with the operation's progress, as it was 45 days behind schedule and $58 million over budget.[182] With this pressure, it is possible that parties involved ignored or overlooked important safety issues that arose. At the very least, disconfirming information about operational risks was not adequately considered.

BP executives were well aware of ongoing "process-safety gaps in the Gulf of Mexico," according to documents from 2008: "It's become apparent," the BP document stated, "that process-safety major hazards and risks are not fully understood by engineering or line operating personnel... leading to missed signals that precede incidents and response after incidents, both of which increases the potential for and severity of process-safety related incidents."[183] This self-awareness did not translate into action, permitting a combination of issues to be overlooked that ultimately sank the rig:

1. The well needed 21 centralizers "to correctly position the casing (the carbon-steel lining inside the drill hole) so the cement could provide a good seal."[184] BP only had six on the rig and ordered more but received the wrong size; they used only six.
2. Cement around the well was needed to keep gas and oil out of the well hole. Both BP and Halliburton knew the cement had failed Halliburton's internal quality tests, and BP did not conduct a follow-up test once the cement was installed. According to investigators with the Presidential Investigatory Commission, had the cement performed accordingly, there would not have been an accident.[185]

---

[181]Hughes, S. and B. Casselman (2010). "BP Took Risk on Well Job: Investigator," *Wall Street Journal*, November 9.

[182,183,184]Elkind, P., D. Whitford and D. Burke (2011). "BP: An Accident Waiting to Happen," *Fortune*, January 24.

[185]Broder, J. (2010). "Panel Says Firm Knew of Cement Flaws," *The New York Times*, October 28.

3. Employees on the rig failed to properly conduct the critical negative-pressure test, accepting non-standard indications that pressure levels were fine. This was despite the fact that there were indications of pressure building in the well.[186]

On the night of April 20, 2010 gas escaped from the well, causing the rig to burst into flames. For a day and a half the rig burned until the entirety of the craft sank, breaking the piping and allowing oil to leak into the Gulf.

Cleaning up and Growing Costs

Tony Hayward's comments ensuing the Deepwater Horizon tragedy only added to the fallout. One of his initial responses to the incident tried to absolve the company from all blame: "This was not our drilling rig, it was not our equipment, it was not our people, our systems or our processes. This was Transocean's rig, their systems, their people, their equipment."[187] He would later recant this statement and attribute full blame to BP but not before the damage was done. He is recalled as also having said such inappropriate things as how he'd "like [his] life back" in reference to the massive resolution effort undertaken.

Congressional hearings and investigations by the Justice Department soon followed, prompting BP to establish a $20 billion escrow fund that would begin payout of damage claims. Much of the payouts would be to local communities along the shores of Louisiana, where the oil leak wreaked havoc on local tourism and fishing industries. It was not until July 15, 2010 did BP close the leak. Hayward resigned, and Bob Dudley, the new American CEO with a Southern accent, took charge. His to-do list included resolving the massive losses related to the spill. BP estimated "the Gulf spill will cost the company and its partners, including Transocean, which owned the blown-out well, $40 billion."[188]

In the January 2011 Report by the National Commission on the BP Deepwater Horizon Oil Spill and Offshore Drilling, the commission writes:

---

[186] "BP Spill Troubles Far Deeper Than First Thought." Available at http://www.msnbc.msn.com/id/41647474/ns/us_news-environment.

[187] Wray, R. (2010). "Deepwater Horizon Oil Spill: BP Gaffes in Full," *The Guardian*, July 27.

[188] Gold, R. and B. Casselman (2010). "Far Offshore, a Rash of Close Calls," *Wall Street Journal*, December 8.

"As a result of our investigation, we conclude:

> *The explosive loss of the Macondo well could have been prevented;*
>
> *The immediate causes of the Macondo well blowout can be traced to a series of identifiable mistakes made by BP, Halliburton, and Transocean that reveal such systematic failures in risk management that they place in doubt the safety culture of the entire industry;*
>
> *Deepwater energy exploration and production, particularly at the frontiers of experience, involve risks for which neither industry nor government has been adequately prepared, but for which they can and must be prepared in the future;*
>
> *To assure human safety and environmental protection, regulatory oversight of leasing, energy exploration, and production require reforms even beyond those significant reforms already initiated since the Deepwater Horizon disaster. Fundamental reform will be needed in both the structure of those in charge of regulatory oversight and their internal decision making process to ensure their political autonomy, technical expertise, and their full consideration of environmental protection concerns;*
>
> *Because regulatory oversight alone will not be sufficient to ensure adequate safety, the oil and gas industry will need to take its own, unilateral steps to increase dramatically safety throughout the industry, including self-policing mechanisms that supplement governmental enforcement;*
>
> *The technology, laws and regulations, and practices for containing, responding to, and cleaning up spills lag behind the real risks associated with deep-water drilling into large, high-pressure reservoirs of oil and gas located far offshore and thousands of feet below the ocean's surface;*
>
> *Government must close the existing gap and industry must support rather than resist that effort;*
>
> *Scientific understanding of environmental conditions in sensitive environments in deep Gulf waters, along the region's coastal habitats, and in areas proposed for more drilling, such as the Arctic, is inadequate. The same is true of the human and natural impacts of oil spills.*"[189]

Case Review

BP became an easy target for the government and those pushing for greater government regulation of the energy industry. The case of BP is odd in that

---

[189] January 2011 Report by the National Commission on the BP Deepwater Horizon Oil Spill and Offshore Drilling.

their risk taking extended to the safety of their assets and employees, with steep fines and employee deaths hardly being a deterrent or reason for pause. Moreover, this level of risk taking was not apparent in the rest of the industry, as BP stood above its peers in both fines incurred and fatalities — so other oil companies were more cognizant of the cost of ignoring safety. One response by the new CEO has been to tie operational managers' bonuses to safety performance.[190] It is unclear whether new enterprise-wide process safety measures will come about.

Billions aside, the full impact of the Deepwater Horizon disaster is yet to be estimated as the Gulf and its inhabitants will no doubt suffer lasting effects of this tragedy for generations. At the time of the accident, plumes of leaking oil were reported where "the top of the plume is... 3,600 feet below the sea surface... three miles wide and as thick as 1,500 feet in spots" and another with "one layer... about 1,200 feet below the surface, and the other... 3,000 feet deep."[191] BP's solution to this underwater catastrophe was to pour toxic chemical dispersants into the Gulf. Many have questioned this decision. Many also questioned the response of the US government and its agencies in response to this spill, too. The fate of BP and its ability to operate in the US and Gulf of Mexico are now on a path wrought with legal, political, and long-term risks.

The tragedy of the 11 men who lost their lives, the damage to the environment, the loss of economic ways of life along the Gulf Coast, and the damage done to the many other constituents to BP (employees, contractors, shareholders, and the like) is that this event was "preventable" and that its causes stemmed from failures in systematic risk management.[192]

The timeline above and the National Commission on the BP Deepwater Horizon Oil Spill and Offshore Drilling list many things that BP and its partners, Transocean and Halliburton should have done in terms of diligence in preventing the accident. The failure of risk management in many ways is evident. Risk information was disregarded or overlooked, and implications of changes in design were not carefully considered. However, getting to the

---

[190] Olson, P. (2010)."BP Ties Bonuses to Safety," *Forbes*, October 19.

[191] Gillis, J. (2010). "Plumes of Oil Below Surface Raise New Concerns," *New York Times*, June 8.

[192] January 2011 Report by the National Commission on the BP Deepwater Horizon Oil Spill and Offshore Drilling.

place where such oversight or disregard could occur in a dangerous activity takes a corporate culture that presses forward in spite of risk signs. BP had long been known for taking larger risks than its competitors. In fact, owing to having lost its Middle East reserves, it has spent decades clawing back in terms of proven reserves and market share.

The culture for risk taking and dangerous risk prevention can be, in part, measured by looking at how firms experience operational risk and prevent it. Those operational risks embedded in the nature of doing business are large and frequent in a business as dangerous and physically and environmentally demanding as energy exploration. One assumes operational losses in this business and should expect to self insure against these losses and or invest in maintenance and upgrades to reduce the risk likelihood and severity. With this reality in mind, it is therefore expected that energy exploration firms should hold cash (as insurance against operational losses) and demonstrate a prudent level of risk prevention and reduction through investments, often seen as operational expenses. Naturally, the level of cash and operating expenses would vary based on the size of the enterprise and the inherent risks taken by it. Still, similarities exist across firms involved in the same industry and exposed to the same base risks.

Consider Table 10.1. It provides the revenue, operating expenses, and cash holdings of BP, Exxon Mobil and Chevron for the period of 2001–2009.

Assuming that operating expenses, cash holdings and revenues are in proportion to the enterprise's size, we can develop ratios such as: 1) Operating Expenses/Revenue, and 2) Cash Reserves/Revenue. In each case, we expect the firms to have similar ratios, given the similar nature of the operational risk which they face. However, the results reveal a difference, consistent with the risk-taking culture at BP. Consider the cash Reserves/Revenues ratio. BP held less cash per unit of revenue than these two competitors, in spite of also having many lawsuits, judgments, and fines over that period of time. Although one might argue that holding less cash shows some fiscal efficiency, the cash position is fundamentally a measure of the firm's ability to absorb shocks and unforeseen impacts. A shareholder in BP would be rightfully concerned that the firm was not sufficiently prepared for catastrophe and operational risk losses that might well manifest in the course of normal operations, based on the cash reserve measure alone. At least, we would expect BP to have similar cash reserves, surely not levels 2–5 times less. It further suggests that in the absence of cash reserves, BP might be forced to liquidate assets (physical or equity) in an effort to meet

Table 10.1. Comparison of BP to competitors on operational risk investments.

	2001	2002	2003	2004	2005	2006	2007	2008	2009
BP (in millions of $)									
Operating Expenses	10,918	12,632	14,130	17,330	21,092	23,793	25,915	26,756	23,202
Revenue	174,218	178,721	169,441	199,876	249,465	265,906	284,365	361,143	239,272
Operating Expenses/Revenue	6.27%	7.07%	8.34%	8.67%	8.45%	8.95%	9.11%	7.41%	9.70%
Cash Reserves	1,358	1,520	2,056	1,359	2,960	2,590	3,562	8,197	8,339
Cash Reserves/Revenue	0.78%	0.85%	1.21%	0.68%	1.19%	0.97%	1.25%	2.27%	3.49%
Chevron (in millions of $)									
Operating Expenses	7,650	7,848	8,553	9,832	12,191	14,624	16,932	20,795	17,857
Revenue	104,409	98,691	120,032	150,865	193,641	204,892	214,091	264,958	167,402
Operating Expenses/Revenue	7.33%	7.95%	7.13%	6.52%	6.30%	7.14%	7.91%	7.85%	10.67%
Cash Reserves	2,117	2,957	4,266	9,291	10,043	10,493	7,362	9,347	8,716
Cash Reserves/Revenue	2.03%	3.00%	3.55%	6.16%	5.19%	5.12%	3.44%	3.53%	5.21%
Exxon Mobil (in millions of $)									
Operating Expenses	17,743	17,831	21,260	23,225	26,819	29,528	31,885	37,905	33,027
Revenue	212,800	200,949	237,054	291,252	358,955	365,467	390,328	459,579	301,500
Operating Expenses/Revenue	8.34%	8.87%	8.97%	7.97%	7.47%	8.08%	8.17%	8.25%	10.95%
Cash Reserves	6,500	7,229	10,626	18,531	28,671	28,244	33,981	31,437	10,693
Cash Reserves/Revenue	3.05%	3.60%	4.48%	6.36%	7.99%	7.73%	8.71%	6.84%	3.55%

the losses of unforeseen risks. Such a loss of assets during a crisis should be a real concern to shareholders.

Speaking of normal operations, it is normal in this industry to invest in maintenance for the purposes of preventing risk. For example the corrosion-driven loss event on the Alaska pipeline experienced by BP, might well have been prevented by maintenance of the pipeline. Such maintenance and other similar maintenance investments appear as operating expenses. Consider the ratios on the before-mentioned table. Again, BP trails Exxon Mobil and Chevron in operating expense as a percentage of revenue. BP's result in this ratio is not as severe as its cash reserves ratio, but when one considers that BP has operations that are inherently more risky, we are left with two conclusions: 1) either BP management exerted excellent judgment in preventing operational risks, or 2) operational risks are not sufficiently addressed. The latter, as the supporting data shows, is more the case. It reminds us that when dealing with risks, the costs cannot be hidden or ignored.

While it is true that some shareholders and financial experts would laud BP for its financial efficiency of holding such low cash levels and for maintaining low operating expense levels, one must question the impact of such extreme financial efficiency. In an industry wrought with risk and high-cost payouts, the financial diligence leads to potentially dangerous operating norms. Preventing risks and being prepared for risks are valuable to shareholders, especially in the long-term. Protection of assets and prevention of risk contagion are important to firms of all levels.

In the process of raising funds to cover the losses from the Deepwater Horizon oil spill, BP had to sell assets. The target was raised in late 2010 from $20 billion to $30 billion. For BP, this meant selling assets in the US, Canada and parts of Asia and Russia to raise the funds. By the end of 2011, BP reported that about $22 billion had been raised.[193] Of course, the long-term persistent nature of risks becomes evident when one considers that the only natural buyers for energy-producing assets are other energy exploration firms. In short, BP's loss become a transfer for assets (albeit for some price) to competitors. BP had worked for decades to overcome its shortfall in reserves relative to competitors and

---

[193]Gismatullin, E. (2011). "BP Sells US, Canada, UK Assets to Meet $30 Billion Target." Available at http://www.bloomberg.com/news/2011-03-03/bp-sells-u-s-canada-u-k-assets-to-meet-30-billion-target.html.

pressed into natural gas and other energy sources. The hit to BP is like a quantum shift. Its reserves, and therefore long-term earning potential are reduced. Its competitors directly benefit, however. Risks can persist for a long time.

After announcing a sale of assets to help fund the $30 billion trust, Dudley said, "safety, compliance, and operational risk management... will be the sole criteria for performance reward for the remainder of the year."[194] The focus on operational risk was clear. BP could not afford to operate in the manner that it had previously operated. The long-term costs were too great.

In positioning BP for a successful future, Dudley has many concerns to address. The full financial impact of the oil spill in the Gulf may not be known for many years. This uncertainty is hard to shake and continues to depress BP's stocks price, which is still some 30% below the pre-spill prices. See Figure 10.1.

BP is exploring a strategy of "shrinking to grow." Some investors are even calling on splitting the firm into pieces to isolate the long-term liability of the oil spill and increase shareholder value. It is clear that the risk is persistent to BP and weighs heavily on the minds of shareholders.[195]

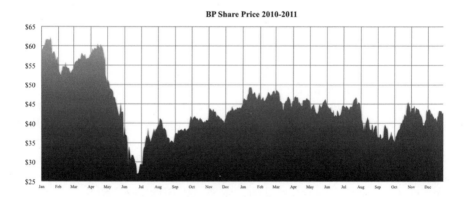

Figure 10.1.   BP stock prices from 2010–2011.

---

[194]Fontevecchia, A. (2010). "BP Sells More Assets to Pad Spill Payback Fund." Available at http://www.forbes.com/2010/10/25/bp-sell-gulf-equities-marekts-marubeni.html.
[195]Pratley, N. (2011)."Bob Dudley Gushes at BP," *The Guardian*, July 26.

The losses at BP are directly tied to operational risk. The ability to prevent, measure, and contain the losses associated with the oil rig operation are inseparable from how the enterprise operates. The failure of the well casing was a physical phenomenon, perhaps predictable, or detectable from early warning signs (such as inconclusive well tests), but the impact to the enterprise is long-term. This single event will cost BP many billions of dollars (its current CEO, Bob Dudley is allocating $30 billion). The potential for long-term liability associated with environmental and economic stress to the Gulf region is high. The ability to operate in deep water, impacts not only BP but the industry as a whole.

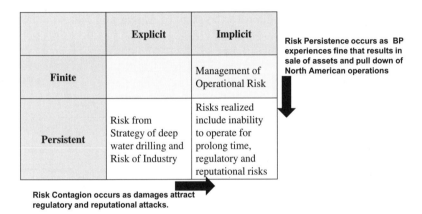

Figure 10.2.   BP's risk leads to persistence and contagion.

Figure 10.2 above maps out how the operational risks of the oil rig failure has grown in contagion and poses persistence. CEO Dudley is wise in making operational risk management a priority for the firm, as it prevents not just operational losses, but the damages to brand, reputation, and the ability to operate that are so critical in a high-profile industry like energy exploration.

Risk Management Lessons

The story of BP offers many lessons for business leaders, especially those operating in high profile businesses with an abundance of operational risk. The political backlash and potential for a long-term liability at BP also provide a lesson that liabilities and expectations from political entities and society have changed to hold corporations liable for longer periods of time and for secondary losses. BP's reputation in the US has been tarnished and its credibility so eroded that Dudley has, as one of his priorities, "rebuilding trust with regulators and our customers."[196]

At the time of this writing, the US government announced that felony charges will be filed against BP and select employees. The impacts from the highly visible catastrophe have seemed to amplify with our high velocity media and entrenched governmental agencies. Consider the impact of the Valdez oil spill of 1989 on Exxon. Although this event was much smaller than the BP event, Exxon, now Exxon Mobil, ultimately paid a $100 million fine to the US government, admitted guilt to various misdemeanor fines, and paid an additional $900 million to the state of Alaska and federal agencies for damage to natural resources. Its stock price was hardly impacted.[197] See Figure 10.3.

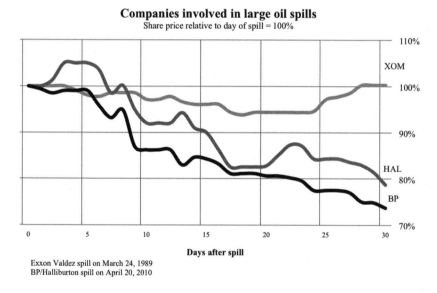

Companies involved in large oil spills
Share price relative to day of spill = 100%

Exxon Valdez spill on March 24, 1989
BP/Halliburton spill on April 20, 2010

Figure 10.3.   Share price of Exxon, Halliburton and BP relative to day of spill.

[196] "Bob Dudley's Speech to the Barclays Capital Energy Conference." Available at http://www.bp.com/genericarticle.do?categoryId=98&contentId=7070829.
[197] "Criminal Charges Are Prepared in BP Spill," *Wall Street Journal*, December 29, 2011.

As of late 2012, many of the claims impacting BP were being settled. A federal judge approved BP's $7.8 billion settlement with businesses and people impacted by the 2010 oil spill. Of this $7.8 billion, BP will pay $2.3 billion to commercial fishermen, seafood boat captains and crew, seafood vessel owners and oyster leaseholders. BP also agreed to pay $4.5 billion in government penalties. Of those penalties, $4 billion will resolve criminal charges. An additional $525 million will be paid to resolve claims brought by the Securities and Exchange Commission on the basis that BP lied to investors by understating the amount of oil flowing into the Gulf. Furthermore, the US Attorney General Eric Holder announced that BP would plead guilty to manslaughter charges from the loss of life in the explosion.

In addition to, and separate from the corporate manslaughter charges, a federal grand jury issued an indictment charging the two highest-ranking BP supervisors on board the Deepwater Horizon on the day of the explosion with 23 criminal counts.

In perhaps the most powerful demonstration of the change in fate for BP and its challenges with the US Federal Government, it was announced that the US Federal Government will not do new business with BP. The Justice Department in September of 2012 also accused BP of gross negligence and a "culture of corporate recklessness," which expands BP's liability. A major civil trial is scheduled in New Orleans in February 2013. The properties of contagion and persistence are heavily shown in this case and remain troublesome for BP. In BP's first attempt to reduce the contagion, it wisely settled out of court. Now, its adversary is the US Federal Government, posing especially dangerous outcomes of judgments that already show BP's long-term presence in the US will shrink.

Examine your company's history for taking risk

In the case of BP, the culture for risk taking was a product of the firm's history. For decades, BP was racing to catch-up with the likes of Shell and Exxon Mobil in the quest to be the leading energy provider. The unlucky losses of its prized Persian reserves left BP hungry for more. BP management focused on growth. The byproduct was a culture that took large risks, not just on new oil fields, but in operations and ventures. The results are a product of its history in many ways.

As an executive leading an enterprise, recognize the impact that the firm's history has had on risk taking. Examine how events in the past have impacted the management and perspective of other constituents like employees, shareholders, and regulators. We saw how the history of management caused a persistent risk for Conseco. Much in the same manner that Conseco created a clean break, executives must do the same when the culture for risk taking is dangerous, reckless or otherwise unacceptable. For BP, the selection of Bob Dudley, an American with a Southern accent, not the typical blue-blood Englishman, sends a message that the company is making a clean break. In his opening comments to shareholders, Dudley stressed the importance of operational risk management in that it is elevated to the first of three priorities leading the firm — "Putting Safety & Operational Risk Management (S&OR) at the heart of the company."[198]

In your organization, recognize when a clean break from a clouded history of risk taking is needed and set the tone for risk management from the top. Emphasize its importance in all decisions and hold your team accountable for risk measurement and risk-adjusted performance.

Examine anomalies in low operating expenses and cash reserves

The financial performance of BP is a symptom of under-investment in risk management. For a long time, BP was heralded as a high dividend stock for investors. Indeed, the shareholders are clamoring for the return of high yield dividends, but recognize that financial performance must be assessed from a risk perspective.

As an executive overseeing many operations, examine the investment in operating expenses and decisions to defer capital expenses. All types of systems require maintenance and investment and show a tendency to fail more over time. For operationally-intensive firms and for key operational systems, examine how and why expenses are being made. Excessive operating expenses may be the sign of aging and failing systems. Emergency repairs are the signs of an unmaintained system. Low operational expenses may be the sign of neglect or disinterest by the team in prevention, and further suggest that risk measurements are not in place.

Cash reserves provide protection against unexpected losses. In general, financial models for firm efficiency suggest that holding cash is unattractive. Those models have merits. Indeed, the availability of cash reserves in

---

[198] "Bob Dudley's Speech to the Barclays Capital Energy Conference." Available at http://www.bp.com/genericarticle.do?categoryId=98&contentId=7070829.

the context of risk is to ensure the long-term survivability of the firm. As the Great Recession of 2008 showed us, many banks failed due to a lack of liquidity and inability to sell assets. In the case of BP, the requirement for raising the funds for the damages was one that required selling valuable assets. It is never attractive for a firm to be in a position where selling valuable assets is required. Such information is known in the markets and generally results in a lower price for the assets. And as such, the sale of assets is almost always to a market competitor. Holding cash against operational risk is largely protection against such contagion and the need to sell assets.

Be mindful of the political process and how it can exacerbate your losses

In the case of BP, the former CEO, Tony Hayward, seemed to have caused greater scorn on the part of regulators. His early remarks which attempted to deflect liability to business partners, like Transocean, only infuriated regulators and politicians. BP, operating in the US, was at an immediate disadvantage. It was viewed as a foreign firm unwilling to take ownership of a catastrophe that would impact the environment and many thousands of Americans. The setting was ripe for political attack.

When operating in a foreign jurisdiction, recognize that you are at greater risk for political attack and regulatory review. This is an unfortunate reality of country-level politics. There are business models that can help mitigate this, such as joint ventures and partnerships, but the risk is never fully removed. It suggests, however, a need to over invest in risk prevention because the risk impacts (post political involvement) are likely to be punitive and expensive.

Set risk management goals for long-term value protection

For BP, the ability to make operational the failed oil well would have been a long-term success. In retrospect, the losses and expenses experienced here are much greater than the savings generated by pushing for a quicker start date or by not examining the well fitting again. True, delays in operating such a complex system as the Deepwater Horizon oil rig will result in high marginal costs, but failures of complex systems involve dangerous catastrophe. In dealing with complex systems, long-term performance and safety must be top of mind. Succumbing to the pressure to be first to market will lead to rash decision-making that might not sufficiently consider risk. In managing complex systems, develop a set of risk metrics for long-term surety.

Examine your risk-taking relative to the industry and your level of readiness relative to the industry

At an industry-wide level, BP should have seen the many warning signs that operational risk management and safety were an issue for the enterprise. Dudley saw it and acted upon it as soon as he was named CEO. The disproportionate number of safety violations, injuries, and deaths in BP were clear signs that something was amiss in safety and operational risk management.

In leading your organization, look to key industry accepted measures of safety and operational risk performance. Ask how your firm compares against the others. Examine changes, especially increases in the risk metrics. Hold your team accountable for reducing operational risk losses, including losses that result in injury or loss of life. A chief risk officer of a major mining firm has a policy that after the death of a worker, the management team and risk team must present the case, lessons learned, and follow-up changes to the board of directors. The level of attention to such events has resulted in a reduction in fatalities for the firm and an overall greater attention to the risk management process.

Case Questions

1. How would you advise CEO Dudley to install operational risk and safety metrics at BP? Provide some examples of metrics that would be useful in preventing the type of catastrophe observed.
2. BP has invested significantly in communicating its response and dedication to returning the Gulf region to economic prosperity and ecological vibrancy. There are many TV commercials and on-line ads to this effect. Survey some of these. Comment on the effectiveness of this strategy. Does it help BP or pose a risk of a higher standard of performance?
3. The US has reinstated deep water drilling in the Gulf, after a moratorium in response to the BP accident. There are many issues related to having a domestic energy supply. Some believe that the need to tap such deep oil reserves is in part driven by our national energy policy and therefore risks should be shared by the country, as a whole. Comment on the risks

that belong to the energy explorers and those that belong to the country as a whole.

4. Many scientific reports question the long-term environmental impact to the Gulf and its fisheries. Should there be a time limit on claims against BP? What is reasonable in your mind?

5. What do you expect the competitors of BP to learn from this event? What impact will this have on deep water oil drilling and the risk and rewards of bring such oil reserves to market? Who ultimately pays for that?

Chapter 11

Toyota: Dealing With Crisis in a Major (Foreign) Market

You must accept the truth from whatever source it comes.
— Maimonides, Spanish Philosopher

In the summer of 2009, Americans learned of an alarming number of accidents involving Toyota vehicles. This proved affronting to Toyota's reputation of producing high quality, safe, and reliable cars. The turning point in this disturbing trend occurred when the Saylor family died after Mr. Saylor lost control of the Lexus vehicle he was driving. It was made more vivid by the harrowing phone call that Mr. Saylor, a California Highway Patrol officer, made to 911 before he lost control. This event, and others before it, showed that Toyota was suffering from operational risk contagion. From a branding and reputational perspective, it was more dangerous for Toyota, as this accident occurred in a Lexus, its flagship luxury brand in the US. In the eyes of many, including regulators, the problem with Toyota vehicles had reached a point of unacceptability. The management of Toyota, located in Japan, was not nearly as responsive as the US government and media expected. There were reports of accidents before this incident and many investigations by the National Highway Traffic Safety Administration (NHTSA). In general, the problem was viewed as driver error or some combination of floor mats jamming pedals and the like. Technically, Toyota was in the clear, at least up until this most dramatic tragedy. For Toyota, what initially appeared as a mechanical glitch, had grown through contagion to impact its ability to operate and sell in its largest market, the US. As a foreign-held entity with non-union labor plants in the US, it was especially vulnerable to regulatory and union activist attack. Toyota enjoyed a lower price for non-union labor and the ability to sell a product viewed as high quality. It was an envious position. However, its response to the latest incident was under review, and the Department of Transportation had even advised Americans on the safety issues inherent in Toyota vehicles in the US.

Toyota faced risk that it had never seen before. It was in an organizational and supply chain shift. It was attempting an audacious growth goal. Let's take a look at how risks were manifested, handled, and ultimately gave rise to additional risks through contagion. The impacts, as we will see, have and likely will persist for Toyota for quite some time.

Toyota Profile and Background

The Toyota Motor Corporation assumed the position of the global leader in automotive market share in 2008. Of course this position does not happen overnight. Toyota was a Japanese success story with a history of over 70 years, founded and led by members of the Toyoda family. As we know today, Toyota is a Japanese owned, managed, and headquartered entity, but it operates in significant ways in almost every continent, with large sales and manufacturing in the US. Its strategy today includes building locally.

Toyota began making smaller, more efficient vehicles in the late 1940s. This strategy allowed Toyota to first enter the US market in 1957 with the Toyopet Crown. Without much initial success with the Toyopet Crown, Toyota made large investments in developing the Corona, which would ultimately provide a strong foothold in the US. By 1967, Toyota became the third-best-selling import brand in the US, and its place in the US automotive industry rose with each subsequent year.

By 1975, Toyota surpassed Volkswagen as the number one import brand in the US, and its place as a quality producer of fuel-efficient cars was established. By the late 1970s, the US automobile manufacturers had taken action to emulate Toyota by offering smaller and more fuel-efficient cars. Toyota had large plans for the US market, and opened its first US production plant in 1985 at the New United Motor Manufacturing facility in Fremont, California — a joint venture with General Motors, in which each had hoped to learn from the other. Toyota led with the Corolla, which quickly became American's most popular small car. It was also the first Toyota car manufactured solely in the US. Toyota's investment in the US continued, and in 1988, Toyota commenced production of Camry vehicles at its first company-owned and non-union facility in Kentucky. Rapid growth was part of Toyota's story and became an expectation for its management.

In 1989 Toyota launched its luxury brand for the US market, Lexus. The brand offered European style luxury at a more affordable price, fortified by Toyota reliability. As we know, it was a great success. Toyota quickly became leader in luxury cars in the US. It was a laggard only in the truck business.

By the beginning of the 1990s, Toyota's reputation as a leader in manufacturing and production was well established. Toyota's famous application of lean manufacturing and just in time production practices provided new advantages to the firm. Toyota saw significant growth and entrenched its operational advantage against other automobile manufacturers. Toyota's highly technical focus on operations allowed for the elimination of waste, inconsistencies, and inefficient processes. Inventory levels were slashed to bare minimums under just in time delivery models. Toyota made supplies adjust to this new set of requirements by supplying only what was needed, when it was needed, and only the quantities needed. The Toyota Production System (TPS) looked more like a supermarket for sales and a laboratory for engineering and process excellence. With this technical approach to operations and business, each process was engineered to only produce what the next process needed, further reducing the need for inventory and providing the financial advantage of minimizing inventory. Surprising to many, the principle of efficient operations practiced in Toyota originated from American thought leaders and businesses. Toyota relates the story that its executives learned of just-in-time operations by observing a US supermarket in the 1950s and heeding the advice of Dr. W. Edwards Deming, the famous American statistician and quality control sage during the US occupation of Japan in the 1940s and thereafter.[199] The irony is that US automobile companies would spend the 1980s and 1990s learning about the same principle of efficient operations from leading Japanese firms like Toyota.

By the late 1990's, Toyota's advantages were translating to growth and market dominance. Its position in the global market share started trending upwards as shown in Figure 11.1. In the US, Toyota was planting seeds for its next forest of the future. Its portfolio approach to product development and sales harkens back to the principles of portfolio theory in practice. American competitors were still focused on creating gas-guzzling SUVs.

---

[199]Deming's 1950 Lecture to Japanese Management. Translation by Teruhide-Haga.

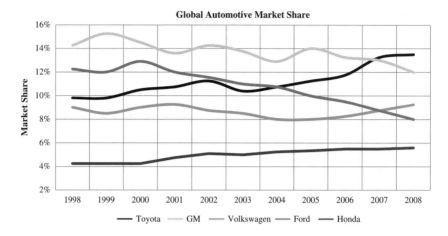

Figure 11.1.   Global automotive market share.

Toyota began development of what it saw as the next generation of vehicles. It placed R&D investment towards the development of more fuel-efficient vehicles, ultimately launching its first hybrid car, Prius, in 1997. Toyota also expanded its offerings to include a full-sized truck, as its luxury line, Lexus, was well entrenched in the US. By 2004, Toyota overtook Ford as the second largest manufacturer of automobiles in the US. Toyota's success continued through 2007 when it overtook GM as the global market share leader. GM was in an uncomfortable position for GM, as it had held the top manufacturing position almost every year since 1931. Success at Toyota was reinforced with more good news with each year passing.

As the global leader in automobile manufacturing, Toyota's brand conveyed positive messages to its customer base. It was synonymous with affordability, durability, and reliability. To US consumers, the vehicles were known to have high resale value and longevity. Toyota was riding a wave of successes. Its US competitors seemed to be struggling with each move by Toyota, and many were contracting in number of plants and market share.

However, Toyota was focused on growth. As we will see, this focus on growth, coupled with overconfidence and a reliance on a highly technical, engineering-based approach to solve operational problems contributed to Toyota's mismanagement of its greatest challenge in the US to date.

The Risk Flashpoint at Toyota

On August 29, 2009, an off-duty highway patrol officer and his family were killed while driving a rental Lexus. The National Highway and Traffic Safety Administration (NHTSA) and California Highway Patrol investigation ultimately concluded that the floor mat snagged the pedal, causing the uncontrollable acceleration. Toyota had been in the midst of numerous investigations about uncontrolled acceleration and failed braking for some years. This event put a face to the growing perception that Toyota vehicles were not safe.

Timeline of Crisis[200,201,202,203]

As much of the benefit of risk management stems from the ability to measure and detect risk early, it is important to consider the timeline of events impacting Toyota and how key information was available, known, yet missed or disregarded by the management. That such important information is repeatedly missed speaks to the culture of risk management at the firm and the management focus at the time. The series of impressive successes in Toyota's history surely provided an aura of confidence too. So, it is important to consider how corporate culture and goals impacted the ability to manage risk.

1998: Toyota sets a goal of achieving 15% market share of world vehicle sales by 2010. This would be an increase of over 50% from the 1998 level of 9.7%.[204]

---

[200]Steinmetz, K. (2010). "Toyota's Safety Problems, a Checkered History." *Time Magazine*, February 9.

[201]MacKenzie, A. and S. Evans (2010). "The Toyota Recall Crisis." *Motor Trend*, January. Available at http://www.motortrend.com/features/auto_news/2010/112_1001_toyota_recall_crisis/viewall.html.

[202] "Timeline — Toyota's Rise and Run-up to Its Recall Crisis," *Reuters*, February 9, 2010. Available at http://www.reuters.com/article/2010/02/09/toyota-idUSN0920267420100209.

[203]Automotive News. "Events Leading to Toyota's Crisis." February 24, 2010. Available at http://stage.autonews.com/apps/pbcs.dll/article?AID=/20100224/OEM/100229936/1147/RETAIL07&template=printart.

[204]Cole, R. E. (2011). "What Really Happened to Toyota?" *MIT Sloan Management Review*, June 2.

2000: Toyota desires to reduce costs in its sourcing and launches a program known as "Construction of Cost Competitiveness for the 21st Century" which promised to cut cost by 30%, saving nearly $10 billion by 2005. Much of the cost savings would come at the expense of suppliers.

February 2004: NHTSA investigates the occurrence of complaints related to the malfunction of electronic speed controls in various Toyota vehicles lines. The investigation is closed in July 2004, finding no occurrence of a vehicle defect and no "trend of defects."

February and March 2004: The large automobile insurance firm, State Farm, notifies the NHTSA of a troubling and surprising trend in claims of unintended acceleration in 2002–2003 model year Lexus ES300s and Toyota Camrys.

December 2004: Toyota vehicles accounted for about 20% of all unintended acceleration complaints filed with NHTSA in 2004, yet its share of the US market was less than 16%. This 2004 volume in complaints was up from just 4% of total claims in 2000.

August 2005: NHTSA investigates the claims of uncontrollable acceleration due to the electronic throttle system on 2002–2005 model year Camry, Solara and Lexus ES models. The investigation is closed in January 2006 with no clear discovery of a defect.

September 2006: NHTSA opens another investigation of 2002 to 2006 model year Camrys and Solaras based on complaints of short duration acceleration without pressing the accelerator. As in previous investigations, no defect was found.

2006: Following a surge in global recalls, Toyota's CEO Katsuaki Watanabe apologizes for "quality glitches." Toyota delays some new models by up to 6 months.

March 2007: NHTSA opens an investigation into pedal entrapment of floor mats in the model year 2007 Lexus ES350. The agency further reexamines this concern in August 2007, after a fatal crash involving a 2007 Camry.

September 2007: NHTSA determines that floor mat entrapment was the cause of the investigated crashes and tells Toyota a recall is required to ensure vehicle safety. The automaker recalls 55,000 floor mats for the 2007 and 2008 model year Camry and Lexus ES350 in response to the NHTSA's findings.

October 2007: Consumer Reports, the highly revered and influential vehicle quality survey drops three Toyota vehicles from its recommended list, including a popular version of the Camry. The verdict: "After years of sterling reliability, Toyota is showing cracks in its armor."[205] The mounting number of complaints and NHTSA investigations weighed heavily on the decision to remove the Toyota vehicles from the recommended list.

December 2007: Toyota's US sales for 2007 hit 2.6 million units. It has displaced Ford as No. 2 in the US market and has its target set on unseating General Motors as the leading automobile produced on a global basis. Toyota was making great progress towards its goal of 15% of the world market share of vehicles, but was still below 14% at the end of 2007.

December 2007: Toyota vehicles accounted for 23% of all unintended acceleration complaints filed with NHTSA in 2007, continuing a trend of increasing numbers and proportions. Meanwhile, its share of the US market was still less than 15%, making the 23% of complaints seem disproportionately large.

April 2008: NHTSA begins an investigation of unwanted acceleration due to trim panel interference on the 2004 model year Sienna minivan. Toyota subsequently recalls 26,501 Sienna minivans to replace floor carpet in response.

June 2009: Akio Toyoda, 53, grandson of Toyota's founder, is named president, replacing Watanabe, 67. Yoshi Inaba returns from retirement to head Toyota's US sales arm, a very key and influential post at Toyota.

August 2009: The fatal crash involving the Saylor family in California makes headlines. The NHTSA and California Highway Patrol conclude that floor mat entrapment led to this horrific accident. Toyota makes the front page and headlines nearly daily thereafter.

September 2009: NHTSA officials tell Toyota that a recall is needed to address the problems with floor mat entrapment, due to possible defects in the pedal and floor mat design. Toyota tells the agency it will recall the pedals in addition to the floor mats.

---

[205]Krebs, M. (2007). "Consumer Reports: Toyota Quality Sees 'Cracks in Its Armor.'" Available at http://www.autoobserver.com/2007/10/consumer-reports-toyota-quality-sees-cracks-in-its-armor.html.

October 2009: Toyota recalls 3.8 million vehicles in the United States in response to the NHTSA request for a recall. The recall specifically addresses the risk that floor mats could trap the accelerator pedal in an open position. The recall ultimately is expanded in January 2010 to more than 5 million vehicles suspected of having similar risks.

December 2009: NHTSA officials meet Toyota executives in Japan seeking increased responsiveness and a commitment to addressing the growing alarm facing Toyota vehicles. Toyota commits to improving its responsiveness.

December 2009: Toyota accounted for 33% of all unintended acceleration complaints filed with NHTSA in 2009, showing a continued increase in both number and proportion from previous years. Its market share in the US was still below 15%, suggesting a more than twice the rate of complaints for its market share.

January 16, 2010: Toyota informs the NHTSA that accelerator pedals made by supplier CTS Corp may have a dangerous "sticking" defect. CTS Corp is a leading part supplier, supplying many parts for other automobile companies. CTS Corp responds by noting that the reported complaints with Toyota vehicles predate the sourcing of parts from CTS Corp by Toyota.

January 19, 2010: At a meeting in Washington including Inaba and US sales chief Jim Lentz, NHTSA asks Toyota to take prompt action. Hours later Toyota tells NHTSA it will issue a recall to remedy this problem with the pedals.

January 21, 2010: Toyota announces a recall for some 2.3 million Toyota vehicles to fix pedals suspected of suffering from poor response and "stickiness."

January 25, 2010: NHTSA tells Toyota to stop selling vehicles that have acknowledged defects, given that it does not have a remedy in place.

January 26, 2010: Toyota halts US sales of eight models, including its best-selling Camry and Corolla sedans. In order to address the manufacturing issues, Toyota says it will halt production of the impacted vehicles for the first week of February.

January 28, 2010: Toyota meets with NHTSA to review its recommendation for fixing the sticky pedals. NHTSA says it has no objections to the fix and suggests an expedited remedy.

January 29, 2010: NHTSA opens investigation into CTS pedals. NHTSA asks CTS if it sold pedals to other carmakers and when it discovered reports of uncontrolled acceleration and lack of responsiveness with the pedals.

February 2, 2010: Toyota reports a 16% drop in January US sales. Monthly US sales drop below 100,000 for the first time in more than a decade. Toyota's US market share falls to its lowest level since January 2006.

February 2, 2010: NHTSA renews investigation into Toyota's electronic throttle control system. US Transportation Secretary Ray LaHood says, "While Toyota is taking responsible action now, it unfortunately took an enormous effort to get to this point. Department of Transportation (DOT) officials flew to Japan in December to remind Toyota management about its legal obligations and followed up with a meeting at DOT headquarters in January to insist that they address the accelerator pedal issue."[206] Toyota says it will cooperate with the probe.

February 3, 2010: US Secretary of Transportation bluntly warns Toyota owners to stop driving the vehicles, while speaking before the US House Appropriations Sub-Committee.

> *My advice is, if anybody owns one of these vehicles, stop driving it.*[207]

He later withdraws his remarks, saying it was a misstatement. Meanwhile, the crisis is spreading to Toyota's latest flagship. Meanwhile, Toyota says it is examining braking complaints about its 2010 model Prius hybrid.

February 4, 2010: NHTSA opens investigations into at least 124 consumer complaints about issues with brakes on Toyota Prius hybrids.

February 5, 2010: After keeping a low profile for nearly two weeks, Toyota president Akio Toyoda appears at a news conference to apologize for the safety problems. He announces plans to bring in a task force, including outside analysts to review quality.

---

[206]Todd, B. (2010). "US Official: Toyota Pressured Into Recall." Available at http://articles.cnn.com/2010-02-02/politics/lahood.toyota.recall_1_cts-pedals-toyota-accelerator?_s=PM:POLITICS.
[207]US Secretary of Transportation, Ray LaHood.

February 9, 2010: Toyota announces recall of nearly 500,000 new Prius and Lexus-branded hybrid cars globally for braking problems. Akio Toyoda says he may visit the United States in the third week of February.

February 22, 2010: Toyota says it received a federal grand jury subpoena from the Southern District of New York for documents related to unintended acceleration in some of its vehicles and the Prius braking system. It also disclosed that the US Securities and Exchange Commission requested documents related to unintended acceleration and subpoenaed documents related to the automaker's disclosure policies and practices.

February 24, 2010: President of Toyota, Akio Toyoda, testified before the US Congress to apologize for his company's poor response to safety concerns. His testimony highlighted the change in priorities that prevented Toyota from being more responsive:

> *Quite frankly, I fear the pace at which we have grown may have been too quick. I would like to point out here that Toyota's priority has traditionally been the following: First; Safety, Second; Quality, and Third; Volume. These priorities became confused, and we were not able to stop, think, and make improvements as much as we were able to before, and our basic stance to listen to customers' voices to make better products has weakened somewhat. We pursued growth over the speed at which we were able to develop our people and our organization, and we should sincerely be mindful of that. I regret that this has resulted in the safety issues described in the recalls we face today, and I am deeply sorry for any accidents that Toyota drivers have experienced.[208]*

May 18, 2010: US regulators impose a record $16.4 million dollar fine on Toyota for their slow response to safety concerns.

Big Risk, Big Costs

Although the fine of $16.4 million dollars from the US was the largest ever to an auto manufacturer, and likely a minor direct cost to Toyota, the cost of the crisis and how it was handled were much more, and would persist with Toyota for some time.

---

[208] Akio Toyoda's testimony to the US Congress on February 24, 2010.

In today's world of rapid information accessibility and immediate reporting, the events impacting Toyota's brand became international news. Bans on selling Toyota vehicles spread to other countries and reports of problems with pedals and braking appeared internationally. Of course, the international interest and alarm translates to financial costs, too. By January 2010, Toyota's sales were down 16% year-over-year at a time when its biggest competitors were experiencing growth after losses stemming from the Great Recession. A portion of the sales decline was self-inflicted, as Toyota halted production and sales during its recall crisis.

By the end of 2010, Toyota recalled 9 million vehicles in the US, Japan, and China in direct response to the quality and perception issues stemming from the crisis in the US. For the 2010 calendar year, passenger car sales in the US were up some 12.8%, but Toyota continued to lose market share to its major competitors. Toyota began to increase sales incentives in response. At least one estimate placed the increased incentives at an additional $800 per vehicle sold. Toyota had once enjoyed one of the lowest incentive costs in the industry, owing to the perceived quality and high desirability of the brand.[209]

Direct costs appeared in other tangible forms for Toyota. Namely, the operational risk that Toyota experienced spread through contagion and was manifested in other costs. A partial enumeration includes:

1. US regulators linked Toyota vehicle incidents to some 51 deaths.[210]
2. Over 109 class action lawsuits in the US and Canada, and additional individual lawsuits were pending against Toyota for issues on its vehicles.
3. Industry estimates put cost for litigation, warranty, and lost sales at $2 billion, $1.12 billion, and $0.895 billion respectively.[212]
4. In the weeks following the January 21st accelerator recall, the automaker lost $25 billion in market capitalization.[213]

---

[209]Szczesny, J. R. (2010). "Another Safety Issue: Can Toyota Ever Bounce Back?" *Time Magazine*, August 25.

[210,211]Ohnsman, A., J. Green and K. Inoue (2010). "The Humbling of Toyota." *Business Week*, March 11.

[212]Fisk, M. C. (2010). "Toyota Recall Cost to Exceed $2 Billion, Lawyers Say." *Business Week*, February 9.

[213]Fackler, M. and H. Tabuchi (2010). "Toyota Posts Profit in Quarter Before Recalls." *New York Times*, February 4.

Toyota's brand equity took a hit, too. The brand had been negatively impacted so much that car values were decreasing due to weakened customer demand for Toyota vehicles. Kelley Blue Book values for Toyota vehicles showed downward trending on both new cars and used cars. In fact, over a two-week period in February 2010, Toyota's Kelley Blue Book values had gone down between 2.5%–4.5%.[214] "It seems the longer Toyota was the subject of daily headlines with the continuing recall news, the more consumers reacted negatively by defecting from Toyota, Lexus, and Scion. We are seeing shoppers on kbb.com lean more toward competitors, especially the domestics like Ford and Chevy who are offering enticing incentives," said James Bell, executive market analyst for Kelley Blue Book's kbb.com. "Toyota is going to have to work extra hard for quite some time to overcome the 'double-whammy' it is seeing with the continuing drop in values and consumer brand consideration."[215]

As Figure 11.2 clearly shows, Toyota's stock price significantly declined relative to its major competitors in the US. This was also a period of growth for the equity markets, with the S&P 500 increasing. The risks manifested for Toyota became opportunities for the other automobile manufacturers. This is best measured by Toyota's US market share in Figure 11.3. Note that Toyota's share of the US market dropped in response to the recall crisis. Ford, in particular, enjoyed an increase in market share.

Earning back market share requires investment and costs. As the operational risks have taken on new forms through contagion, they have also persisted. Toyota responded to the loss in market share by increasing incentives to dealers and consumers, but also in launching Toyota Care, a new warranty and maintenance coverage program for buyers of new Toyota vehicles. It was the first of its type in the industry. Previously, Toyota relied on its reputation to sell vehicles. Now, it was fighting for market share alongside its competitors, hoping to win back customers, and paying dearly to do so.

[214,215]PR Newswire, "Toyota Brand Consideration, Vehicle Interest, Values Continue to Decline," *Kelley Blue* Book (February 2010). Available at http://media room.kbb.com/kelley-blue-book-toyota-brand-consideration-vehicle-interest-values-continue-decline.

Figure 11.2.   Toyota stock performance relative to competition and S&P 500.

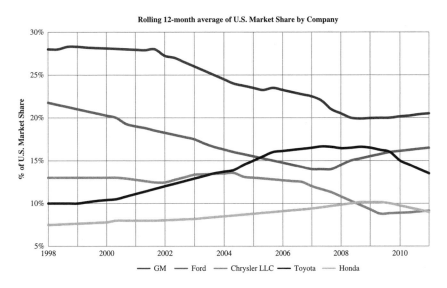

Figure 11.3.   Share of US automobile market by manufacturer.

Controlling for Risk Contagion in Practice

The chronology of events suggests that Toyota missed or disregarded many early warning signs. Perhaps, the downgrade by Consumer Reports in 2007 should have been a wake-up call. Still, the damage done to Toyota's reputation and stock price was as much a product of its poor handling of the crisis as the technical issues with the vehicles. So, it is important to consider how a firm might easily measure the media climate and look for early warning signs to suggest that contagion in risk is present.

In a research effort with a team of Kellogg MBA students,[216] we assembled a set of all media articles about Toyota from the Wall Street Journal, The New York Times, The Washington Post, and CNN from September 2009 through the peak of the crisis in March 2010. We chose these widely accessible media outlets as fair measures of the pulse of the media and the presence of a brand in news. Our logic was that these outlets would also ultimately capture the sentiment developing against Toyota, even if these might not be the first media outlet to report on an issue. To strengthen this work and increase the detection of contagion in risk, one might have added internal documents, US DOT filings, industry-specific articles, blogs, and social media. In considering the daily media articles, we simply measured the volume of message being written about Toyota in these four widely viewed media outlets. As you might guess, most of the articles written about Toyota during this period were generally investigative or negative in sentiment. Upon personal reflection of my daily readings, I find few articles about corporations that are otherwise. This suggests that any media presence in major outlets should be a trigger to management that a contagion in risk may be developing.

Using IBM SPSS, we developed a graphical representation of the impact of the number of daily articles about Toyota (in the before mentioned outlets) and the stock price. The results are revealing and are presented in Figure 11.4.

The early warning signs evident in the graph of Figure 11.4 are quite telling. Toyota saw a great deal of media attention after its initial floor mat recall in October 2009. However, these early warning signs were not recognized at Toyota. Moreover, a concerted effort to protect the brand and control contagion was not undertaken by Toyota. It was the opinion and public assertion of Toyota, after the floor mat recall, that the issue was largely based on customer or driver error. In the months before the Saylor accident and the crisis in February of 2010, Toyota had an opportunity to engage the media, its customers, and it missed that opportunity. It should have noted the large media coverage of the floor mat issue and recognized

---

[216] Josh Carpenter, Shital Chheda, Peter Jaeschke, and Nipesh Patel.

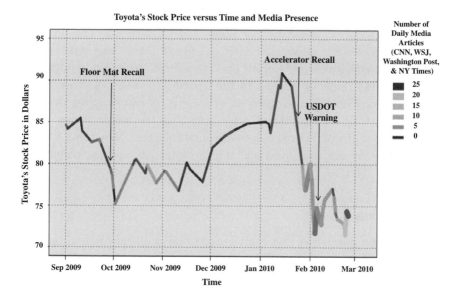

Figure 11.4.   Toyota's stock price versus time and media presence.

the opportunity to protect the brand against further attack and work to reduce the perception of reduce quality and safety with Toyota vehicles. Perhaps even changing or softening its stance on the cause of vehicle issue, away from blaming customers, would have been beneficial in October 2009.

The impact of the number of media articles on the stock price shows that analysts and the investment community are clearly looking to the media for guidance on the performance of a firm, and that in our high velocity world, there is no lag in media reporting and impact to a stock's price.

There are many open questions raised by graphical analysis. The analysis, of course, does not sufficiently capture lost future sales. Perhaps we can argue that some investors in the stock have considered this in pulling the stock price down. It is not clear that we selected the best media outlets (although these do not seem unreasonable). For an international firm like, Toyota, the presence in other countries would also be a concern. And as mentioned before, the analysis could have been strengthened with the addition of industry-specific media, too.

Tracking a firm's presence and occurrence in the media is a powerful means for detecting the contagion posed by an operational risk. Doing so also helps separate some important concepts in dealing with risk contagion. It was tempting for Toyota to offer technical rebuttals in defense of the claims against it. However, what is technically right is not the same as what is widely believed by customers and constituents. The presence of media articles is a measure of what is believed (or at least written and read). The technical aspects of an operational risk are rarely reported in the media and rarely of interest to the writers or readers. A story about how a corporation failed to meet its promise is, of course, great newspaper fodder. Corporations should take note that the media serves as an agent to move an operational risk to a reputational risk. Measuring a firm's presence in the media is a critical step in detecting and containing risk contagion.

Case Review

There are many activities that contributed to the contagion and persistence of operational risk at Toyota. There were many warning signs and opportunities for intervening. Toyota's case offers an important lesson on how risk management and its measurement can be lost by management in the sea of other priorities.

Toyota ends the high-level quality control task force[217]

In research by Robert Cole, he uncovered that Toyota management "had come to believe that quality control was part of Toyota's DNA and therefore they didn't need a special committee to reinforce it.[218] A special task force formed in 2005 to serve at a high level in the organization and resolve quality glitches that impacted the firm was dissolved in early 2009, just as the accelerator crisis was building up. It is ironic because it was Toyota that developed the "Toyota Way" and its much-lauded approach to quality and efficiency. Toyota had lost its way. Although management was credited for having the right commitment in its DNA, its focus had moved to growth and profits. Presumably, this quality team was disbanded in an effort to reduce costs, redundancy and rework, all in the name of cost cutting and efficiency.

More interestingly is that Toyota experienced a large-scale recall and crisis with engine oil sludging on many of its vehicles in the late 1990s and

---

[217,218]Cole, R. E. (2011). "What Really Happened to Toyota?" *MIT Sloan Management Review*, June 2.

early 2000s in the US. After much resistance and customer and industry paper criticism, the issues were resolved. Toyota even enacted a customer service team to address this issue. However, the risks posed by engine oil sludging did not result in dramatic loss of life. That impact to loss of life creates a victim. In the context of risks to brands and reputation, overcoming the loss of a victim is difficult. Consider the case of Conseco as an example, where the brand was ultimately changed due to the disproportionate impact to victims.

Management focus on high growth

As the Toyota Motor Corporation shifted management away from the Toyoda family, the founding family of the firm, the firm's goals and aspirations became less rooted in the underlying principles of the firm. Toyota set a goal of increasing world market share by 50% over a 12-year period from 1998–2010. Specifically, Toyota was set to go from 9.7% market share in 1998 to 15% market share by 2010. This period corresponded with the period of massive recalls, as well as the move to outsource some manufacturing to reduce costs throughout the supply chain.

It is a common tale that companies seeking rapid growth experience increased operational risk. Much research suggests that operational risk increases with growth, leading us to realize that operational risk is the unfortunate byproduct of how a company does things.[219] There are many logical explanations. During rapid growth, details may be overlooked, products may be approved without the needed review or rigor, facilities are operating at extreme utilizations, employees may be doing more overtime, contractors and new employees (who lack the internal experience) may be added, and of course, management may be focused more on growth measures than risk metrics.

Setting audacious goals may be required by management in setting strategy. Operating in a dangerous manner, however, endangers all constituents in the business. When audacious goals are needed, it is best to ramp up risk measurement and to increase focus on operational risk.

---

[219] "Asian Growth May Mask Operational Risk Problems." Available at http://www.risk.net/asia-risk/feature/1800399/asian-growth-mask-operational-risk.

Development of more complex products

Consistent with its history as a product and technology leader, Toyota was in the midst of launching new and advanced products, namely the Prius brand in the US and Japan. It is almost certain that the complexity of such new products and the importance in terms of future market share growth attracted a disproportionate amount of attention from the engineering teams and management. Developing new and complex products always poses that risk. The average vehicle includes over 2,000 components assembled from over 30,000 separate parts. Each car would have over 10 million lines of computer code, and all vehicles would have to comply with new and ever changing regulations on safety, environmental regulations, and part sourcing to comply with contracts and trade treaties.[220]

Stretched supply chain

The economics of the international automobile industry reward those that can manufacture products at a low price. Toyota knew this, and as part of its cost initiatives leaned more heavily on single source suppliers for parts. In such a model, parts are used in many vehicle platforms. Parts might even be industry standards used by other automobile manufacturers. The result is that a technical problem or a perception of one impacts many vehicles. The dangers and benefits of single-supply sourcing are evident in the Nokia-Ericsson case. The remedy is, of course, more detailed measurement and quality assurance, because the impact of an operational risk is magnified under single-source supply.

Change in management and US operations

Although much can be lauded about Toyota's success in manufacturing and management, the US market was more or less managed as a sales operation with select manufacturing. Important engineering, design, and finance decisions remained in Japan. Of course, it caused some level of friction with US employees at the factories and may have even attracted unwanted political attention from the US Congress. This separation of key responsibilities was noted by Toyota president Akio Toyoda, when he stated

---

[220]MacDuffie, J. P. and T. Fujimoto (2010). "Why Dinosaurs Will Keep Ruling the Auto Industry," *Harvard Business Review*, June.

in an open letter to the Washington Post that:

> *"... I have launched a top-to-bottom review of our global opera-*
> *tions to ensure that problems of this magnitude do not happen*
> *again and that we not only meet but exceed the high safety stan-*
> *dards that have defined our long history. As part of this, we will*
> *establish an Automotive Center of Quality Excellence in the United*
> *States, where a team of our top engineers will focus on strength-*
> *ening our quality management and quality control across North*
> *America..."* [221]

Research by Greto *et al.*[222] and Quelch *et al.*[223] indicated that former Toyota executives reported an organizational structure that required design
and engineering decisions be approved by headquarters. In this manner,
the manufacturing model of Toyota did not include local decision-making.
Although there are many key benefits to centralized decision-making in a
large firm, there is a need for information to flow to the decision makers.
In the case of Toyota seeing an increased number of quality complaints and
investigations in the US, it is easy to see that details related to this risk
might not have flowed to the decision makers. Moreover, the physical separation, cultural and political differences pose a bias to the decision makers.
It is a reminder that managing from afar requires an over-investment and
emphasis in risk measurement, as well as a requirement to respond and
acknowledge the information in order to create a culture that is forthcom-
ing with such information.

In Figure 11.5, we see that Toyota's inability to contain the operational
risk arising from technical issues with braking and acceleration caused contagion and ultimately impacted the firm's ability to operate over a long
period of time.

Once an operational risk has moved into the realm of media, the tech-
nicalities no longer represent the reality or "truth" of the problem. The
"truth" is what your customers believe and what is represented in the
court of public opinion. This can be frustrating for a firm wrongly accused

---

[221] Open Letter to Washington Post by Toyota President Akio Toyoda, February 9,
2010.

[222] Greto, M., A. Schotter, and M. B. Teagarden (2010). "Toyota: The Accelerator Crisis," *Thunderbird School of Global Management Case # TB0243*, December 15.

[223] Quelch, J., C.-I. Knoop and R. Johnson (2010). "Toyota Recalls (A): Hitting
the Skids," *Harvard Business School Case #511-016*, October 19.

	Explicit	Implicit
Finite		Management of Operational Risk: Technical Issues
Persistent	Risk from Industry	Risks realized include inability to sell for prolong time, regulatory and reputational risks, costs to recover market share

Risk Persistence:
One time event impacts firm for prolonged period of time and result in loss of market share

Risk Contagion
Technical issues become reputational and regulatory issue

Figure 11.5.   Toyota's risk leads to contagion and persistence.

or otherwise in the right. However, perception is truth and in our world of sensational news, it is wise for firms to err on the side of caution when dealing with reputational issues.

In late December 2012, the courts granted preliminary approval to a $1.1 billion settlement towards claims that recalls for unintended acceleration hurt the value of US customers' vehicles. Final approval will be determined in mid 2013. To be clear, this payment was just for lost value in vehicles due to the reputational impact that Toyota vehicles took after the acceleration crisis. In early 2013, lawsuits claiming personal injuries and deaths caused by such incidents remain pending, with the first federal trials set in the first half of 2013. The settlement for $1.1 billion shows the contagion feature of risk. Toyota is addressing loss in value, not even injury from the acceleration issue. There is no doubt that this concern that Toyota vehicles are worth less, due to acceleration concerns, will plague Toyota for some years, showing also the persistent nature of risk once victims are involved.

Risk Management Lessons

Perception issues can linger

For Toyota, the largest loss was that of their brand reputation for quality and reliability. It will take time and money to overcome this hit. The danger here is that competitors have an opening to gain market share as was the case of Ford taking some market share from Toyota during the crisis. The dangerous nature of operational risk leading to persistent impairment is at work here for Toyota. In your organization, pay careful attention to the long-term impacts of risks.

The management of long-term impacts of risks are challenging for organizations, as often the CEO and other senior management have short-term pressures and even short-term outlooks that reflect their likely tenure in the role. The discussion of linking CEO pay to long-term performance is one way to remedy this, but perhaps incomplete. The fate of the enterprise and its ability to earn profits can be materially impacted by a systematic shock or mishandling of the enterprise. Management must look at long-term impacts in terms of making decisions about risk.

Correcting a damaged brand is more difficult and expensive than a technical correction

Toyota ultimately realized the impact to its brand. In order to overcome this crisis, it had to pay billions, but ultimately worked to overcome the perception issues at an even greater expense. The error is in many ways rooted in how organizations look at risks. For a highly technical firm like Toyota, complaints (especially after investigations proved no defects) were more or less a nuisance and an anomaly. The technical nature of the organization provided a bias in how the growing number of events might impact the organization. Perhaps, Toyota should have heeded the downgrade of Consumer Reports earlier. The lesson is that when an organization is built, it has inherent strengths and biases in how to solve problems. For Toyota, the approach was technical. The consideration of impact to brand did not register until much later. In your organization, consider who is responsible for maintaining the brand and its value proposition to constituents. That might be the CEO or a team of executives. Does that team have the right risk metrics to consider? Many firms now track media sentiment and articles on the Internet as a measure of such risk. For Toyota, there were many such measures available including its frequent and high rate of complaints. Any one of these should have been a metric considered by a brand steward, working to prevent the contagion of operational risk to reputational risk. Develop a set of metrics for your firm's brand steward to allow detection of such risk contagion.

Early identification and remedy of risks is best

The timeline outlines how there were many early warning signs. Indeed, in retrospect, the Toyota crisis highlights more about how information is often missed or disregarded in organizations. The complexity of having a headquarters in Japan, making decisions for the US operations, and different cultural norms in terms of reporting disconfirming information are surely at work, too. These elements are often with us, but require an overinvestment to insure that information is shared across the organization and leveraged to the benefit of the firm. Bad news needs to be shared. Sharing it earlier allows for containment. Waiting allows for the risk to grow. For Toyota, a vehicle's safety is perhaps the most critical element to consider. Similar standards exist for companies producing food or pharmaceutical products. Impacts to the assumed standard of safety are generally high and disproportionate. In your organization, develop processes that discover and report disconfirming information. Move that information to teams that can address the problem or perception of a problem. In the case of Toyota, a pedal and floor mat fix earlier might have solved this and saved the firm much damage.

In an effort to contain risk contagion, consider a process for measuring and reporting your firm's presence in the media and other industry-specific media outlets. Evaluate the trending of your presence in the media and the reporting of operational risks. Such media occurrence is an early warning sign that a reputational or legal risk, more complex and dangerous, may be developing. Know what is being said about your firm, track it, measure it, and report. Do not disregard it.

Rapid growth (and profits) exacerbate operational risks

Recognize that when you are moving quickly as a firm, there are more things that can go wrong. It is exciting to be part of a rapidly growing organization, and as such, disconfirming information is often unwelcome. However, as a leader of such an organization, provide and develop a culture that reports such information and brings it to the attention of decision makers. There is a need to over-invest in measurement and quality assurance during rapid growth. Be willing to do that. Be willing to question new contractors and suppliers and train new employees. Although those costs may seem unattractive, when weighed against the risks or operational failure during a period of high growth, the trade-off is worthwhile. In the case of Toyota, consider the value that a high-level, quality assurance task force offers. The costs of having such a team, in retrospect, seem like a real bargain. Protect your growth by investing in similar assurance. In the long run, that is money well spent.

Beware of risks that include a potential victim

For Toyota, the impact to its brand and reputation was made worse by the fact that the issues with braking and acceleration ultimately and tragically included the loss of life. Virtually every automobile manufacturer has recalls and technical issues. These risks are embedded in the operations of making vehicles. Reasons for recalls vary, and risks to the firm vary. Those that are linked to loss of life or victims are dangerous to the firm. For Toyota, the severity of these risks in creating a class of victims should have been a red flag. For Toyota, it was ultimately not about a recall or even the underlying technical issue; it was about victims (perceived, real, or possible). It is difficult to regain credibility when challenged by a victim. In your firm, examine disconfirming information and ask if the victim class can be defined. If so, take careful action to prevent the risk from growing, as impacts to victims have a negative feedback to the firm.

Case Questions

1. How do you think Toyota failed to consider early information in the measurement of the number of complaints? What information should have most startled the management?
2. Consider the decision to disband the high-level task force on quality assessment. Develop your cost estimates for operating such a team. What is that cost, relative to the losses experiences by Toyota?
3. Examine the role of victims in this case. How does that change the impact to the brand and the promise to customers? How does it activate the political and legal process?
4. What information would you recommend that Toyota (or other such firms) consider as risk metrics in determining whether an operational risk (say technical issue) is growing? Consider measures in the media and society.
5. How do you think this crisis and the long-term risk will impact Toyota in the US?

Chapter 12
Communicating Risk Information in the Enterprise

Necessity is the mother of taking chances.
— Mark Twain, American Humorist, Writer and Lecturer

The risk of a wrong decision is preferable to the terror of indecision.
— Maimonides, Spanish Philosopher

In the cases that have been previously presented, it is clear that firms that fail to link operational data to enterprise risk experience more severe impacts to profit. In the examples of Nokia and JP Morgan Chase, where advantages were gained from the treatment of risk, it was also the case that processes for communicating risk information were in place. How organizations communicate risk and support risk decisions with information is indeed a key differentiator in the fate of firms.

Organizations that excel at communicating about risk do not simply adhere to a pre-defined process or copy formula from a text, but rather craft processes that are specific to their business and identify metrics and qualitative assessments that are key in understanding and exposing risk. Enterprises today have the ability to produce large amounts of data, especially operational data. Surveillance of markets, customers, and competitors offers additional sources of data. Transforming this data into risk information requires relating the data ultimately to the profit function of the firm. In short, answering the question, "What does this new data say about my ability to earn a profit in the future?" In the cases of Nokia and JP Morgan Chase, the organizations were able to answer that question and realize that changing the course was needed. Doing that requires discipline to examine new risk information and test assumptions about the business.

Risk information, as needed in the context of business decisions, should be considered in various categories or dimensions to make it most useful.

First, the risk must be definable on specific metrics or units that describe the operation, market, or transaction. Next the risk should be communicated in terms of outcomes and scenarios, especially as it relates to the profit impact of the firm. What might happen? What does realization of the risk bring? And third, risk information should be communicated in terms of what has changed since the previous measurement. Focusing on the change in risk metrics allows one to examine the dynamic reality of risk. This suggests a call for action or decision. When brought together, these dimensions of risk offer a holistic view on risk information, allowing the enterprise to consider the full weight of a risk decision.

Risk Specifics

Each risk has a unique profile. It is fundamentally a risk if it can impact the profit function of the firm in the future. Consider the following categories for communicating the nature of the risk.

Description — For any identified risk, the nature of the risk, its path, and form should be identified. In the case of BP and Ericsson, detailed understandings of their operational risks would have likely made the decisions clearer to management that failure was imminent and prevention of the risk worthy of some additional efforts. For Ericsson, the supply chain was not linked to the profit function of the firm, making understanding of the path of the risk and impact to the profit unknown. For BP, well performance data was not considered in the context of a failure and resulting liability.

Relativity and Scale — When examining any metric, it is appropriate to ask for a scale. Is the score high or low? How does it compare to others in the industry? Is it dangerous or safe? Risk metrics require the same scale. Consider the case of Toyota where it regarded the number of complaints as minor and a result of simply making many vehicles. When one considers that Toyota had a greater fraction of complaints made to the US DOT than it did market share of vehicles sold, it becomes clear that Toyota had an issue. Bringing such scale and relativity to the metric of complaints changes the impact of the information. Similarly, let us consider BP, with its history of violations in the US. At first pass, the number of violations seems a product of operating in a risky business like oil exploration. However, in the comparison to its competitors, BP stood out for having the most safety violations in the industry. Such scale reveals the alarming reality of BP's safety violations, suggesting that BP was far from "normal."

It is often the case that business metrics are presented without scale or relativity. This is the case for simple things like profit, loss, and more likely the case for internal measures where external constituents like investors are not demanding explanations. It is therefore imperative to demand that the business metrics be scored. It is ideal to score metrics against others in the same industry, so noted as bench marking. If bench marking is not possible, consider comparisons with similar industries. Also, consider how you have scored against previous years and/or quarters.

Likelihood — The measurement of anything uncertain must deal with the most uncomfortable question of likelihood. Will it happen? I don't know, is the general answer. How likely is the risk? For those questions, we have statistical tools. Statistical measures are well positioned to measure likelihood, but poorly positioned to project what will happen next. Probabilities let us know the chance of an event in some series of random draws. However, the next year of business is not purely a random draw or statistical process. Its outcomes will be driven by conditions that are presumably measurable.

As humans, we process information about likelihoods (probabilities) poorly — hence the phenomena of gamblers and daily umbrella totters, each mis-estimating the risk that concerns them. However, we do generally understand processes and cause and effect. Therefore, we should use logical processes to present probability information.

In the assessment of likelihood, present the factors that contribute to the likelihood assessment. Identify the drivers that you understand to increase or decrease the likelihood. State your assumptions about these drivers and the impact on the likelihood. More critically, examine how you might be wrong. Develop the counter argument to likelihood assessment. For instance, if you believe that the likelihood of a risk event is down, develop the logical process for why one might conclude that the risk is increasing. Attempt, with logic and information, to disprove the counter argument. If the counter argument cannot be disproved, you have identified disconfirming information in the form of a counter argument and should reassess the likelihood. If you can defeat the counterargument, then you have found affirming information to your likelihood assessment.

This rigorous process brings us some increased comfort and confidence in assessing likelihood. It does not make the prediction of the future any easier. Hence the quote attributed to many, "Making predictions is hard, especially about the future."

Severity — Although risk, especially operational risk, can challenge us to fully understand the severity of a risk event, we have physical limits to operational risk but many examples in the world of business to use as guides. When assessing hazards, the severity is resolved by quantifying the assets at risk and estimating the percent of assets damaged in the risk event. Although our estimates may suffer from optimism bias and underreporting, in many businesses it is relatively clear which specific assets are directly at risk. More specifically, we might have clarity on the direct or short-term impacts. However, what is not clear is how the risk, especially an operational risk, may spread through contagion and lead to persistence in the enterprise. Such measures of contagion and persistence should be considered in conjunction with outcomes. Severity should be viewed with these two dimensions: 1) direct assets (or value) impacted, and 2) additional loss from contagion and persistence from the risk. In all of these assessments, the severity should be related to the business strategy and its ability to earn profits in the future.

Drivers to the Risk — The path to the risk is highly related to understanding the likelihood and severity. In fact, examination of the drivers provides a more fundamental understanding on how the risk arises. In the case of BP, consideration of the well testing information may have increased the assessment of likelihood of well failure. Presenting risk information in the context of understood risk drivers also asks the questions if the risk drivers are changing over time and if the understanding of the drivers on risk should be reconsidered.

Outcomes — In general, estimating the outcome of the risk event is just that — an exercise in estimation. It is not realistic to expect precision in predictions of the outcome. We do have to deal with some uncertainty. However, there are particular outcomes that are especially unattractive for an enterprise: a contamination of the brand, a liquidity crisis, a loss of life, and change in the perception of product quality. Such outcomes, even if anticipated with low likelihood should be called out in particular, given the high aversion to these. Risk information that relates to these high aversion outcomes is therefore especially valuable.

Scenarios — A rather useful way to communicate risk is to develop scenarios and present the results of such scenarios, given the most recent risk information. A scenario is a path to an outcome. It provides some estimation of the outcome and how the outcome was reached. Again, using scenarios helps determine the weaknesses in the understanding of risk facing the enterprise. Scenarios are helpful when the risks are related to the financial performance and profit earning ability of the firm.

Impacts to Victims — When considering new risk information, especially with regards to operational performance, it is important to ask if a victim can be impacted by a failure in the operation. In the case of Conseco, there were early warning signs to indicate that customers were waiting longer than expected to receive payments. In the case of BP, loss of life at the Texas City facility and operational challenges in the Gulf of Mexico suggested that future accidents would directly impact victims. The presence of victims, as noted previously, not only presents an undesirable liability, but creates a difficult recovery path for the enterprise. The damages to the victim must be recognized and remedied. The solution going forward must demonstrate that the victim is protected. Such victim impacts also attract regulation and brand attacks.

Impacts to Regulation — Consider if the new risk information says something about the potential for regulation. In the case of Société Générale, there was a rise of new regulatory scrutiny. The Financial Crisis of 2008 had given the banking world new regulation. Conseco realized that its operational challenges and unfortunate media attention would also attract regulatory investigation. Being a first mover on regulation is a huge advantage.

Impacts to the Brand — When a business process, product, or system fails, and a customer is impacted, it ultimately says something about the promise and brand of the firm. Protection of the brand is paramount, as damage to the brand is hard to overcome. When risk information suggests problems that might give rise to victims, invalidate the enterprise's promise of quality and undermine its brand, it is important to note that damage to the brand is damage to future profits. Consider the challenge that Toyota faces in overcoming the safety perceptions that plague it. Had the operational risk been resolved earlier, it would have protected lost sales that Toyota had experienced.

Change in Trends and Call to Action — Decision makers in business look to their teams for insights and recommendations. The presentation of risk information, even as related to profit, is especially powerful, but it still does not make clear what to do next. In the context of risk-based decisions, it is important to address the following:

Timeliness of a Decision — Identification and communication of the urgency of a decision. In the case of Ericsson, a decision was needed in relatively short order. Urgency and importance are often confused in business. See Figure 12.1. We gravitate to solving urgent problems by delaying and even ignoring important ones that are not urgent.

	Not Urgent	**Urgent**
Important	Firms can overlook these decisions and the embedded risks, hoping to decide later.	Firms rarely miss these and provide great attention. Urgency is often the call to action.

Figure 12.1.   Dimensions of decisions with risk.

For an organization that has many urgent and important decisions, it is often a relief that some are not urgent and can be postponed. This triage of decisions is dangerous in that important decisions can be delayed and optionality in the management of risk lost. Recognize when decisions, especially those involving risk, are important yet not urgent. Make time and schedule resources to address these important decisions.

Alternatives Identification — When presenting risk information and a decision is suggested, it is most valuable to present a set of reasonable alternatives so that the decision is placed in appropriate context.

Consider the case of Ericsson and Nokia, when one suggested using a secondary supplier in the market to resolve the chip shortage. Nokia's decision to buy all of the supply seemed less risky. Ericsson's mistake of not linking the decision to take action on its supply chain was clouded by not having alternatives presented along side the risk information of delayed shipments.

Presenting alternatives in the light of new risk information also helps focus on the ensuing fate of the firm. Alternatives almost always require short-term adjustment to the status quo and may even require an investment or strong call to action. Sometimes the call to action can run counter to the conventional opinions of the industry. Consider the case of JPMorgan divesting of subprime mortgages because it had insights that a credit reversal was likely, even while the market was still liquid. Such a bold move was possible when considering alternatives. It would not have been an alternative to sell the mortgages after any credit reversal. In that regard, alternatives are really only options with a window of viability. As we know from financial markets, options have peculiar properties in terms of value and attractiveness. Alternatives are most valuable well before an impending event and have a window of time in which they are usable. This is important to consider because the pressure to delay decisions when urgency is not felt may in fact be a result of not considering that alternatives may expire. Risk decisions are ultimately about protecting firm profits and moving through a series of events so that the option to preserve and gain profit is best identified. In that manner, presenting risk information along side alternative decisions makes for a complete consideration of the risk.

Chapter 13
Benefits of Competing on Risk

There is a tide in the affairs of men, which taken at the flood,
leads on to fortune. Omitted, all the voyage of their life is bound in
shallows and in miseries. On such a full sea are we now afloat. And
we must take the current when it serves, or lose our ventures.
— *William Shakespeare, The Tragedy of Julius Caesar*

In many organizations, risk management has been viewed as a corporate requirement, and such organizations have often positioned it along with audit and regulatory functions. It might even be part of "compliance." Some have even empowered and titled corporate groups to "manage risk" along these lines and ensure that the firm is in "compliance." For many firms this has historically involved the management of insurance policies and the impact of financial decisions on bond ratings. Historically, risk management functions often focused on managing insurance policies and reviewing reports from rating agencies, which suggests that risk management was viewed more as the hedging of certain risks and the overall outsourcing of critical risk analysis, especially as related to credit risk.

Risk Management and the Great Recession of 2008

The Great Recession of 2008 has taught us that risk management cannot and should not be outsourced. Many bankers and investors alike relied on rating agencies and the reputation of financial firms in considering the credit risk of securities. Implicit risks in such securities were not accounted for in ratings. Investors' long mortgage securities were implicitly long the US real estate market and job market. The ability to recognize and separate implicit risk from those explicit in an investment is key. This requires surveillance and a response to the dynamic market place. It is not a tasked fulfilled by compliance.

The firms who performed best during and coming out of the Great Recession are those who integrated risk management as a more comprehensive part of corporate strategy, recognizing that risk management is about selecting those risks that are most desirable and preventing or containing those risks that have unfavorable characteristics, such as contagion and persistence. Firms that applied the traditional approach to risk management for the sake of compliance only did not do so well in the Great Recession. Reliance on credit rating agencies for evaluation of mortgage-backed securities burned many investors. The importance of risk management is especially true in financial services, where decisions and investments are explicit and pose credit and market risk. Operational risk in financial services and other industries is even more problematic, and exposes firms to risk that can grow and spur new risks. Our examples from Ericsson, BP, and Toyota show that small operational risks can balloon to large-scale enterprise risks that cost billions of dollars in liability and impact the ability of the firm to operate according to its strategy. Fundamentally, such risks impact the profit function of the firm for a protracted period of time.

Operational Risk Dominates

Outside of financial services, the importance of risk management is greatest in preventing and containing operational risk. Lessons learned from Conseco and Société Générale might suggest that operational risk, because of its properties of contagion and persistence, are far more dangerous than the more obvious credit and market risk decisions of financial services. In non-financial services firms, operational risk is far more common than credit and market risk, and indeed operational risk is the source of many a firm's ending. We can expect to see firms experience larger operational risk related losses as they become more interconnected with external constituents, reliant on centralized business systems for operational execution, dependent on broad-scale IT systems, and extended across complex global operations. We can also see that the opportunity to differentiate on risk management and gain competencies in operational risk management will produce superior firms that win at the expense of less prepared firms.

The cases that we have explored highlight not only the importance of risk management in business, but also key lessons on, and key behaviors of, risk management as a competitive advantage. First and foremost, sound risk management requires senior executive involvement and accountability.

Where the management is not deeply committed towards risk management, there are sure to be gaps in risk reporting and risk identification. Consider the example of Ericsson and its mishandling of its supply chain risk. Next, there must exist a culture and climate for openly communicating risk in the organization, which includes an acceptance and acknowledgement of disconfirming information. Pressures against discovering and reporting disconfirming information can destroy a firm. Consider the impact of risk information in the Toyota and BP examples. There were early signs of increasing risk, but it was disconfirming of the firm's goals and its outlook on the situation.

Developing Risk Metrics

Additionally, communication of risk must be focused on risk metrics and measures that have scale. Decisions must be driven from such risk data. The discipline for such data-driven decisions must be in place. Lastly, but perhaps most critically for the preservation of the enterprise, is that the enterprise must have a "ready response" to known risks and lookout for key risk indicators that it might signal that their imminent presence.

The examples that we considered looked at how firms in many industries addressed risk, and how the risk management (or lack thereof) impacted the strategy and long-term destiny of the firms. The example of JPMorgan is especially telling in that its risk management allowed it to not only miss the impacts of the US real estate crisis, but benefit when a competitor's assets became available for sale. Of the major US banks, JPMorgan brilliantly executed a strategy that was rooted in understanding its risk and adapting to the market, as risk metrics and risk information suggested the US real estate market was approaching a downturn. The win in terms of risk management for JPMorgan was finally realized in their acquisition of Bear Stearns at $10 a share and their purchase of Washington Mutual (formerly the largest savings and loans operator in the US). Jamie Dimon, unlike many a CEO, took an active role in regular risk briefings, requiring risk metrics and risk information for decisions. The direction and discipline towards risk-based, decision-making culture within JPMorgan allowed it to examine decisions with long-term goals in mind. Had that level of attention to risk metrics been in place for operational risks at Toyota and BP, we would have different stories to write. There are no wins for Toyota and BP. Sadly, for them, their competitors are the winners for the risks taken.

Measuring the Market and Competitors

Therefore, winning with risk management requires monitoring the competition and recognizing when there will be an opportunity to acquire assets at a discount. The assets gained might be physical in nature, as in an acquired factory. Usually, the impact of differential risk management is manifested as the transfer of market share from one participant to another. Recovering customers and market share is difficult, gaining it from a competitor because of a difference in risk readiness is a superb opportunity. Assets therefore should not be limited to the physical or tangible. Consider the risk impact on Toyota, where it lost market share in the US and is fighting to win it back from a resurgent Ford, while also trying to repair its damaged brand. BP is facing a long-term liability of unknown size and is now forced to sell off valuable assets to fund the claims. Assets include the loss of market share and the platforms to operate, which may not immediately come to mind as bank branches and factories.

The shocks that impact firms disproportionately due to risk readiness ultimately result in the transfer of value from one firm to another. We might observe it in the form of accounting measures or it might be disguised as an inability to grow or protect a market position. It is often the case that the impacts (loss of market share and assets) occur a great deal of time after the operational risk was identified or even realized. This unfortunate linkage means that risk decisions are prone to errors in the assignment of impacts to risks realized, making forecasting and planning even more challenging.

It is hard to fathom that companies might allow operational risks to mount and grow to a level that the firm's existence and ability to operate are impaired, but the examples we have seen show that senior leadership can often be caught up in short-term goals and audacious growth plans, allowing risks to build up and impairing the long-term viability of the firm at the expense of short-term gains. Therefore, just as executive involvement is important in setting corporate strategy, it is equally important in risk decisions.

In creating an organization that is cognizant of, and focused on risks, there must be honesty and openness in communicating risks, which means providing the processes for reporting and investigating disconfirming information. It makes us wonder how and why BP and Toyota did not examine early disconfirming signals. Additionally, the example of Société Générale, which did not follow-up on market warnings, suggests that corporate hubris or disregard for disconfirming information can be entrenched and even intentional. Consideration of the human component, the incentives of employees, and the reward mechanism in place are also critical in building a sound risk management effort.

Focus on the Details in Risk Management

In the case of the US real estate boom and bust, it has become clear that the market was, in part, fueled by a field of mortgages that were, in various forms, deceitful, incomplete, or otherwise untraditional. The underlying risk data was suspect. Indeed, the best-trained credit risk managers signaled these mortgages as high credit risks. Looking into the details of the mortgages was of little interest to many banks. In fact, many banks had outsourced the credit risk management to rating agencies and accepted their opinions as good as gold. If only the banks had been holding gold instead of mortgage-backed securities.

The challenge for many organizations, focused on short-term earnings, is encouraging and permitting the climate for reporting risk metrics without raining on the parade. There is a natural reaction to silence the unwelcomed information, especially if it suggests bad news. It is difficult, if not impossible, for the leadership of an enterprise to detect or become aware of all risks. Indeed, it is the task of the greater team to research and evaluate risk for reporting. The senior leadership must create decisions standards that demand data and revisit decisions when new data become available. As the trader's adage goes, "If you are not selling you are buying." This means that you are never without action. By not acting you are accepting implicit risks. Requiring and developing a culture that reexamines its decisions is powerful and leads to the type of success enjoyed by JPMorgan and likely would have saved Société Générale, BP, and Toyota each billions.

In the modern world of large enterprises operating across many lines of businesses and continents, this sharing of data must be proactively encouraged. Otherwise, it is sure to fail from inertia alone. Where firms are ever more reliant on business partners and outsourcers for services, this flow of information must even cross the business boundary to include such partners. Without this sharing, the linkages and insights needed to alter the course of the firm are not seen by management. Practically, risk management must be in place before risk happens, otherwise it is risk response or damage control. Risk management requires examining risk information when times are good. It also suggests that an enterprise must be willing to communicate about risk before the risk has yet to be realized.

Develop Intra-Business Risk Management Functionality

Separate businesses lines should take time to learn what other lines are doing given the interconnectedness of risk within an organization. This suggests making time to join other team meetings and to provide the same opportunity to colleagues. The importance of disconfirming and disconnected information in risk management should not be understated. In wake of the Great Recession of 2008, many risk managers and even politicians question how the traditional risk management models failed to predict the crisis, and why the events were more extreme than would have been predicted. As we know, a great body of thought and science has gone into the development of the risk models and techniques that have been used to conventionally manage risk. The greatest attention has been given to the problems of credit and market risk, where measurement of risk is perhaps easiest (not that credit or market risk are easy to manage). In that convention resides the problem: we are not just limited by our risk management tools, but the information that we consider appropriate. In the case of Toyota, it looked to a history of investigations where no defects were officially found, but missed that it had one of the highest complaint rates in the industry, and that the perception of its vehicle reliability and safety was trending downward by customers and external reviewers, like Consumer Reports. Risk management must involve the discovery process to bring new and even unconventional information to the table.

Consider Contagion and Persistence in Risk Decisions

Conventions of risk management often restrict us to examine the outlook for the future within what has previously been observed. Conventional risk management techniques use historical data to make projections about "worse cases" or statistical anomalies that might happen with some likelihood. It is the highest form of statistically driven risk management, and it is indeed helpful in credit and market risk. In operational risk, where risks are predominantly internal and not market driven, the approach fails to capture the nature and path of the risk. Additionally, the traditional statistically-driven process does not adequately incorporate risk contagion and persistence. What model would have projected the loss to BP based on previous oil spills? None had ever been seen before. And no such statistical model would have predicted the political strife and public anger that ensued. However, an operational risk model that examines the complexity of stopping a leak at such extreme conditions might have suggested that risk was at a level never seen before, but likely would have still been low in its estimate of what came to pass. Such operational models are more complete in that the nature of the risk can be examined beyond its manifestation as a statistical deviation. Indeed, in statistical models, unseen negative outcomes are unknown to the models and unseen "failure paths" are unincorporated in the models. This provides a call for a more explanatory approach to risk, as most of the employed risk models are poor at incorporating new information and even worse at new types or sources of information. In the case of Toyota, perhaps it should have considered customer perceptions versus technical measures. In the end, the customer's opinion (and perception) is the most valuable. In the case of BP, answering the question of how a spill might be stopped at such depths would have put the risk in a new light.

Develop Proprietary Risk Information

Seeking out new risk information is therefore critical. We see that JPMorgan created new risk information by seeking signals from their mortgage accounts. This proactive approach incorporated information on mortgage payments that was unconventional for the evaluation of portfolios of mortgages by the investment bank. The success came from identifying such novel information and realizing that it challenged conventional thought. For Nokia, similar information on shipping delays proved valuable. In the case of BP and Toyota, similar operational risk metrics would have suggested increasing levels of risk, too. These cases suggest that relying on conventional risk models is highly questionable and even say harmful for dealing with operational risk and the contagion and persistence that result. Risk management at the enterprise should be customized to reflect the nature of risk encountered. The function of the risk manager should not be focused strictly on quantification (as in the execution of conventional risk models), but on the identification and incorporation of information, especially from new sources in order to determine direction and changes that drive risk. The process of managing risk must involve a healthy level of inquiry and investigation. Risk management is inherently a process of investigation, driven by learning and examination. It is ultimately rooted in unraveling the complexity of the unknown and should be focused on understanding how the unknown impacts the enterprise, and how the unknown can be minimized or avoided, if possible.

Given a world reliant ever more on global partners, international financiers, and operating under the attention of a rapid-response media, the risks facing organizations are more complex and tightly connected than ever before. The complexity of risk is additionally driven by technological advances and the need to innovate and bring new products to market more rapidly. Business leaders should look to data to make decisions in such challenging situations. Assumptions about markets, customers, and operations should be openly questioned and verification pursued. This provides a means of breaking down the complexity of business and bringing clarity to the embedded risks.

The international market crashes during the Great Recession and failures of various investment banks showed us the dangers that product innovation can bring to financial markets. For many organizations, there was a reliance on securitization or swaps to transfer risk to counter parties. This provided a "new tool" in managing risk that was unwanted or unacceptable. This was heralded, and in fact, there are many benefits to these instruments, when properly deployed and used. In practicality, the swaps served as a form of insurance, yet the buyers of such swaps were not necessarily qualified or even financially guaranteed (as is required by many insurers worldwide). The value of an insurer, of course, is that the insurer is financially resilient to the risks that have been transferred. Every business partnership and sourcing arrangement involves some level of risk transferability. However, it is important to ask if the counterparty is actually able to absorb the risk in the ways assumed. Consider the assumptions implicitly made by Ericsson in accepting the supply from Philips, or in TJX in accepting the operational risks of processing credit card payments. Just as buyers and sellers of novel financial instruments became painfully aware of the risks implicit in such instruments after the financial crisis, non-financial service firms become aware of the operational risk implicit in partnerships, supply chains, and other complex systems.

Examine Complexity and Market Interconnectedness

The current financial crisis in Europe reminds us that risks in the markets are inherently interconnected. German and French banks hold large numbers of Greek and Italian bonds and fear a write-down and subsequent liquidity issues. Nobody seems to want to open up the problems building up in Spain. In the unwinding of AIG, the US government learned of the complex web of risk trades that proved virtually impossible to track.

It showed that even a large and diversified firm can struggle to fully understand its obligations and risks. It is little surprise that Toyota found it hard to identify technical risks in its supply chain or that BP might have missed risk signs.

Monitor Your Counterparty

In the case of Toyota, reliance was on a partner to source the pedal, and in the case of BP, reliance was on Transocean and Halliburton to manage the oil rig and well. In each of these examples, Toyota and BP hoped to transfer the operational risk to its partner in some form. On paper perhaps each did, but in practice, the risks, especially the reputational and regulatory risks came back. The reputational and regulatory risks cannot be transferred. It is an important lesson in outsourcing. Your business partner may actually be less prepared than you for the operational risk that it is taking, yet you can be ultimately left with the crisis and losses.

The assumption that risk is perfectly transferred means that one's counterparty is perfectly resilient, too. We have seen that this is not the case, of course. The assumption that counterparties can absorb risk fully is a naïve view and one proven wrong repeatedly. However, this view demonstrates how a few assumptions about risk can drastically impede a corporate strategy, especially one that assumes risk has been transferred to a partner through instruments or through contract.

Align Risk Management With Corporate Strategy

The setting of a corporate strategy is largely rooted in selecting those risks that are to be accepted, namely and ideally those risks which management believes hold some attractive opportunity. Balancing risk and reward is tied to the investments of the firm and selection of markets, customers, and even employees. Confirming the corporate outlook and changes to markets and customers becomes a key step in active risk management. Firms should focus on the data and early warning signals of the risk accepted. Implicit or embedded risks can be difficult to spot and many times impossible to separate from the business opportunity. Reducing the implicit risks becomes a key part of active risk management.

As risk management is a process of investigation and study, it is interesting that may firms have engaged outsourcers for the purposes of risk management. Not only have many companies worldwide accepted credit ratings data at face value, we have seen outlooks on the price of commodities, energy and real estate prices vary wildly across forecasters. Such uncertainty in markets suggests a need for more information and a willingness to prepare for a host of outcomes. Consider the fleet decisions being made of US automobile manufacturers. It is now clear that the US automobile industry overall was not prepared for rapid increase in the price of oil and the ensuing impact on vehicle desirability. The "Big Three" manufacturers were largely working with a view that oil would remain inexpensive to the US consumer. However, using the same market information, the likes of Toyota and Honda were making calculated investments in hybrid vehicles and other high efficiency vehicles to be positioned for the scenario of higher energy prices. In many ways, Toyota and Honda, had already "readied their response" to the risk posed by higher oil prices and the subsequent impact on their customers. Should such a high oil price scenario develop, they would be winners based on their approach to preparing for this risk. This approach reflects a treatment of risk by Toyota and Honda integrated with their respective corporate strategies.

This forward thinking about risk in the context of corporate strategy is key. Toyota and Honda were not immune to the trials of the recent recession. Nor did they forego the lucrative SUV market in the US. But each examined the scenarios and considered that it must take action to be better positioned than the major US manufacturers for a situation of high oil prices in the future. They identified a risk, took action in a way that would allow their corporate strategy to adapt to an environment with lower consumer interest in large vehicles. The emphasis is on "readying the response," much in the same way that militaries conduct simulations to prepare for a yet unseen conflict. Companies that ready a response for various situations are not necessarily better at predicting the future; they are just more prepared for what comes to pass. This continuous preparation often makes them better at understanding factors predictive of a risk. So, being ready is not preparing for doomsday, but rather being able and prepared for tomorrow.

Diligence in Risk and Diligence in Savings — Avoiding Liquidity Risk

It is interesting we have heard the phrase "liquidity risk" come to describe the woes of many a firm recently. BP is off selling assets to raise funds for its claims; it is looking for liquidity, of course. Liquidity risk is a more polite way of saying that an organization ran out of money or cash. The seeds of today's liquidity risks were set a few years ago, during more prosperous times, when companies dispersed excess cash through dividends, share buy backs, and undertook a wave of high-priced mergers. Banks were guilty of that, but the behaviors cut across all industries. High dividend-paying firms, like BP, might wonder if such pressures amplified the risks at hand. Indeed, shareholders and the investment community clamored for this sharing of wealth and punished those firms that held "excessive cash reserves." Yet, today those organizations that hoarded a bit of cash can protect themselves against "liquidity risk" and can purchase competitor assets at significant discounts. JPMorgan picked up a few choice assets. Warren Buffett's Berkshire Hathaway also serves as a wonderful example in this case. Its history and policy of not paying a dividend has drawn naysayers in the past. Yet, this has provided a strategy that positioned the firm to have cash when it was most needed. It has allowed Berkshire Hathaway to follow a strategy of long-term value to investors. Liquidity risk is not best prevented during a crisis but well before a crisis. Preserving cash, personally and at the enterprise level, is also a rare discipline, but one often rewarded by buying opportunities when others have "liquidity events."

The World Has Changed

It is fair to admit that the recent economic situation has altered many assumptions about business, markets, and risk management. We have seen massive intervention by governments in corporations. We wonder if this level of investment and protection is available the next time around. This government involvement will surely bring new risks to corporations and governments alike. The level of accountability that BP must meet for its oil spill will surely surpass that of Exxon's from 1989, driven largely by government dictate and new governmental standards for the environment. Governments and corporations have different strategies and goals, of course. Although we can more or less agree that corporations are driven to return profits to investors, the role and even mission of governments as major shareholders in banks, mortgage-holding firms, automobile manufacturers, and insurance firms is less clear. Do the governments wish to see these firms prosperous? The answer may depend on the firm and its nationality. Consider BP's and Toyota's fate in the US. Would Ford or Chevron (once protected by the US against Chinese take-over) have experienced a better fate? In part, the governments of the world participate in markets and corporations in order to stabilize their respective national markets. But don't expect that level of attention to be applied equally or without bias.

There are many secondary consequences to governmental involvement. But such investments by the government come with a price tag, generally paid for by the consumer. We have already seen the US Congress and UK Parliament adjust and limit banks' pricing on credit cards, impacting the strategies and profits of banks in the US and UK. Banks in both countries are furthermore restricted in taking action on defaulting mortgages, as part of accepting the government funds. So, the risks that are accepted and embedded in the business operation change as the corporate strategy changes. Governments and politicians seem much more sensitive to reputations and public outcries than corporations, suggesting that firms facing government involvement will likely be addressing a new list of risks and responding to a growing group of constituents. Toyota and BP for example had to address not only the crises but also the concerns of many Americans and politicians alike. The risk of regulation is high for many industries, and firms should develop risk metrics that track constituent discontent and adjust their corporate strategies accordingly.

In driving corporate strategy, we see that risk management is much more than a set of best practices and tools for the transferring of risk. Instead, it involves clear identification of those risks accepted, both explicitly and implicitly. Factors that are believed to drive risk and the risk metrics that are predictive of risk should be openly communicated. Such measurement should not be strictly internally focused, but should look at competitors customers, and markets. Let's not forget, "Profit is reward for taking risk," as so wisely put by the famous American economist Frank Knight.[224] Therefore, firms should not only be selective in which risks to take, but willing to pounce when the opportunity presents itself to acquire market share or seize assets at a discount. This involves tracking the risk position of competitors in order to understand competitive disadvantages. The best time for a price discount is when your competitor can least afford to match it. This explains Ford's successful and aggressive marketing coming out of the financial crisis (when it did not take US governmental investments) and in reaction to Toyota's crisis. So, risk management is not an exercise in

---

[224]Knight, F. H. (1921). *Risk, Uncertainty, and Profit*. New York: Houghton Mifflin.

paranoia, but rather a thoughtful approach to understanding uncertainty, exposures, opportunities, and limits in order to make educated investments. Risk management requires executive involvement, an emphasis on making data-driven decisions, open communication about risks, and a discipline to think through scenarios and ready responses. Indeed, a great many of the winners of the future will be those that not only hold a bit more cash, but have a bit more information and are quicker to connect information in novel ways than their competitors.

These lessons show that risk management is really about the identification of key information and its use in the decision-making process. It is not about guidelines or the execution of conventional mathematical models. Risk management is more important than ever, as preparing for the unknown requires having the best information, not just the industry accepted "best practice." This all signals that the risk management team belongs on the corporate strategy team. Leading with risk management and developing an approach for winning with risk ultimately leads to winning in business.

Risk Management Lessons in Review

Develop proprietary risk information

1. **Develop a dynamic and investigative nature to your risk management approach**

   - Encourage the investigation of the unknown, misunderstood, perplexing, and complex. Insights gained from that inquiry become valuable company information and ultimately lead to competitive advantages.

2. **Early Identification and remedy of risks is best**

   - Use risk information to identify scenarios that impact future profits. Investments earlier to prevent such losses are so many times less expensive than investments later to recover loss market share.

3. **Proactive information gathering**

   - *Investments in information systems.* Be willing to develop information platforms that allow for the tracking of risk. Although such systems appear as costs, the value will come in many improved risk decisions.
   - *Data collection and creation.* It must be a discipline in the organization to measure and collect data. The value of data often is not clear until it is amassed or given scale or relativity. Firms that create data do so as a discipline and a standard way of doing business.
   - *Development of risk metrics.* Create metrics that focus on how operational data links to the profit function in your firm. Risk metrics must ultimately link back to the profit function of the firm.
   - *Authority of individuals to respond to information.* Develop a culture that is metric and information driven. Require decisions to be based on risk-information. Empower individuals to act on risk information without escalation.

4. **Measurement of the competitive landscape**

   - *Examine your risk-taking relative to the industry.* Be able to answer how you fare against your competitors in risk taking. Understand how your risk taking is different than theirs. Differences in risk identify not just vulnerabilities but opportunities.
   - *Examine your level or readiness relative to the industry.* Understand how you would fare relative to competitors for a market-wide shock. Examine how your firm is expected to fare. Consider the long-term game. Identify how your firm wins in a market-wide shock.

Ready the response for risk

1. Identification of alternatives

   - Recognize alternatives as options that have windows of usability. Early identification of alternatives often results in risk management solutions that are less expensive in the long run.
   - Presenting alternatives in the context of risk information also defines urgency in decision making and makes clear the future path of the firm.

2. **Focus on preventing persistence and contagion in risk**

   - Risks, especially operational risks, may grow and persist at the firm, impacting profits over a long period of time. Work to isolate operational risks from impacting large parts of the enterprise. Provide safeguards in place. Protect against risks that can create victims or impact the brand. Examine the operations for processes that have "high leverage" and monitor those processes intensively for disconfirming information.

3. **Protection of the firm's profits**

   - When examining any risk information, examine what the information says about future profits. Protection of existing profits is critical and often more important than seeking additional profits in the short term. Remember that risk loss events ultimately erode profit in the form of asset transfer or market share transfers.

4. **Examine anomalies in low operating expenses and cash reserves**

   - Question if the firm is prepared for the unexpected. Answer if the firm can survive a storm better than the competitor. In such an examination, the path to failure is identified as well as the path to gaining market share over a competitor.

Set risk management goals for long-term value protection

- Risk management goals are often made on annual decision cycles. Consider goals for the firm over many years or decades. For long-term growth and asset protection, understand what threats and risks are likely. Develop a plan to address such risks.

Focus on operational and technological risks

1. **Rapid growth (and profits) exacerbate operational risks**

   - Rapid growth brings many positive things to a firm, but it also brings the vulnerability that operations may be taxed or insufficiently examined. Human systems and suppliers can be operating outside of norms. Rapid growth can often disguise and make difficult the reporting of disconfirming information. Extra effort and focus is required to overcome these forces.

2. **Operational risk and embedded risk require attention to detail**

   - The devil is in the details. The time spent understanding means of operations leads to opportunities for improvement and understanding the means of failure in operations. In a world where operations are complex and governed by many electronic systems, remember that small things can bring down the firm. Focusing on the seemingly small details in operations is critical.

3. **Technology has made operational risk highly levered**

   - The movement to large scale platforms has brought great efficiencies. The downside is that small disruptions can result in large-scale impacts. Develop capabilities that can contain operational failures. Focus intensely on those processes that touch all customers, transactions and pose the highest leverage risk.

4. **Recognize your competencies and partner to transfer operational risk**

   - Although risk transfer is never perfect, leverage best in class technology, best practices and expert partners to handle operations that are outside of your core competencies. However, measure and track your partners' risks and have in place key risk indicators to manage partners.

5. **Look beyond laws for what is best in dealing with technology and operational risks in technological processes**

   - The ultimate judge and jury for any firm is the customer. As companies move to larger digital footprints, the impact to customers' privacy becomes greater. Remember that in the absence of laws and legal direction, your actions, especially with customer data and information will be tried in the court of public opinion. The same holds true for other socially sensitive issues.

Lead with a culture for active risk management

1. **Scale risk management policies and measures across the enterprise**

   • Risk management must be embedded in the firm's culture and way the firm operates. Risk management and the communication of risk must be a discipline and norm for the firm.

2. **Examine your company's history for taking risk**

   • Know if there are risk aversions or risk-seeking tendencies in the history of the firm. These behaviors are built over time and may lead to faulty risk decision-making. Recognize the history and make a clean break if the history is problematic.

3. **Risk management is important during prosperous times**

   • Umbrellas are least expensive on sunny days, goes the old adage. Investments to protect or grow future profits are similarly less expensive when there is not a crisis brewing.

4. **Develop an ability to question data, not to dismiss it**

   • Overcome institutional bias and confirmation bias. Drive decisions from a thoughtful consideration of data. Develop and examine counter arguments. Understand how the counter argument fails. If the counter argument does not fail, examine your assumptions and treatment of data.

5. **Be willing to take bold decisions but look to data for guidance**

   • No action is an action. It is acceptance of the implicit risk to not act. Taking actions offers other risks, however decisions should be fact-based and driven by measurement and insights.

6. **Employees are your greatest asset ... and risk**

   • Your firm will go as far as your people are willing and able to take it. Developing a positive and rewarding work culture is of course necessary. Rogue employees and motivated agents are real threats to undermining a firm's operations. Perfect surveillance is never possible, so develop a culture that affirms the enterprise and welcomes disconfirming information.

Develop redundancy for information in processes and systems

1. **Develop a risk management culture that has multiple layers of safeguards in place**

   • Risk information and risk decisions should not be driven by one person or one process. Consider redundancy in risk information gathering and redundancy in making risk decisions.

2. **Recognize moral hazards — Take steps to reduce motivated agents and the attractiveness of targets**

   • Motivated agents are a product of society. Consider your firm's hiring standards and the impact on creating motivated agents. Moral hazards are a creation of the firm, often a by-product of poor process design. Reduce moral hazards in your firm and reward your team for risk-based decisions.

3. **Work to overcome optimism bias in your team**

   • It is not that optimism is bad, but optimism bias impedes the treatment of disconfirming information. As a discipline, require that your team develop and defeat the counter argument to their recommendation. This rigor removes many of the trappings of optimism bias.

4. **Learn from previous risk lessons — Remind your team**

   • Risks realized are not simply losses, but they are opportunities for the firm to learn and improve. Having open and honest discussions about what went wrong and how the firm failed in the wake of a risk realized encourages your team to examine their work and even bring new information forward.

5. **Verify results**

   • In an information-rich world, the integrity of the information has never been more important. Verification can come from internal audits or redundant measures. Verification ensures the integrity in the risk information but also works to identify new information.

Measure and manage your brand and reputation

1. **Perception issues can linger**

   • Impacts to the customer experience and brand are hard to erase. We are likely to remember highly negative customer experiences well, and in fact often remember and consider those four times longer than positive experiences. Remember that your brand and message are always at risk and damages are inherently felt over a long period of time. Work vigorously to protect the brand and customer promise at all times. Proactively measure risk information that suggests trends in the health of your brand and validity of your customer promise.

2. **Correcting a damaged brand is more difficult and expensive than a technical correction**

   • When faced with operational challenges and operational investments, it is important to examine if such challenges or investments against them are worthy of protection for the brand. Damages to the brand are expensive if not nearly impossible to overcome. Operational investments to protect the customer experience and brand promise before a risk event are often far less expensive. Firms often fail to link these two types of decisions.

3. **Beware of risks that include a potential victim**

   • In business, it is seemingly easy for the customer to become a victim or perceived victim, given the failed processes of the firm, or worse its negligence. Recognize that operations which impact customers negatively can activate victim status in the customer and pose a unique risk to the firm. These processes should be especially understood and managed.

4. **Be mindful of the political process and how it can exacerbate your losses**

   • In the US, we often hold a naïve perspective that decisions in regulation are strictly for the protection of customers. However, recognize that governments, regulatory bodies, and even individual regulators have agendas. Firms, due to their operational model, ownership, success, failure, or history can become targets for governmental bodies. Staying away from such attention is of course best but not entirely possible. When faced with regulatory scrutiny, take proactive measures to reduce the impact to the firm.

Bibliography

Chapter 1

Apgar, D. (2006). *Risk Intelligence: Learning to Manage What We Don't Know.* Boston, MA: Harvard Business School Press.

Hurst, H. E. (1951). "The Long-Term Storage Capacity of Reservoirs," *Transactions of the American Society of Civil Engineers,* 116, 770–808.

Hurst, H. E. (1955). "Methods of Using Long-Term Storage in Reservoirs," *Proceedings of the Institution of Civil Engineers,* 5, 519–590.

Kedar, B. Z. (1970). *Again: Arabic Risq, Medieval Latin Riscum. Studi Medievali.* Centro Italiano Di Studi Sull Atlo Medioevo, Spoleto.

Mandelbrot, B. B. (1963). "The Variation of Certain Speculative Prices," *Journal of Business,* 36, 394–419.

Mandelbrot, B. B. (1999). "A Multifractal Walk Down Wall Street," *Scientific American,* 280(2), 70–73.

Markowitz, H. M. (1952). "Portfolio Selection," *Journal of Finance,* 7(1), 77–91.

Merna, T. and F. Al-Thani (2006). *Corporate Risk Management.* West Sussex: John Wiley & Sons.

Taleb, N. N. (2007). *The Black Swan: The Impact of the Highly Improbable.* New York: Random House.

Chapter 2

"Why CEO Tenure Varies: Are You at Risk," *Chief Executive.net,* June 3, 2011. Available at http://chiefexecutive.net/why-ceo-tenure-varies-are-you-at-risk.

Chapter 4

"A Survey of Logistics: When the Chain Breaks," *The Economist,* June 17, 2006.

"Beyond the Bubble," *The Economist,* October 11, 2003.

"A Finnish Fable EspoO," *The Economist,* October 14, 2000.

"Ericsson Gets Alarm," *Financial Times,* October 23, 2000.

"Nokia/Ericsson," *Financial Times*, April 29, 2000.

"Top-5 Mobile Phone Vendors Lost Market Share in 2009," *Cellular-News.com*. Available at http://www.cellular-news.com/story/42084.php.

Brown-Humes, C. and D. Roberts (2001). "Ericsson Nears Surrender in Handset Battle," *Financial Times*, January 26.

Brown-Humes, C., R. Budden, and A. Gowers (2002). "Nokia Forecasts Rise in Handset Market," *Financial Times*, November 18, 17.

Brown-Humes, C. (2004). "Vote Ollila," *Financial Times*, January 9.

Daniel, C. (2000). "Ericsson Faces More Than Just a Test of Fire," *Financial Times*, July 24, 19.

Eglin, R. (2003). "Can Suppliers Bring Down Your Firm," *Sunday Times*, November 23.

Guyon, J. and P. Hjelt (2002). "Nokia Rocks Its Rivals; Flawless Execution Put Nokia on Top. Will Customer Love Keep It Growing?" *Fortune*, 145(5), 115.

Handfield, R. (2011). *How Do Supply Chain Risks Occur? A Managerial Framework for Reducing the Impact of Disruptions to the Supply Chain.* Available at http://scm.ncsu.edu/public/risk/risk3.html.

Harvard Business School Cemex Cases 308-022, 308–023.

Latour, A. (2001). "Trial by Fire: A Blaze in Albuquerque Sets off Major Crisis for Cell-Phone Giants," *Wall Street Journal*, January 29, A1.

MacCarthy, C. (2000). "Ericsson Handset Side Hit by Fire," *Financial Times*, July 22, 17.

Mukherjee, A. S. (2009). "The Fire That Changed an Industry: A Case Study on Thriving in a Networked World," in *The Spider's Strategy: Creating Networks to Avert Crisis, Create Change, and Really Get Ahead.* Upper Saddle River, NJ: FTPress.

Rapoport, M. (2000). "In the Money: Now It's a Wireless Bubble That's Popping," *Dow Jones News Service*, July 27, *Factiva*.

Sheffi, Y. (2007). "Building a Resilient Organization," *The Bridge*, 37(1), 30–36.

Chapter 5

"Retailer TJX Suffers Data Breach; PCI Compliance Unknown," *Warren's Washington Internet Daily*, 8(12), January 19, 2007.

"Security Expert Believes Banks, not Merchants, Should 'Own up' to Responsibility to Protect Data," *Cardline*, 7(3), January 19, 2007.

Arar, Y. (2003). *Better 802.11 Security.* Available at http://www.pcworld. com/article/111330/better_80211_security.html.

Berg, G., M. S. Freeman and K. N. Schneider (2008). "Analyzing the TJ Maxx Data Security Fiasco: Lessons for Auditors," *The CPA Journal*, 78(8), August 1.

Condon, S. (2009). "Retailers: Credit Card Data Inadequately Protected," *CNET News.com*, March 31.

Gjelten, T. (2010). "Cyber Insecurity: US Struggles to Confront Threat," *National Public Radio*, April 6.

Goodison, D. (2007). "TJX E-Mails Tell the Tale; Execs Knew of Info Security," *Boston Herald*, November 28, 23.

Greenemeier, L. (2007). "Data Theft, Pushback, and the TJX Effect," *Information Week*, August 13, 36.

Holmes, E. (2010). "TJX's Profit Rises 58%," *Wall Street Journal*, February 24.

Pereira, J. (2007). "Breaking the Code: How Credit-Card Data Went out Wireless Door — In Biggest Known Theft, Retailer's Weak Security Lost Millions of Numbers," *Wall Street Journal*, May 4, A1.

Ponemon Institute. *Why We Are Unique.* Available at http://www.pone mon.org/about-ponemon.

Ponemon Institute (2009). *2009 PCI DSS Compliance Survey.* Available at http://www.ponemon.org/local/upload/fckjail/generalcontent/18/ file/PCI%20DSS%20Survey%20Key%20Findings%20FINAL4.pdf.

Ponemon Institute. *Ponemon Study Shows the Cost of a Data Breach Continues to Increase.* Available at http://www.ponemon.org/news-2/23.

"SAS: The Royal Treatment," *CBS 60 Minutes*, October 13, 2002.

Shreft, S. L. (2007). "Risks of Identity Theft: Can the Market Protect the Payment System?" *Economic Review*, Federal Reserve Bank of Kansas City, 4th Quarter, 26.

Stone, B. (2008). "A Global Trail That Revealed a Cyber-Ring," *New York Times*, August 12, A1.

Sullivan, R. (2007). "Risk Management and Non-Bank Participation in the US Retail Payments System," *Economic Review*, Federal Reserve Bank of Kansas City, 2nd Quarter, 28.

Vijayan, J. (2007). "Breaches Pushing Retailers to Adopt PCI," *Computer World*, 32, August 6.

Visa, Inc. *Compliance Validation Details for Merchants.* Available at http://usa.visa.com/merchants/risk_management/cisp_merchants.html.

Zetter, K. (2009). "4 Years After TJX Hack, Payment Industry Sets Security Standards," *WIRED*, July 17.

Chapter 6

"Sub-prime Lenders — Trailer Trashed," *The Economist*, April 11, 1998.
"Conseco's Third-Quarter Net Income Drops 43.1% on Long-Term Care Policies in Run-off," *Best's Insurance News*, November 2, 2006.
"The Drawing Board," *Best's Review*, February 1, 2010.
Brown, J. R. and A. Finkelstein (2004). "The Interaction of Public and Private Insurance: Medicaid and the Long-Term Care Insurance Market," Working Paper No. 10989, NBER, Cambridge, MA.
Genworth Financial 2009 Cost of Care Survey, April 2009.
Hagen, S. (2004). "Financing Long-Term Care for the Elderly," Congressional Budget Office, Washington, DC. Available at http://www.cbo.gov/doc.cfm?index=5400&type=0.
Hallinan, J. T. and M. Pacelle (2003). "Turn of Fortune: In Collection Battle, Conseco Ex-CEO Is Fighting Back," *Wall Street Journal*, December 5, A1.
Levitz, J. and K. Greene (2008). "States Draw Fire for Pitching Citizens on Private Long-Term Care Insurance," *Wall Street Journal*, February 26, A1.
McQueen, M. P. (2008). "Insurer Casts-off Long-Term Care Policies," *Wall Street Journal*, December 3, D1.
Mulvey, J. (2009). "Factors Affecting the Demand for Long-Term Care Insurance: Issues for Congress," May 27, Congressional Research Service, R40601. Available at http://assets.opencrs.com/rpts/R40601_20090527.pdf.
Wall, J. K. (2007). "Long-Term Care a Long-Term Problem for Conseco," *Indianapolis Business Journal*, 28(14), June 11.
Zawacki, T. P. (2004). "Basic, Complex Flaws Block LTC Expansion," *SNL Insurance Daily*, September 10.

Chapter 7

"A Matter of Principle," *The Economist*, February 13, 2010.
"A Better Black-Swan Repellent," *The Economist*, February 13, 2010.
"JPMorgan: Dimon Effect Paying off," *Crain's New York Business*, October 2, 2006, 1.

Barr, A. B. (2008). "Dimon Steers JPMorgan Through Financial Storm." Available at http://www.marketwatch.com/story/dimons-tactics-help-jp-morgan-benefit-from-crisis.

Benmelech, E. and J. Dlugosz (2009). "The Credit Rating Crisis," NBER Working Paper No. 15045. Available at http://www.nber.org/papers/w15045.

Cohan, W. D. (2009). "Inside the Bear Stearns Boiler Room," *Fortune*, March 4.

Dash, E. and A. R. Sorkin (2008). "Government Seizes Washington Mutual and Sells Some Assets," *New York Times*, September 25, A1.

Dash, E. (2010). "JPMorgan Chase Earns $11.7 Billion," *New York Times*, January 15, B1.

Federal Deposit Insurance Corporation. Testimony of Jamie Dimon, Before the Financial Crisis Inquiry Commission, Jamie Dimon (Washington DC: January 13, 2010), 2. Available at http://www.fcic.gov/hearings/pdfs/2010-0113-Dimon.pdf.

Guerrera, F. (2010). "Dimon Days," *Financial Times*, February 25.

Kadlec, D. (2004). "Jamie Dimon: JP Morgan Chase," *TIME Magazine*, December 17.

Kassenaar, L. and E. Hester (2008). "The House of Dimon," *Bloomberg Markets*, June.

Lanchester, J. (2009). "Outsmarted: High Finance vs. Human Nature," *The New Yorker*, June 1.

Lattman, P. (2008). "Washington Mutual Fall Crushes TPG," *Wall Street Journal*, September 27, B1.

Lim, P. J. (2004). "Banking Bonanza: JP Morgan and Bank One to Merge," *US News and World Report*, January 18.

McDonald, D. (2008). "The Heist," *New York Magazine*, March 24.

Mildenberg, D. (2008). "JPMorgan Chase's Market Value Tops Bank of America." Available at http://www.bloomberg.com/apps/news?pid=20601087&sid=aIlEBDZG3kFU&refer=home.

Onarn, Y. (2010). "JPMorgan Tops Goldman in Investment Banking as Fees Swell 13%," *BusinessWeek*, March 4.

Sidel, R., D. Enrich and D. Fitzpatrick (2008). "Washington Mutual Is Seized, Sold Off to J.P. Morgan, in Largest Failure in US Banking History," *Wall Street Journal*, September 26, A1.

Sidel, R. (2009). "Profit Solid, JP Morgan Aims to Repay TARP Funds," *Wall Street Journal*, April 17, C1.

Sorkin, A. R. (2009). "JP Morgan and 9 Other Banks Repay TARP Money," *New York Times*, June 17.

Tett, G. (2009). "How Greed Turned to Panic," *Financial Times*, May 9, 20.

Tully, S. (2008). "How JPMorgan Steered Clear of the Credit Crunch," *Fortune*, September 2.

Chapter 8

IMD International Cases on "The Barings Collapse" (1995), Cases #IMD001, #IMD002.

"After JK," *The Economist*, May 29, 2008.

"Biting the Hand That Feeds It," *The Economist*, January 31, 2008.

"France Faces the Future," *The Economist*, March 30, 2006.

"Davos 2010: Sarkozy Calls for Revamp of Capitalism," *BBC News*, January 27, 2010.

Bennhold, K. (2008). "Société Générale Case Hears From Options Specialist," *New York Times*, October 16.

Clark, N. (2010). "Rogue Trader at Société Générale Gets 3 Years," *New York Times*, October 5.

Gauthier-Villars, D., C. Mollenkamp and A. MacDonald (2008). "French Bank Rocked by Rogue Trader," *Wall Street Journal*, January 25.

Guernigou, Y. L. and S. Kar-Gupta (2008). *BNP Paribas Says Will not Bid for Société Générale*. Available at http://in.reuters.com/article/2008/03/19/us-socgen-bnpparibas-idINL1267801220080319.

Hollinger, P. (2008). "Hard Hitting Lagarde Points up SocGen's Lack of Control," *Financial Times*, February 5.

Hughes, C. (2008). "France's Derivatives Assembly Line," *Financial Times*, January 30.

Matlack, C. (2008). "Jerome Kerviel — In His Own Words," *Business Week*, January 30.

Matlack, C. (2008). "Why Conspire When Nobody's Looking?" *Business Week*, March 14.

Parasie, N. (2007). *French Banks Reportedly Setting up Conduit to Help Asset Managers*. Available at http://www.marketwatch.com/story/french-banks-reportedly-setting-up-conduit-to-help-asset-managers.

Viscusi, G. and A.-S. Chassany (2008). *Societe Generale Plans Offer to Raise EU 5.5 Billion*. Available at http://www.bloomberg.com/apps/news?pid=newsarchive&sid=aY1ywT_wCWUM&refer=home.

Chapter 9

Knight, F. H. (1921). *Risk, Uncertainty, and Profit*. New York: Houghton Mifflin.

Chapter 10

"Back to Petroleum," *Financial Times*, July 7, 2009.

"BP Spill Troubles Far Deeper Than First Thought." Available at http://www.msnbc.msn.com/id/41647474/ns/us_news-environment.

"BP Operating Management System." Available at http://www.bp.com/sectiongenericarticle.do?categoryId=9032650&contentId=7059902.

Bob Dudley's Speech to the Barclays Capital Energy Conference. Available at http://www.bp.com/genericarticle.do?categoryId=98&contentId=7070829.

Broder, J. (2010). "Panel Says Firm Knew of Cement Flaws," *New York Times*, October 28.

Cowell, A. (2007). "John Browne Steps Down Abruptly From BP," *New York Times*, May 1.

Elkind, P., D. Whitford, D. Burke (2011). "BP: An Accident Waiting to Happen," *Fortune*, January 24.

Fontevecchia, A. (2010). *BP Sells More Assets to Pad Spill Payback Fund.* Available at http://www.forbes.com/2010/10/25/bp-sell-gulf-equities-marekts-marubeni.html.

Fowler, T. (2011). "Criminal Charges Are Prepared in BP Spill," *Wall Street Journal*, December 29.

Gillis, J. (2010). "Plumes of Oil Below Surface Raise New Concerns," *New York Times*, June 8.

Gismatullin, E. (2011). *P Sells US, Canada, UK Assets to Meet $30 Billion Target.* Available at http://www.bloomberg.com/news/2011-03-03/bp-sells-u-s-canada-u-k-assets-to-meet-30-billion-target.html.

Gold, R. and B. Casselman (2010). "Far Offshore, a Rash of Close Calls," *Wall Street Journal*, December 8.

Hoffman, C. (2010). "Investigative Report: How the BP Oil Rig Blowout Happened," *Popular Mechanics*, September 2.

Hughes, S. H. and B. Casselman (2010). "BP Took Risk on Well Job: Investigator," *Wall Street Journal*, November 9.

January 2011 Report by the National Commission on the BP Deepwater Horizon Oil Spill and Offshore Drilling.

Kolmar, P. (2007). "A Standard of Excellence," *The BP Magazine*, 4.

Lyall, S. (2010). "In BP's Record, a History of Boldness and Costly Blunders," *New York Times*, July 12.

Olson, P. (2010). "BP Ties Bonuses to Safety," *Forbes*, October 19.

Olsen, L. (2004). "BP Leads Nation in Refinery Fatalities," *Houston Chronicle*, May 15.

Pratley, N. (2011). "Bob Dudley Gushes at BP," *The Guardian*, July 26.

Tharoor, I. (2010). "A Brief History of BP," *Time Magazine*, June 2.

US Chemical Safety Board (2007). "Investigation Details: BP America Refinery Explosion." Available at http://www.csb.gov/news room/detail.aspx?nid=205.

Wray, R. (2010). "Deepwater Horizon Oil Spill: BP Gaffes in Full," *The Guardian*, July 27.

Chapter 11

Deming's 1950 Lecture to Japanese Management. Translation by Teruhide-Haga.

"Asian Growth May Mask Operational Risk Problems." Available at http://www.risk.net/asia-risk/feature/1800399/asian-growth-mask-operational-risk.

"Events Leading to Toyota's Crisis." Available at http://stage.autonews.com/apps/pbcs.dll/article?AID=/20100224/OEM/100229936/1147/RE TAIL07&template=printart.

Akio Toyoda's testimony to the US Congress on February 24, 2010.

Cole, R. E. (2011). "What Really Happened to Toyota?" *MIT Sloan Management Review*, June 2.

Fackler, M. and H. Tabuchi (2010). "Toyota Posts Profit in Quarter Before Recalls," *New York Times*, February 4.

Fisk, M. C. (2010). "Toyota Recall Cost to Exceed \$2 Billion, Lawyers Say," *Business Week*, February 9.

Greto, M., A. Schotter and M. B. Teagarden (2010). "Toyota: The Accelerator Crisis," *Thunderbird School of Global Management Case #TB0243*, December 15.

Krebs, M. (2007). "Consumer Reports: Toyota Quality Sees Cracks in Its Armor." Available at http://www.autoobserver.com/2007/10/consu mer-reports-toyota-quality-sees-cracks-in-its-armor.html.

MacDuffie, J. P. and T. Fujimoto (2010). "Why Dinosaurs Will Keep Ruling the Auto Industry," *Harvard Business Review*, June.

MacKenzie, A. and S. Evans (2010). "The Toyota Recall Crisis," *Motor Trend*, January.

Ohnsman, A., J. Green and K. Inoue (2010). "The Humbling of Toyota," *Business Week*, March 11.

"Toyota Brand Consideration, Vehicle Interest, Values Continue to Decline," *Kelley Blue Book, PR Newswire*, February 2010. Available at http://mediaroom.kbb.com/kelley-blue-book-toyota-brand-considera tion-vehicle-interest-values-continue-decline.

Quelch, J., C.-I. Knoop and R. Johnson (2010). "Toyota Recalls (A): Hitting the Skids," *Harvard Business School Case #511-016*, October 19.

"Timeline — Toyota's Rise and Run-up to Its Recall Crisis," *Reuters*, February 9, 2010. Available at http://www.reuters.com/article/2010/ 02/09/toyota-idUSN0920267420100209.

Steinmetz, K. (2010). "Toyota's Safety Problems, a Checkered History," *Time Magazine*, February 9.

Szczesny, J. R. (2010). "Another Safety Issue: Can Toyota Ever Bounce Back?" *Time Magazine*, August 25.

Todd, B. (2010). "US Official: Toyota Pressured Into Recall." Available at http://articles.cnn.com/2010-02-02/politics/lahood.toyota.recall_1_ cts-pedals-toyota-accelerator?_s=PM:POLITICS.

Index